Wars at Work

AN ACTION GUIDE FOR RESOLVING WORKPLACE BATTLES

Kaveh Mir

authorHOUSE®

AuthorHouse™ UK Ltd.
500 Avebury Boulevard
Central Milton Keynes, MK9 2BE
www.authorhouse.co.uk
Phone: 08001974150

Published by AuthorHouse 10/17/2012

ISBN: 978-1-4772-3415-0 (sc)
ISBN: 978-1-4772-3416-7 (e)

TABLE OF CONTENTS

DEDICATION

This book is dedicated with affection and respect to my many guides, coaches, teachers, mentors, and awakeners who helped me to awaken at many levels.

ACKNOWLEDGEMENTS

Many people have supported me in writing this book, both professionally and personally.

Many thanks to Lisa James for assisting me during this journey, to my beautiful wife Saghar for her constant energy and support, to my wonderful sons Barsa and Basim for teaching me about life with their innocent questioning.

INTRODUCTION

There is nothing that war has ever achieved that we could not better achieve without it. ~**Havelock Ellis**

Late Friday afternoon found me hunched over my desk, exhausted – both physically and mentally. Stress washed over me in waves like a rising tide. My heart rate was elevated; I felt emotionally vulnerable, scared, and shaky. Suddenly I recalled a World War II film I had watched just a few nights before. In that moment it struck me that I felt just the way soldiers must have felt in the aftermath of a bloody, brutal battle. My work life had begun to simulate full-scale war.

As I stared dazedly at my computer monitor, whatever image actually appeared on the screen faded away. In its place the last five years of my career played out before my eyes like a movie. Battles – one after the other – replayed themselves across the screen, dredged up in vivid detail from the film-reel archives of my memory.

Five years before I was running a software house, and we had just decided to merge the software business with a consultancy firm. The merger had made perfect sense: we would not only distribute software but also teach people how to use it. Combining the expertise of our separate staffs would make us more visible, more approachable, more successful, and inevitably richer. But little did I anticipate the struggles, control issues, and interpersonal strife that would be part and parcel of our decision. Merging companies means bringing together groups of people, intermingling work styles and work ethics, expanding the mix of personalities that the workplace comprises. Conflict was unavoidable. Now I realised that those battles had become the one constant in my inconstant world: almost daily I was either called out to fight or called in to resolve others' battles.

After five years of constant war, I was exhausted, defeated. I could take no more. Yet as I gazed towards the projection of my remembered battles, another idea broke into my mind like light into a tunnel: *I can change this.*

For fifteen years I had been studying psychometric personality measures. I'd started this course of study as something of a hobby, but somewhere in the back of my mind always simmered the idea that personality measurement could make a profound difference in the workplace. I'd learned that the majority of issues – whether at work, home, school, the gym, wherever – can be solved simply by better understanding ourselves and other people. That may sound deceptively simple, but it's what personality research is all about. Personality measures are designed to tell us how people are likely to behave and feel in a given situation. Psychometric analyses can help improve communication, relationships, teamwork, decision-making, leadership, learning, career choice, and much, much more. Alone in my office that Friday afternoon, I realised that here lay the answer to my dilemma.

I could put my knowledge to its best use. Using my understanding of the behavioural sciences and their psychometrics, I could help my software and consultancy colleagues resolve their battles. But I didn't have to stop there. I could guide any individuals, or entire companies, to bring their workplace wars to a satisfactory end. I could help transform corporate cultures from polarised war zones into top-performing, productive teams at peace and battle-free.

My Friday-afternoon epiphany was the beginning of this book. I resolved to turn my idea into a gift for others, to spread my knowledge in the world. I decided to find a way to teach others that understanding and honouring personality differences, then practically applying that understanding to positive problem-solving, can win lasting peace at work, foster camaraderie, and engender personal satisfaction.

The ideas behind this book

I don't think it's unreasonable to say that everyone who ever works with others at a job will at some point encounter conflict. And humans, social beings that we are, approach conflict from as many different sides as there are countries in the world. The fact that many of us define our personal identities by our professions just fuels the fire. It's little wonder that a workplace misunderstanding can so easily escalate into what feels like a civil war.

No matter what your industry, no matter your position, you will one day find yourself in a disagreement. Whenever two or more people combine forces to accomplish a project, misunderstandings will occur. Battles will be joined. War will break out.

Work is arguably the largest component of a typical human life. Think about it: the average UK citizen will spend more than 99,000 life hours – the equivalent of 11.5 years – at work. Most of us spend more time at work than we do with our spouses, our children, or our religious communities. And there's no question that work is our primary source of anxiety. When we wage workplace wars, our home lives suffer too. Relationships with family and friends become strained; spousal bonds sometimes break. Anxiety brings emotional and mental distress, even physical illness or incapacity.

Fallout from work problems travels beyond the individual and the home. Work battles translate into huge amounts of wasted efficiency and lost productivity. That damages not only a specific company and its bottom line, but the employee workforce and our society as a whole. Work war is bad for everyone.

But there's hope. Conflicts can be settled, and peace can prevail. You may not be able to *win* the workplace war (like pacifist and US Congresswoman Jeannette Rankin once said, "You can no more win a war than you can win an earthquake"[1]). But battle flames can be doused; work problems can be addressed and solved successfully. Sometimes the onset of war can be avoided altogether.

How? We can learn to understand the personalities of each individual involved and apply that understanding to identify a solution – a solution that satisfies everybody. It may sound too easy, but it works.

That is the promise of this book: to help you discover and comprehend the practical toolkit of psychometric measures, methods to characterise and define personalities, and to illustrate how those tools can be applied to resolve workplace conflicts. So to accomplish my purposes, this book's premise is simple: if we become aware of and learn to understand the personality differences between ourselves and others, we can build a conceptual framework within which we can solve workplace problems constructively.

Defining "personality"

First we need to clarify what's meant by the word *personality*. It's a complex notion. Many great minds have pondered the nuances of human personality for centuries – Freud, Jung, Adler, Odberg, and Allport are just the tip of the iceberg. That's good news for us because those same minds have produced tools *we* can use both to understand our own personalities and to comprehend the facets of others'. And in the workplace, learning how the aspects of one personality mesh with those of another give us the power to make peace.

---

1   James J. Lopach and Jean A. Luckowski, *Jeannette Rankin: A Political Woman* (Boulder, CO: University Press of Colorado, 2007).

What does personality mean to you? In our everyday conversations, we might say, "Paul is so unapproachable; he's got no personality", or "Ruth is so easy to talk to. What a nice personality she has!" Over the years many psychologists have developed models that try to quantify and qualify personality using scientific methods. Gordon Allport, an American psychologist who became one of the first to delve into the personality realm, described it as "the unique organisation of characteristics that define an individual and determine that person's pattern of interaction with the environment."[2] Personality psychology has emerged as the pursuit of learning not only the differences among individuals (what makes a person unique) but also the characteristics of human nature (how people are alike).

So different minds have come up with different models, and each distinct theory contributes something unique to our understanding of how an individual personality can be described. Yet there are many commonalities among personality theories. Each of the various models bases the definition of personality on one (or a combination) of the following ideas:

- Individuals play *roles* (like actors in a film) within each situation.
- Each human has a permanent entity at the heart of his or her being (the *self*).
- People exhibit *preferences* for behaving in certain ways.
- People behave in certain ways in order to *adapt* to their environments.
- One can calculate the *probability* that a given person will behave in a particular way.

In the chapters that follow, you will be introduced to the ideas of several different psychological theorists and how they define and characterise personality. As you read, consider how each theory resonates with your comprehension of the personalities you encounter in your day-to-day life, as well as with your own self-perception. You may develop your own theory from the models which seem most accurate and useful for your everyday situations.

Objectives of this book
This book is for everyone who has ever encountered a problem at work. In other words, this book is for *you*.

---

2   Gordon W. Allport, *Personality: A Psychological Interpretation* (Oxford: Holt, 1937).

Almost every workplace issue can be traced back to a clash between differing personalities. If we come to understand and eventually to honour our own and each other's personality traits, we can bring peace to our workplaces and solve problems often before they arise. We can detect and analyse personality issues using a toolkit of psychometric measures proven to be reliable and valid through years of stringent research. This book will show you how psychometric personality tests might be applied to practical workplace problem-solving and to positive interaction among colleagues. This book also will provide managers, who are held responsible to handle work-related issues, with a viable framework within which they may learn to define, describe, and resolve such issues.

One drawback of much personality research has been over-reliance on a single measure to guide decisions. What I seek to do here is bring together a large number of psychometric measures and show how they can complement each other and work in tandem. That creates a bigger toolkit, increasing the potential for success.

I have two words of caution to accompany this book. First, as you read the descriptions of personality measures, please note that one personality trait or type should never be considered better or worse than another. They are simply different. We must learn to accept and honour our differences, to recognise and respect the qualities of others if we really want to avoid or resolve the workplace wars. That's the beauty and strength of psychometrics.

Second, most psychometric personality measures require some training – often a certification process – in order to interpret their results reliably. Although you may be able to find a website that allows you to take a personality test and receive the results online, that doesn't automatically mean you'll understand the implications and nuances of those results. This book is not meant to replace the study and experience involved in becoming an expert at personality measurement. Your best bet is to consult with an educated professional, preferably one certified to administer and analyse the specific measure of interest. In this book I introduce **the Admiral** as the qualified professional who helps the characters understand their test results. Not only does the Admiral lend his substantial expertise to the psychometric analyses, he provides an objective third-party point of view to counterbalance those of the battling parties. Should you seek to apply psychometric tools to your own organisational or individual interactions, I highly recommend that you seek out professional guidance to ensure that you can put the measured results to the best possible use.

This book is designed as a prelude to action. What good are tools when you don't know how they function? Each chapter presents a scenario designed to illustrate one of the common battles that people often fight at work. Now, it's impossible to write a book that captures all possible battles; the page count alone would be infinite. But over my twenty-year career, I've been exposed to a lot of battle experiences. (And I do mean *a lot*.) So while I don't intend this book to represent a complete description of every possible conflict, I believe my experience has helped me illustrate battle scenes to which a wide range of people can relate – creating recognisable characters, at least one of whom will fit with your perceived reality as well. You probably won't completely relate to any given character or situation, but you should recognise qualities of the personalities described and components of the battle scenarios that you've encountered in your own work life. I'm trying to raise your awareness about common issues and to inspire you to compare and contrast them with your own experience.

I also do not intend to say that psychometric measurement is the answer to *every* work-related issue. Certainly some battles can be successfully handled using different strategies. And in other situations much more stringent measures may be required – for example, in cases of harassment or gross employee misconduct. My aim here is just to introduce you to multiple psychometric tools and to show you how their models build a safe vocabulary that recognises, accepts, and accommodates a wide variety of personality styles. Such a vocabulary helps clarify the analysis of workplace battles and expands one's toolkit for problem resolution.

Why use war as a metaphor?

The metaphor of war for workplace difficulties is appropriate for several reasons. First, a conflict at work – no matter how small – tends to divide individuals into distinct factions, like nations or alliances in a war. Many of the differences arising in the workplace can be defined as "turf battles," that is, employees will fight over responsibility, recognition, credit, or blame. One party perceives that another party is infringing on his or her turf, the first party fires verbal shots, and war is engaged. Those outside the front lines commonly will choose sides, opting to stand behind one party or the other.

Second, no one ever really wins a war. There are always casualties on both sides. In a traditional war, two sides enter into combat; soldiers are killed or wounded. Similarly, workplace wars can kill projects, enthusiasm, teamwork, and creativity. They result in wounds like lost work hours, decreased productivity, and reduced efficiency. And in addition to the wounds suffered by the company as measured by its profit-and-loss statement, the employees involved also suffer mental and emotional wounds that can prove detrimental to their psyches and to their lives.

Finally, throughout history wars have been remembered in terms of individual battles: the Charge of the Light Brigade, the Battle of Verdun, the Battle of the Bulge. In like fashion, the work war can be broken down into specific battles, as I have done in the chapters that follow.

How this book is organised

This book is divided into nine chapters. The first eight chapters each describe a different work battle, a typical conflict that co-workers commonly encounter:

1. The Battle of Leadership
2. The Battle of Career
3. The Battle of Communication
4. The Battle of Decision-making
5. The Battle of Conflict
6. The Battle of Team
7. The Battle of Learning
8. The Battle of Change

Each chapter begins with a vignette, an illustration of the problem using characters and a fictional setting. After each vignette, I will introduce the book's central character: *the Admiral*. For this book's purposes, the Admiral is the wise man. He has access to all the tools – the psychometric measures and knowledge of how to interpret and apply their results – to solve each workplace battle. The Admiral's role is to analyse and explain what's happening behind the scenes. He offers insights, tactics, strategies, and action steps for the characters to follow to deal constructively and positively with each fictional battle.

The ninth chapter provides a more in-depth description of the psychometric tools at the Admiral's disposal, including their history, a summary of their features and applications, and references for further reading.

The Johari Window model

So let's get started! But before I launch into the individual chapter illustrations of workplace battles, I'd like to introduce a communication model that has helped members of many types of groups to improve mutual understanding. This model is called the ***Johari Window***, and I use it as a framework within which individuals can reach greater self-awareness and corporations can resolve their internal wars.

The Johari Window was developed in the mid-1950s by psychologists Joseph Luft and Harrington Ingham.[3] They named their brainchild *Johari* by combining their nicknames: "Joe" and "Harry". This simple model can be a useful problem-solving tool. Basically, information about a person (such as feelings, ideas, experiences, attitudes, skills, and motivation) is analysed in relation to the larger group from four perspectives (or areas), based on what a person knows about him- or herself (self-awareness) and how that compares to what others know about the person. The model is dynamic because people can take various actions to enhance or reduce any given area (for example, they can share specific information about themselves with others, or they can ask others for specific feedback).

This diagram illustrates the model:

Johari Window

	Known to self	Not known to self
Known to others	Arena	Blind Spot
Not Known to others	Facade	Unknown

So the four areas of the model can be described like this:

1. The **open** (or "free") area contains what the person knows about him- or herself that others also know.

---

3   Joseph Luft and Harrington Ingham, "The Johari Window: A Graphic Model of Interpersonal Awareness", *Proceedings of the Western Training Laboratory in Group Development* (Los Angeles: UCLA, 1950).

2. The **blind** area contains those things the person does not know about him- or herself but that others do know.
3. The **hidden** area contains things the person knows about him- or herself that others do not know.
4. The **unknown** area contains what is unknown about the person *both* by the self and by others.

We can think of the Johari model like a window with four panes. The size of each pane can vary based on how much the person knows about him- or herself in proportion to how much others know about that person. The goal is to increase the size of the open pane of the window, or open area. Here's an example. Consider an organisation in which the open window is small. That is, the people in the organisation know little about themselves or about each other. There will be a great chance for battles to occur within that organisation. Increasing the self-awareness of the individuals involved, along with their realisation and understanding of the qualities of their co-workers, will increase the size of the open pane and reduce the risk of battle being engaged.

This book will illustrate tools and strategies for widening that open pane. Striving to make your open pane larger can improve understanding between you and your work team, between your team and other teams in your organisation, and between your organisation and other organisations with which you do business.

The Uncomfortable Zone of Debate (UZOD)

There's a lot of talk out there about "comfort zones" – the phrase has become part of our current social buzz. We're admonished that accomplishing anything worthwhile requires that we step outside those zones – as Robert Allen, author of *The One Minute Millionaire,* puts it, "Everything you want is just outside your comfort zone." Don't we all know someone who is unwilling to step outside? That friend who wallows in stress and has an excellent excuse against trying any suggestion, programme, or strategy to improve his or her situation? Misery becomes a comfort zone for many. Comfort zones become ruts within which we avoid living full, extraordinary, joyful lives.

In the workplace world, those with narrow open Johari Window pane – a lack of awareness of self and others – would find stepping outside the comfort zone extremely difficult. Yet this is the only way to achieve maximum performance. I like to call the area outside one's workplace comfort zone the **Uncomfortable Zone of Debate (UZOD)**. That's the zone where you face up to possible workplace conflict in order to tackle the tough problems. It's the place where you allow yourself to trust and have confidence in others – enough trust and confidence that you're willing to raise those issues upon which you might disagree. I illustrate the UZOD like this:

Figure 2 – The Uncomfortable Zone of Debate
From Johnson G & Scholes K (1999).
Exploring Corporate Strategy: Fifth Edition.
Harlow, UK: Prentice-Hall.

The UZOD model was developed by Gerry Johnson and Kevan Scholes.[4] In Zone A, the agreement levels are extremely high – everyone agrees about everything. In order to maintain this harmonic façade, we only discuss topics upon which we're very likely to agree. Thus in Zone A people talk about the weather, sports results, TV programmes, common allies, or common enemies. All our focus is trained on agreement rather than on efficiency, productivity, or results. We sacrifice results in favour of maintaining that agreeable illusion. If we remain in this zone, the problems we'll face include stagnation, lack of innovation, and low performance.

In Zone B, on the other hand, agreement is absent – we disagree about everything. Tensions run high. Ideas are killed before they can even be brought to the table for proper evaluation. We focus on scoring over each other; winning is the most important goal. We evaluate others' ideas based on our own emotional, personal, and political preferences rather than on potential benefits or results. We engage in long meetings and debates; stress and exhaustion are rampant. It's interesting that the problems faced by those stuck in Zone B are quite similar to those found in Zone A: lack of change, innovation, or ability to think creatively and low performance and productivity.

In Zone A agreement levels are high but difficult to maintain – the pressure is on to keep the peace, and it's only a matter of time before pent-up

---

4   Gerry Johnson and Kevan Scholes, *Exploring Corporate Strategy, 5ᵗʰ ed.* (Harlow, UK: Prentice-Hall, 1999).

disagreements erupt like a volcano. Too long in Zone B, and the stress will destroy you.

To achieve ultimate performance, we need to move into the middle zone (the UZOD) and stay there. In the UZOD we are willing to entertain appropriate agreement and disagreement levels about the subjects under discussion. In this zone the emotional, personal, and political interferences are minimised in favour of a focus on results. People have adequate trust and confidence in themselves and their work relationships to raise questions and challenge ideas, as well as a willingness to have their own ideas challenged and questioned. Moving from Zone A to the UZOD requires an increase in self-awareness. Zone B dwellers are generally self-aware, but moving from Zone B to the UZOD requires increased awareness of others.

Put a different way, there are four different scenarios when people communicate with one another:

- When the parties focus on what they're comfortable talking about: "Shallow" talks.
- When the parties focus only on those topics about which they disagree and follow any statement with a counter-statement: "Warrior" talks.
- When the parties agree that they can have different points of view, but they don't have the behavioural capability or desire to disagree: "Eye-rolling" talks.
- When the parties agree that they can have different points of view and they know how to behave and have the capabilities and desire to enter into healthy debate: "Roll up sleeves" talks.

Can you see how this model relates to the Johari Window? Increasing one's awareness of self and others to the point where ideas – even those which may prove unpopular with colleagues – can be brought into the light, discussed, challenged, improved upon, and finally adopted will serve to widen the company's open windowpane. The ideas in this book are designed to help you become more comfortable straying outside your personal comfort zone and able to roll up your sleeves and enter into productive debate.

As this book's battle scenarios unfold, the Admiral will revisit the UZOD and the Johari Window model frequently. These ideas form an important part of the conceptual framework within which the psychometric personality assessments can be analysed and applied.

Summing up

This book is for you. You are sure to compare at least one or two of the battle situations to those in your own personal war room. In some of the characters, you may see qualities of yourself. In other characters, you're likely to recognise people you know. The battle characterisations can be generalised to a wide variety of workplaces, people, and events. Wouldn't it be wonderful if, every single day, you could feel a sense of engagement, enjoyment, and accomplishment at work? This book can help you build the confidence to wave a white flag of truce. The ideas herein contribute to a kit of tools that help workplace soldiers lay down their arms and work together in alliance, camaraderie, trust, and hope for a peaceful future.

CHAPTER I

What qualities make a good leader? Effective leaders absorb and use available information to direct their work relationships in ways consistent with their values, goals, and well-being. They use data to track how things are going and alter direction when needed. Good leaders evaluate options and use their knowledge to manage change, give feedback, enhance employee performance, resolve conflict, and develop cooperation and trust. The best bosses lead by example: they exhibit the qualities they want to encourage in their employees. Competence, courage, honesty, independence, inspiration, loyalty, self-control – these are some of the traits we seek in the people we're most willing to follow and serve.

Leadership quality underlies the success or failure of any company or group. Even today's trends towards cooperative and collaborative arrangements are just another way to distribute the responsibilities of leadership. Organisational greatness is achieved when the organisation's focus is highly trained on execution; when its leaders exhibit the great qualities outlined above by choice, rather than by requirement; and when its ranks are composed of great people who contribute to the organisational mission and focus.

The Battle of Leadership ensues when leaders cease to be effective. For example, a leader might be misunderstood by his or her followers, offer no clear direction, or lack visionary skill. A leader might fail to recognise a follower's potential. A leader might become distracted by details and ignore the big picture or might neglect important details in favour of a larger vision. Decision-making ability might hinder the pursuit of interpersonal relationships, and vice versa. Some people land in leadership roles without truly knowing how to lead. Can you see how personality might come into play in causing a leader to succeed, or to fail?

In the two scenarios that follow, you'll be introduced to some characters who end up fighting the Battle of Leadership. You'll learn how the Admiral negotiates peace using personality measurement and interpretation, increasing the open pane of the Johari Window and helping the characters move into the UZOD.

Scenario I: Tradition vs. Innovation

It will always be a battle a day between those who want maximum change and those who want to maintain the status quo. ~Gerry Adams

Monday morning's staff meeting got underway right on schedule. The marketing team of Smith Management Consulting (SMS) seemed, for the most part, eager to get started with a busy workweek.

Department Manager John Leader opened the meeting in his typical level, well-organised style. "Let's talk through our lead strategies," said John. "We need to attract several new clients before fiscal year-end." SMS, a provider of business-to-business consulting services, generally relied upon traditional in-person marketing approaches. Since their success depended upon in-depth assessment of a client's organisational structure and unique needs, the conservative John had always steered his team towards generating client leads from face-to-face settings.

"I'm running a station at the AdvansTek Consulting Trade Show next month," offered Sam Taylor. "We've had a presence at that show for the past two years, and it gives us a good deal of exposure. I'll be doing a featured presentation on centre stage on the Saturday, and we'll have a lot of chances to meet potential clients. I think it's a great opportunity."

"Good," said John, nodding approval. He turned to Joe Marks, the team's tech advisor. "Joe, is information about the AdvansTek show up on our website?"

"Yes," responded Joe, "there's an article with a few photos from last year's show, and a link to the trade show's page."

"Fantastic," said John. "This is just the kind of networking opportunity we need."

It was bright young Ella Explorer's turn to chime in. "I'm glad you brought up networking," she said. "I have an idea."

Inwardly, John rolled his eyes. Ella had joined his team less than a year ago, and although John worked hard to conceal his feelings, he had trouble accepting her maverick persona. She never failed to interject some harebrained scheme into his well-ordered agenda. His strategies had worked stunningly well for the past twenty years, had they not? In fact, his marketing tactics were the prime impetus behind SMS's establishment as a recognised leader in the consulting community, John was proud to say. But Ella seemed to think the company should make a complete strategic turnabout – mostly centring on increasing their presence in cyberspace. Her persistence in pressing her views had become a thorn in John's side. But she was a member of the team, so he had to allow her the floor – at least for the moment.

"Go on," he said.

"I've been doing some research on social media, and I believe we could use that avenue to our advantage. We could launch an email marketing campaign, and we could use Facebook and Twitter to spread the word about our services." Ella became more animated as she spoke, her eyes lighting up with enthusiasm. "We could even start a company blog. I read recently that companies with blogs receive 55 per cent more website traffic than companies without blogs.

"Social media provide a whole new frontier for networking and client contact," Ella continued. "We need to tap into that!"

John sighed audibly. "Well, Ella," he said, "what can you tell us about the bottom line?"

"I haven't worked up specific figures yet," said Ella, "but online marketing can be quite inexpensive. You see, all the social media platforms are interconnected. We could use our email campaigns to drive readers to the blog. And then we could use a Facebook page to get subscribers to our newsletter, or to get followers on Twitter!"

"And who, exactly, will be doing all this work?" asked John. "Our team is overloaded as it is."

"I expect we'd need to hire someone to head up the effort, someone who's a social media expert. Or maybe we could find existing staff with those skills." Secretly Ella hoped to undertake the role herself. She had been researching social media as a marketing tool for several months, and the more she explored the possibilities, the more excited she became. With an undergraduate degree in journalism, she had the writing skills to create an excellent blog, and her marketing MBA gave her the instincts to know that social media marketing was the wave of the future.

John shook his head. "I like to see the financial impact before I jump into new territory like this. You need to think it through completely, Ella."

"But I have done," objected Ella. "I know online marketing content has to be constantly updated and search-engine optimised to be effective. That's why we need someone dedicated to the task – to curate the content and ensure SEO. Maybe the marketing department could serve as the central hub for the blog and collect entries from authors all over the company. That would spread the work around and give us some content variety."

"I'm sure the consultation and accounting staff have plenty of work to do," snapped John. "Do we have to ask them to do our work too?"

Ella fell quiet for a moment, choosing her words. "No," she said carefully, "I was just trying to identify a way to keep costs to a minimum." Her voice rose again. "But we shouldn't pass up the chance to expand our horizons! It's time we brought SMS into the twenty-first century!"

"I've heard horror stories about negative posts that show up on blogs," countered John. "Our competitors might even post fake reviews as a way to undermine our image. It's far too risky, Ella, especially until you can demonstrate a solid return on investment."

"But we can't show return on investment until we try it," Ella protested. "If we don't take advantage of new marketing avenues, we're missing out. Twitter and Facebook, these are the media everyone's talking about. We're shooting ourselves in the foot if we don't keep up."

John had heard enough. "We must revisit our marketing goals, Ella," he said. "I fail to see how social media serve the objectives of a small service business like ours, with its intimate clientele. Ella, virtually all our business is conducted face-to-face. Instead of spending so much time on the Internet, maybe you could attend the meetings of that business network I asked you to join."

Ella said nothing, but her face betrayed her feelings. She kept her eyes trained on the table and blushed. John could read her frustration and anger. For the good of the team, he decided to throw her a tiny line of hope – just enough to keep her happy, without having to commit the company's scarce resources to her wild schemes.

"I appreciate your enthusiasm, Ella," he said, "so I'll tell you what. Why don't you design a survey and ask our existing clients whether they even *use* the Internet? Find out where our customers go online, whether they use social media, and if they're open to receiving online information about our service. Compile the results and do a cost-benefit analysis. Then maybe we can consider your proposal." His tone left no opening for further discussion, and the group moved on to talk about their weekly tasks.

Ella left the meeting hurt and fuming. She couldn't believe how readily and thoroughly John had shot down her ideas. And in a public meeting, too! The man was impossible – he had no appreciation for creativity. He stifled any attempts at innovation before they could even get off the ground. Ella had tried to introduce online marketing tools several times before today, and his response had been the same. It wasn't that she minded criticism; she was used to being made aware of her mistakes, and she could take it. But this time she knew she was right. John was such a good old boy! He thought the only way to reach customers was at a Chamber of Commerce meeting. And now she had to design a customer survey, tabulate the results, and calculate the cost-benefit ratio? She *hated* that kind of work. If he would only let her unleash her creative potential, Ella knew her ideas would prove fruitful – giving SMS a global presence far beyond John Leader's limited capacity to imagine.

John returned to his office, partly satisfied with his adroit handling of the situation yet faintly annoyed at having his marketing expertise challenged yet again. Ella's repeated attempts to introduce new technology into the SMS marketing plan always felt like personal criticism aimed directly at him. He was old, that's what she was saying, and his ideas were outdated. Never mind that they'd worked great for the past twenty years. Never mind that he was recognised as one of the great marketing minds in his community; never mind that he'd dedicated his career to building strong client relationships and trust over time. Ella was all emotion and no substance, he thought; she was too independent. She must get on board with the team instead of striking out on her own to do unsolicited research the company didn't even need. Well, once she completed this survey task, the results would put her silly ideas to rest. John was as sure of it as he was sure of his own ability to run his marketing department with a firm, constant hand. The concrete evidence would back him up.

Over the next few weeks, John and Ella's relationship deteriorated further. Ella pursued the customer survey listlessly, and her half-hearted efforts failed to yield results. John was only too happy to let the matter drop. Yet he nursed a nagging suspicion that Ella was acting behind his back, dividing the marketing staff into factions based on their allegiance to either him or her. The weekly staff meetings suffered from the split created by the divergent beliefs of these two strong personalities. Staff members who agreed with John remained vocal, continuing to report accomplishments made via the traditional methods he advocated. Ella and her supporters stopped communicating at meetings altogether. Behind the scenes, they continued researching new marketing avenues; Ella and at least one of her colleagues began searching for new employment where their creative inspirations would be entertained. Neither faction would help the other, and the company was losing market share. The brief clash between John Leader and Ella Explorer had escalated into full-on war.

Eventually SMS's CEO became aware of the situation. After reviewing both sides of the issue, he decided it was time for the management consulting firm to consume some of the services they were used to selling. He had met the Admiral at a club meeting a couple of months ago and learned that he used psychometric personality tests to help solve corporate leadership issues. He decided to give the Admiral a call.

What do *you* think?

Before reviewing the strategies the Admiral chooses to help win peace at SMS, I want to ask *you* to take a good, hard look at the situation. Consider the impressions you've formed about the personalities involved. Maybe you see some qualities you recognize in these characters. They may be qualities you possess or traits you've observed in your co-workers. Perhaps you have even chosen a side – you may feel more affinity for John's views or for Ella's. Have you begun to form some ideas about how you might deal with a situation like this one? Take a moment to answer a few questions:

1. How would you describe John Leader's personality? Just think of a few adjectives you would use to characterise John as a colleague and as a supervisor.
2. How would you describe Ella Explorer's personality? Assign a few descriptors to Ella as a co-worker and as an employee.
3. In your opinion, where does the root of the problem lie?
4. Think back to the Johari Window I discussed in the introduction. Remember, the size of the **open** pane in the model is based on what people share about themselves as well as what others know about each person. What do you think the Johari Window between John Leader and Ella Explorer looks like?
5. What do you think John and Ella might do to increase the size of their open windowpane?
6. Consider the two characters in relation to the UZOD. Which zone does John occupy? How about Ella?
7. Think of a similar situation that may have happened to you. How did you deal with the problem? Could you use your own experience to advise John and Ella how to constructively resolve their arguments?

Enter the Admiral

After the Admiral spent time talking with the entire marketing team, both individually and as a group, he decided to accept SMS's CEO's plea for help. He began attending staff meetings and soon observed that the group had split nearly equally into two sides. It also became clear that the differences between John and Ella were the driving force behind the staff division and ensuing warfare between the two factions. After carefully noting his observations, the Admiral drew this Johari Window to represent the current state of affairs between John and Ella:

Open Area	Blind Area
Hidden Area	Unknown Area

As you can see, the Admiral perceived the **open** area between the two colleagues to be quite small, indicating a need for John and Ella to communicate more fully and clearly, disclosing their feelings and ideas about themselves and about each other. In addition, the **unknown** windowpane was quite large, which reflected the Admiral's opinion that there was room for self-discovery on both John's and Ella's parts and that each could undertake efforts to listen to and understand the perceptions of the other. To help them defuse the ticking time bomb that threatened to blow up SMS's marketing operations, the Admiral knew it was time to employ some psychometric tools to help these two individuals work towards increasing that open pane. He could see that widening the open area would benefit not only the two individuals but also the marketing team and thus the whole organisation. He believed that personality assessments could both locate the root of the problem and sow the seeds of a solution.

The 16PF

The Admiral began his evaluation by asking both John Leader and Ella Explorer to complete the **16PF** instrument. The 16PF, which I will describe in more detail in chapter 9, was developed by British psychologist Raymond B. Cattell in the late 1940s. The instrument has been updated over the years, and the current version is the product of more than fifty years of research. Cattell, who was deeply influenced by the horrors of World War II, became driven by a strong belief that deepening our understanding of human nature could bring humankind closer to solving its global political and economic problems. His definition of personality was behaviour based: "That which permits a prediction of what a person will do in a given situation."[5] Cattell used factor analysis – a statistical technique for identifying a small number of underlying *factors* that serve to describe characteristics of a larger set of variables – to come up with a list of *traits* that could predict all aspects of human behaviour. Thus, like most of the personality assessments the Admiral uses, the 16PF is a *trait-based* measure.

Cattell believed that personality and behaviour are determined by a set of underlying traits that everyone possesses but that are maintained at different levels within each person. The 16PF instrument assigns a person to a position along scales describing the sixteen factors Cattell believed were the sources of personality, including Warmth, Dominance, Privateness, and Openness to Change. Using a consistent model to describe the factors that comprise personality allows the interpreter to compare one person with another based on where each factor falls along a scale. Since traits are straightforward to measure, the 16PF interpreter can make reasonably accurate predictions of a given person's behavioural choices across a range of situations.

The Admiral chose the 16PF as a starting measure for three reasons. First, since the 16PF predicts people's future behaviour, it can be readily applied to team development problems. Second, the Admiral felt that the strife between John and Ella could be clearly represented by a map of the differences in where their characteristics fell along the 16PF scales. The measure offers a good global overview of how two people might reasonably be expected to interact with one another, and thus can point up areas in which their communications may be improved. Finally, the Admiral believed Ella had potential which her role at SMS left untapped, and as the 16PF is well suited to guiding both management and career development, he believed the measure would reveal ways in which the company could put her particular talents to mutually beneficial use.

John's Interpretive 16PF Report: John's 16PF report yielded several interesting results to inform the Admiral's analysis. First, in the Relating to Others section, someone with John's profile would lean towards being more

---

5   Raymond B. Cattell, *Personality: A Systematic, Theoretical, and Factual Study* (New York: McGraw-Hill, 1950).

task-focused than spontaneous and would tend towards seriousness rather than lively interaction. His results indicated he probably had a personal interest in colleagues that was likely an effort to seek the stimulation they provided, rather than a desire to form close emotional ties. In fact, although probably socially confident, a person with John's results would probably be less likely than most people to disclose personal information in the workplace. As regards Influence and Collaboration, the Admiral perceived that John might like to exert influence and express his opinions confidently yet might strongly prefer to lean on traditional values. A person with this profile seldom would be open to new ideas or sweeping change; instead, he would opt for well-tested methods with demonstrated consequences.

Also pivotal to the situation at hand were John's scores in the Structure and Flexibility area. The Admiral knew that people who scored as John did here probably found a structured, rule-driven environment important. They were unlikely to be spontaneous or impulsive but would carefully weigh the consequences of each decision prior to taking action. The Thinking Style section of John's profile was logical and objective, which indicated someone who kept his emotions out of the decision-making process. Based on the scores, someone like John might be highly focused and detail oriented, concerned about achieving observable results that met clearly defined guidelines.

The results indicated that a leader like John would have many strong points. His responses were consistent with high productivity and successful problem solving. A person with John's scores was likely loyal and committed to the firm, setting clear direction for employees while holding them to high standards. On the flip side, John's colleagues might perceive him as overly critical, inflexible, or dogmatic. John was more likely to seem rigid and exacting than trusting and warm. While probably a clear communicator himself, John might sometimes appear to dismiss others' ideas without due consideration.

Ella's Interpretive 16PF Report: One of the first relevant things the Admiral noticed about Ella's 16PF analysis appeared in the Influence and Collaboration section. He perceived that a person with Ella's profile would lean towards independence and openness to change. Ella's results indicated someone comfortable expressing her views, holding to them regardless of whether others agreed. An employee like Ella might have a tendency to personalise her disagreements, directing hostility away from the issue and towards the person expressing an opposing view. Ella was likely to perceive herself as unconventional and to view active pursuit of new experiences and unique solutions as important. Her responses in the Thinking Style portion of the 16PF also showed openness to new ideas and desire for active change. Ella's indicated approach to solving problems by questioning might lead her to notice new ways to improve a situation, yet it also might cause her to overlook or reject the positive aspects of existing methods. A person with Ella's profile tended towards abstract and conceptual thinking rather than embracing concrete and traditional methods.

The Admiral saw another point important to the matter at hand in Ella's score in the Structure and Flexibility area. He deduced that someone like Ella was probably highly imaginative, recognising an interconnection of ideas that might not be apparent to others. Such a person's level of abstract thinking might train her focus so much on her own ideas that her colleagues might believe she was not giving due attention to other, equally important issues.

Ella's scores showed that she probably brought many positive attributes to her work at SMS. She was likely to be objective and independent yet gregarious and confident when interacting with others. She would tend to approach work with enthusiasm and energy yet remain capable of exerting great focus on any project in which she was deeply invested. Ella's responses indicated that she might communicate assertively and approach challenges with optimism, adventurousness, and creativity. Her thought processes were probably abstract and her attitude towards change and self-improvement positive; she was likely to accept criticism well.

Mapping the Differences: Now the Admiral put the two 16PF charts together to map out the differences between John's and Ella's profiles. This exercise proved most revealing. John and Ella exhibited major differences across several of the 16PF factor scales. The combined 16PF chart on the following page paints a picture of those differences.

Initially the Admiral was less concerned with those items where John's and Ella's scores overlapped or were close together on the chart, because those would indicate areas where their communication styles were compatible. He was most interested in those places where the two personalities appeared to differ widely. Here are the points where John and Ella reported the greatest trait disparity: Serious (John) versus Lively (Ella); Traditional (John) versus Open to Change (Ella); Expedient (Ella) versus Rule-conscious (John); Grounded (John) versus Abstracted (Ella); and Reactive (John) versus Emotionally Stable (Ella). Looking at these differences, the Admiral made some interesting conclusions.

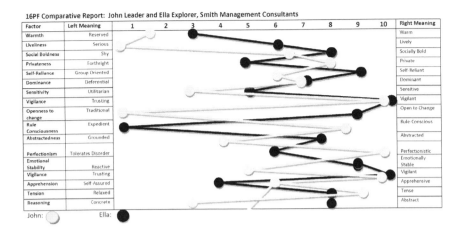

16PF Comparative Report: John Leader and Ella Explorer, Smith Management Consultants

Factor	Left Meaning	1	2	3	4	5	6	7	8	9	10	Right Meaning
Warmth	Reserved											Warm
Liveliness	Serious											Lively
Social Boldness	Shy											Socially Bold
Privateness	Forthright											Private
Self-Reliance	Group Oriented											Self-Reliant
Dominance	Deferential											Dominant
Sensitivity	Utilitarian											Sensitive
Vigilance	Trusting											Vigilant
Openness to change	Traditional											Open to Change
Rule Consciousness	Expedient											Rule-Conscious
Abstractedness	Grounded											Abstracted
Perfectionism	Tolerates Disorder											Perfectionistic
Emotional Stability	Reactive											Emotionally Stable
Vigilance	Trusting											Vigilant
Apprehension	Self-Assured											Apprehensive
Tension	Relaxed											Tense
Reasoning	Concrete											Abstract

John: ◯   Ella: ●

Although Ella's score on the Liveliness scale fell mid range, the Admiral thought this area was important because John's score fell at 1 on the scale, the extreme, showing a strong preference for Seriousness over Liveliness. Thus a person like John was likely to approach every task cautiously, thinking things through before speaking or taking action. He would tend to be persistent and self-disciplined, always considering the consequences of a decision with extreme care. His deliberate, methodical thinking process might cause him to appear pessimistic and resistant and also might lead to missed opportunities. Ella, in comparison, would probably exhibit a greater balance between spontaneity and self-restraint. While someone like Ella was sometimes enthusiastic and expressed herself confidently, in some situations she would tread more carefully to remain in control of how she came across to others.

The Admiral was also quite interested in the two people's disparity on the Openness to Change scale. Here, he believed, lay the root of the current problem, the underlying cause of the war. John's extreme position showed that he might place high value on traditional ideas, established methods, and maintenance of the status quo. Ella's natural tendency to notice how things might be changed and her enthusiasm for new ideas and experiences were sure to clash with John's caution. John's indicated need for proof that change would work before trying something new was likely to seem inflexible and stodgy to an employee like Ella, whose ideas John probably perceived as maverick and chancy.

The remaining data points on the 16PF map rounded out the Admiral's assessment of the situation. He saw that John would tend to prefer following an established set of rules to the letter, while a person like Ella would choose an expedient route towards task accomplishment regardless of those rules. John's profile indicated someone grounded in down-to-earth details and practicality; in contrast, Ella's scores were consistent with the pursuit of abstract theories and creative solutions. John was likely to deal with ups and downs calmly in the moment, while Ella might take more initiative to solve problems proactively.

But That Wasn't Enough: Many interpreters would stop here and simply use what they'd learned through the 16PF comparison to drive their recommendations. Not the Admiral. He recognised that no test is perfect. Results on a single measure will be greatly enhanced when interpreted in the context of other measures, direct observation, and the individuals' self-perceptions and their perceptions of each other. The Admiral's style was always to start with a global personality measure and then to use supplemental psychometric tools to home in on factors more specific to the individual case.

The MSCEIT

In this situation the Admiral saw that while the 16PF drew an excellent overall picture of personality differences, more information about communication skill and emotional motivation would give him a much clearer notion of how John and Ella could work together to widen that open pane of the Johari Window.

The Admiral decided to take a look at a concept known as *emotional intelligence*. He felt that John and Ella, who diverged in areas of creativity, impulsivity, and tradition, might vary significantly in emotional perception and application. Analysing these differences might turn up ways to negotiate their conflict and help them reach a compromise on a model for change.

For this purpose the Admiral turned to a measure called the **Mayer-Salovey-Caruso Emotional Intelligence Test (MSCEIT)**. This tool, named for the three psychologists who developed it, assesses a person's ability across four domains: *recognising, using, understanding,* and *managing* emotions. It's a performance test – that is, it asks takers to solve emotional problems and measures their skill at doing so. People who take the MSCEIT complete two tasks for each of the four domains. Then they're presented with a score for each domain and finally a total MSCEIT score (Total EIQ).

The Admiral asked John and Ella to complete the test independently. He calculated their scores. The following tables present each person's MSCEIT results.

John's MSCEIT scores:

	DEVELOP	IMPROVE	COMPETENT	PROFICIENT	EXPERT
TOTAL EIQ 94					
RECOGNIZING 103					
USING 89					
UNDERSTANDING 81					
MANAGING 119					

Ella's MSCEIT scores:

	DEVELOP	IMPROVE	COMPETENT	PROFICIENT	EXPERT
TOTAL EIQ 125					
RECOGNIZING 115					
USING 108					
UNDERSTANDING 135					
MANAGING 105					

Again, the exercise was more than telling to the Admiral's trained eye. He briefly summarised their test results as follows.

John: John's Total EIQ fell within the *Competent* range, indicating that emotions were probably a resource to him but that development might be useful in certain areas. He exhibited basic competence in his emotional read of himself, people, and the environment; usually he picked up important clues about how others were feeling, but at times he might miss those cues. John might be closed to emotional information when making a decision or solving problems. He might have a limited emotional vocabulary and might find predicting people's emotional responses to a given situation difficult. Understanding how emotions are likely to change and progress over time may have tended to escape John, at least in part; in short, he might often miss the point. John's particular strength with emotions might lie in his ability to manage them. The Admiral found it interesting that John's score was *Proficient* in the managing domain, showing that he was probably open to emotions and could choose effective emotional management strategies across a variety of situations. He could achieve goals by effectively integrating his emotions with his thoughts, behaviours, and each situation.

Ella: Ella's overall MSCEIT score indicated *Expertise*. Emotions were a decided resource to someone with her profile, and she probably could trust those skills with confidence. However, the Admiral thought some fine-tuning might be useful along the way. Ella was likely to pay appropriate attention to the emotions of others and read them accurately. Her scores indicated that she could probably incorporate emotional information into her decisions and solutions and shift her own emotions in order to capitalise on their effects; her profile indicated capability to seize inspiration and motivate others, sometimes getting breakthrough ideas. Ella was likely highly skilled at understanding emotions behind complex feelings and predicting people's emotional responses to events. Someone like Ella usually can achieve a reasonably good emotional balance, with some exceptions – meaning at times she might not choose emotional strategies that prove to be effective.

The white flag of truce

It was time for the Admiral to take what he had discovered and put his knowledge into practice. First he met with Ella and John separately to discuss and interpret their individual scores on the two measures. Then at last he brought the two together under the white flag of truce, to parley for peace.

"I've talked with each of you about your 16PF and MSCEIT measures," the Admiral began. "Now it's time to talk about your potential differences, strengths, and areas where communication might improve. Before we start, I want to remind you that when you score differently on a personality measure, it doesn't mean one of you is better or worse than the other. It just means you're different. Our society is conditioned to think that a high number on a scale is better than a low number. Please throw those preconceptions out the window for this discussion. There are no rights or wrongs in personality; each style has its advantages and disadvantages.

"John," the Admiral continued, "someone with scores like yours is likely to be a strong leader who enjoys exerting influence. That person will probably make objective, logical decisions. Your responses indicate a tendency towards being detail oriented and focused and getting a lot of work done. Generally people with this profile will leave emotions out of decisions and be good at managing and controlling both their own emotions and other people's. Your scores show that you might like to organise, plan ahead, and be well prepared for contingencies. Do any of those analyses match your own beliefs about yourself?"

"Yes, pretty well," replied John. "I sometimes think my employees let their emotions get in the way of doing good work. I like to have a strong set of guidelines in place for everyone to follow, which takes emotion out of the equation."

"A person with scores like yours often likes to be rule driven," said the Admiral. "But blocking out emotions doesn't always serve leadership well. It might help you to think of emotions as another data source – just like any set of facts you have at your disposal. Emotions affect your problem-solving skills and your perceptions of situations, and they help you empathise with others.

"Based on the measures and my discussions with your colleagues, I would guess that empathy might be an area where you could improve. People sometimes view you as cold and inflexible. Your co-workers think you seldom seem open to new ideas, and at times you may jump in too quickly to criticise or correct your staff."

"I'm working on exercising more patience," said John. "I think sometimes I come off as intimidating when I'm really just trying to help."

"That's good," said the Admiral. "Someone like you probably recognises other people's emotions easily, but it might help you to work towards seeing a situation from another person's perspective and truly feeling what they're feeling. Going back to emotions as data, you might focus on being more open to emotions at work. I'm talking about your moods as well as those of other people here. Trying to suppress emotion doesn't work – so let yourself feel whatever you feel, and let others do the same. That doesn't mean you have to act on emotions. Just use them as another source of information."

Now the Admiral turned to Ella. "Ella, your scores are consistent with someone who is confident and at ease with expressing opinions," he said. "A person with your profile usually likes to pursue new ideas that challenge the status quo and looks for ways to make things work better. Someone like you might be likely to strike a good balance between being careful and taking risks. A person with your scores often brings a lot of energy and enthusiasm to the workplace and carries a good view of the big picture. Does that sound like you at all?"

"Yes," said Ella, "but I've been frustrated lately because I haven't been allowed to pursue my ideas – even though I know they would work."

"Maybe to others it seems like you're trying to circumvent the rules, pushing your ideas at any cost. You may appear disruptive or rebellious. You might have a hard time trusting people, and people who respond like you don't always pay attention to negative feedback."

"That's possible," Ella admitted. "I like to see my labours yield fruit, and all the rules around here seem to get in the way. Plus, I don't like to be criticised in public."

"But if you disregard negative input, you may miss a learning opportunity," said the Admiral. "John and Ella," he continued, "you have different personalities, but that just means you have strengths that complement each other. If you learn to work together in harmony, you will create a balanced force that will be much stronger than either of you alone. John, you seem to value tradition and want to see concrete proof that a strategy will work before you act on it. Ella, you apparently value new ideas and seek unconventional paths to a goal. I believe this is the crux of the battle the two of you are fighting.

"Ella's evident abstract thinking skills give her a broad view of the future and the ability to conceptualise problems in unique ways. John's thinking probably leans towards the concrete, so his concern is usually the bottom line. Let's try to figure out how you can balance these two strengths and find a solution."

Moving into the UZOD: The Admiral showed John and Ella the diagram illustrating the Uncomfortable Zone of Debate. He explained how placement on the chart depended on the level of agreement between parties and how productivity and results would suffer based on distance from the optimal centre zone. "Ella, where do you think John is on this chart?" asked the Admiral.

"In Zone B," replied Ella. "He won't listen to any ideas different from his own."

"John," the Admiral said, "Where do you think Ella falls on the chart?"

John thought for a moment. "Ella's in Zone B too," he said. "She refuses to do things my way, and she insists on pushing her ideas at meetings even though they don't meet my guidelines."

"Okay," said the Admiral. "I agree with both of you. You're stuck in Zone B, where you disagree with every idea the other has. You've become more focused on winning the battle than on your company's success. And because John's the official leader and Ella is perceived as a leader by her peers, you're encouraging the rest of the marketing staff to remain in Zone B too.

"I've showed you tools that help demonstrate how the two of you are different. What could you do to understand and accept your differences?"

"I just wish John could accept that my ideas have value," said Ella.

"Acceptance is a powerful word," said the Admiral, "because it implies a willingness to be open. John, you seem to lean towards perfectionism, so you probably have a tough time letting yourself make mistakes. But self-acceptance, giving yourself the freedom to make mistakes and have a unique point of view, helps you accept others. Ella, acceptance doesn't mean you have to adopt another person's point of view. It means you grant others the right to have opinions different from your own. I think you both could become more accepting of each other's ideas, and that's how you move into the UZOD, where you'll get your best work done.

"Let's try something. Ella, what are the five qualities you appreciate most in John?"

It was Ella's turn to think. "John seems really confident speaking in a group," she said finally. "I've always been amazed by his great relationships with customers. He holds people accountable, but he meets his own standards. He has a lot of integrity. And he's focused."

"John, what are the five things you most appreciate about Ella?"

"She's got a huge amount of energy," replied John. "And she's outgoing; almost everyone seems to like Ella. She produces high-quality work. If she says she's going to do something, she almost always does it."

"Following through on a promise is a good description of integrity," said the Admiral. "It's interesting that each of you perceives integrity in the other. Knowing you can count on someone's integrity is a path to building trust.

"I'd like you both to look at your 16PF maps again," the Admiral continued. "This time, instead of focusing on the areas where you differ, look for places where your scores are close together."

"Wow," Ella observed, "we're both at 10 on Vigilance."

"Right," said the Admiral. "You both have scores of people who tend to be vigilant and find it hard to trust others. You're likely to question other people's intentions, and you might often feel that you're being treated unfairly.

"Going into the UZOD will require that you learn to trust each other. Now that you know some things you appreciate about one another, how could you make time – let's say, five minutes a day – when you each just listen to one another, with interest and without interruption?"

John and Ella sat silently for a moment, thinking. John was the first to respond.

"Maybe I could go with Ella to her business networking meetings," he said. "It's about a ten-minute drive. On the way, she could tell me her thoughts about prospective clients who attend and how we need to approach them."

"I like the idea of you two working on a project together," said the Admiral. "That would be a good way to combine your strengths and build trust. But, John, the networking meetings are one of your strategies, something you've asked Ella to do for you. What one thing are you prepared to offer Ella in return?"

John drew a blank. "I have an idea," said Ella. "How about if I teach John how to use one of the social media platforms, like, say, Facebook? Then he might be able to see firsthand how we could use it to the company's advantage."

"John, what do you think?" the Admiral asked.

"I probably could do that," said John, "as long as it wouldn't take too much time. It's hard to hear that people think I'm inflexible, and I guess I *have* fallen a little behind the times when it comes to new media."

"Good," said the Admiral. "I think you've made a start. If you spend some time working one-on-one with each other, you'll learn more about each other's thought processes. This is a creative way to compromise and to accept that each of you is a valuable colleague with good ideas.

"As you try this, your goal is not to agree on everything – that would put you into Zone A. Instead, when you do disagree, try to trust each other enough to bring the disagreement up, and talk it over. Remember that trust doesn't come easily to either of you. Start by spending five minutes a day just listening to the other person with an open mind. And remember, too, that each of you recognises integrity in the other. That may help you build trust and confidence."

This discussion formed the beginnings of a solution. John and Ella agreed to work together on their two projects: the business network and Facebook. They planned to spend a small amount of time – one to two hours per week – on each project. Both John and Ella had found their results on the psychometric instruments eye-opening, especially in learning how they were viewed by the other. They took the assessments and the Admiral's interpretation to heart. Both would think carefully in the weeks to come about how their words and actions might be perceived by others.

The Admiral had one more task before moving on to his next assignment: scheduling a follow-up session. "Let's set a time about two months from now," he said, "when we can check in to see how your solution is progressing. It's important to regroup occasionally and talk about how things are going, with an objective third party to serve as a sounding board. If you have ideas between now and then, jot them down. We can use them as a starting place for getting into the UZOD."

Now what do you think?

With the Admiral's help, John and Ella were able to reach a compromise. Instead of one side or the other winning the war, they came up with a third alternative to their dilemma – one that gave both of them a small piece of what they wanted. How do you think the solution will work?

Are you beginning to see how psychometric tools can help people understand and resolve a problem? Did you feel surprised by any of the results generated by the two assessments the Admiral used? How do you think your own assessment would have looked on either of the two measures? I hope it has become evident that combining multiple tests yields a much richer, more supportive information set – both to describe the participants' possible qualities and to illuminate a possible path to resolution – than relying upon one measure alone.

What do you think John and Ella's Johari Window looks like now? Where might they fall on the UZOD chart? Now think back to a similar situation you've encountered with your colleagues. Spend a few minutes thinking about a possible solution you might have reached that looks something like John and Ella's.

Scenario II: Don't Make Waves

> *The hardest battle you're ever going to fight is the battle just to be you.* ~**Leo F. Buscaglia**

Jane Sample bustled into the Mammoth Insurance offices early that Thursday morning, heading straight to the espresso bar for a double latté.

Rodney Rivers was sitting in a corner, reading the *Daily Union* on his tablet computer. "Morning, Rodney!" called Jane. "Is there any news worth hearing?"

"Not really," replied Rodney. "Just looking at the Chelsea box score."

"Oh!" said Jane. "I didn't know you were a sports fan. But now that I think about it, your son is a football player, isn't he?"

"Yes," Rodney responded. "Johnny's first goaltender for his school team."

"That's just wonderful," said Jane. "It's so important for our children to stay active. You must be very proud of him. Well, I must get to work. I'll see you in the telecomm meeting later?" said Jane. "Ciao!"

"Sure," Rodney said. "Have a good one." Watching Jane walk briskly towards the elevators, he wondered – not for the first time – how she had gotten where she was within the Mammoth ranks. Six years ago Jane Sample had been just a claims representative, wearing a headset and fielding calls inside a nondescript cubicle. Now she managed the whole Claims Centre. She'd made lots of social contacts, Rodney speculated; certainly she was a nice, personable woman. People liked her. And she was unlikely to make waves – which probably carried more weight with the powers that be than her managerial skills ever would.

"Oh, well," Rodney sighed to himself. "If we can just get her to decide on a telecomm system, I shouldn't have to deal with her much longer." It had been nearly four months since Rodney had been designated project manager of the Claims Centre telecommunications system upgrade. In that time, the Claims Department had gone round at least three times trying to settle on a list of features for the new system. Each time the task had landed on Jane Sample's desk, and there it had stalled. She'd been bubbling over with ideas at the outset, but every time she was asked to follow up on choosing the details, nothing seemed to get done. Now Rodney's own boss was breathing down his neck to finish the upgrade so he could tackle the pile of work backlogged on the telecomm list. Well, maybe today was the day Jane would get her act together and make some decisions. Rodney certainly hoped so.

En route to her private office on the Claims Centre floor, Jane stopped at Rebecca Ames's desk. Rebecca was Jane's administrative assistant extraordinaire – a capable young woman with a calm demeanour and a ready smile.

"Hello, Rebecca," said Jane. "How are you coming along with polling the Claims Centre staff for user requirements on the new telecomm system?"

Rebecca looked up. "Good morning," she said. "I'm sorry; I thought I gave you the user requirements list two days ago."

"I gave it back to you, remember?" replied Jane. "I asked you to include Valerie Thomas and her staff in the poll." Valerie was VP for operations and Jane's boss. Rebecca assumed Jane wanted Valerie included for political rather than practical reasons; the Operations Department was already on Mammoth's executive telecomm network. "All right," she responded. "I'll try to have it back to you this afternoon. In the meantime, though, I have a question for you. What level of web conferencing capability will you need the system to have?"

"Hmm," said Jane, vaguely. "That's not really my area. Oh, I have an idea: why don't you ask Human Resources about that? They might be able to flesh out the details."

An hour later, Rebecca had a moment to pop by HR, where she was greeted with surprise and a tinge of annoyance. "We're happy with the web conferencing we have now," she was told. "So we'll be fine as long as we have at least that level. You really should ask Jane Sample. She's the one who may need to expand web conferencing services, in order to conduct webinars and so forth."

Rebecca nodded her thanks. Jane was not in her office, so Rebecca headed back to her desk. Late in the morning she caught up with Jane, back at the coffee bar for reinforcements. "Oh, by the way," Rebecca said, "HR says all they need is the web conferencing capability we have now, so the ball's back in your court."

Jane hemmed again. "I'm really not familiar with that area. Why don't you research what's available and bring a list to one of our meetings? Let's say, by two weeks from today."

By the telecomm meeting that afternoon, Rebecca had been unable to reach Operations for input, but she had brought a partial features list to get the ball rolling. "Here it is," she said, handing the list to Jane. "I gathered input from everyone in the call centre, including the daytime and night-shift supervisors and all the claims administrators; I'll add the operations staff as soon as I can."

"I'll need some time to digest this," said Jane, scanning down the page. "There's a lot of information here. But I can approve a couple of things right now. I know we'll need three-way conference calling, and I'm sure we'll need computer networking so we can send faxes through the system things like that."

"That's a step in the right direction," said Rodney. "But I need to know everything you want from your telecommunications system, and soon. Then I can suggest a few alternatives so we can move forwards."

"Well, as I said, I need some time to prioritise this list," said Jane. "But in the meantime, why don't you tell me what the Telecomm Department can do?"

Rodney was stunned. How did they get back to square one? He'd tried very hard to clarify the process from the outset: Jane would give him the user requirements; he would identify three systems that met those needs best; Jane would choose a system; he would install it. Mission accomplished. As a project manager, he had never worked with anyone so wishy-washy. When, if ever, was Jane going to make up her mind?

"We should continue to have these weekly meetings," said Jane as the meeting moved towards adjournment. "It's so important for us to have a forum where we can share ideas. I feel very optimistic that we'll be able to work together to get an excellent new telecomm system in place."

Neither Rebecca nor Rodney shared Jane's enthusiasm. Both of them left the meeting feeling they were no further along than before the hour began. Jane apparently loved meetings; she insisted on holding several each week, and she spent a good deal of time planning how to facilitate discussion at each conference. Yet even the most productive discussions Jane led seemed to fall apart when it came to the implementation stage. As soon as she became responsible for handling the details of follow-through, Jane lost interest.

Unlike Rebecca and Rodney, Jane returned to her office after the meeting quite satisfied. She left the list of user requirements on a stack of similar papers, promptly forgot about it, and went to the break room to join a warm, lively conversation with some other colleagues about the antics of their children and grandchildren.

Two weeks later, Rebecca came to the meeting armed with her research on web conferencing features. "What's this?" asked Jane. "I thought we decided we didn't need any more web conferencing capabilities than the current system provides. Rebecca, you're usually so good about talking things over with me. You really should have consulted me before you started doing all this research."

Rebecca said nothing, holding her feelings inside. Of course she remembered Jane's specific request to complete the web conferencing research. But experience told her that Jane either honestly didn't remember or would deny it upon confrontation.

Likewise, Rodney had drawn up information about two systems that supported three-way conference calls and computer networking. "Why did you focus on these?" asked Jane.

"You approved those features at our meeting two weeks ago," said Rodney.

"Oh, I'm sorry," said Jane. "I've changed my mind. I discussed it with the call centre leads, and we envision needing more robust conference calling than just three-way. We also might have to network with satellite offices. I'll have to consider those along with the web conferencing features.

"I can't choose now," Jane continued. "We're going to need more user feedback. I asked Valerie's assistant to collect user requirements from the ops staff, Rebecca, since you obviously didn't have time."

Rebecca said nothing. At adjournment she went back to her desk shaking her head, confused and frustrated. She'd undertaken the task of helping Jane with the telecomm system assignment because she wanted to develop the decision-making skills she would need to move into management one day. Then she'd spent five months watching Jane avoid any decisions at all. Now Jane had taken the task away from Rebecca and given it to the operations assistant. It felt like a slap in the face.

For Rodney, today's meeting was the last straw. "I can't work with Jane Sample anymore," he told his boss back in the telecomm office. "We'll never get a system in place at this rate. It's making me look bad. It's making the whole Telecomm Department look bad."

Rodney's boss agreed, and his next move was to pay a visit to Valerie Thomas. Jane Sample's indecisiveness finally had sparked a declaration of war.

After he left her office, Valerie heaved a deep sigh. Mentally chalking up another mark on a growing list of complaints about Jane Sample's management expertise, she picked up the phone and called Mammoth Insurance's on-call consultant for personnel issues: none other than the Admiral.

What do *you* think?

What do you believe may be happening at Mammoth Insurance? Jane Sample got her management job by not making waves. Now her indecision is getting in the way of progress and closure. Here are some questions to consider:

1. How would you describe Jane Sample's personality?
2. What aspects of Jane's personality are holding up the telecomm project?

3. What does the Johari Window look like in the Mammoth Insurance telecomm project group?
4. Where does Jane fall on the UZOD chart?
5. What steps could Valerie take as Jane's supervisor to help resolve the issues? What steps should Jane take?
6. Have you encountered a situation like this one? Were you in Jane's position or one of her colleagues'? What did you do, and how well did it work?

The first step

Valerie called Jane Sample into her office and asked the Admiral to be present. "Jane, this is the Admiral," Valerie began tactfully. "I've asked him to help us work through an issue that's arisen.

"I've just spoken with Rodney Rivers and his supervisor," she continued. "The Telecommunications Department has a large backlog of requests, and they really need to finish your system upgrade so they can get moving on other tasks. Rodney has become quite frustrated with progress on the project, and both he and his supervisor seem convinced that the problem lies at your door.

"I prefer to listen to everyone's opinion before I take steps. Jane, you're an excellent communicator, so maybe you can help me understand why the telecomm project is not yet complete."

"I've had lots of good ideas," said Jane defensively. "I just need time to make sure I get input from everyone who's important, everyone who will be using the system.

"I thought I was the project leader," continued Jane. "Shouldn't I be the one who sets the timeline?"

"As Claims Centre manager, you're the person with most interest in the project's success," said Valerie. "But you also need to consider how your actions affect your colleagues and other departments in the company." She turned to the Admiral. "Admiral, how can we move towards closure on this?"

"Let me ask Jane a question," said the Admiral. "Jane, what resources do you need to help you make final decisions on the telecomm features? By 'resources,' I mean external things like time and information, but I also mean internal aspects – like self-confidence or courage."

Jane pondered his question. "Like I said, I have a lot of very good ideas," she said. "When I envision the system I want, I get really excited. But when I have to consider each little detail, I get bogged down."

"I think there are measurements that might help us work through this issue," the Admiral said. "Jane, would you be willing to fill out a couple of questionnaires?"

Jane agreed, and in the ensuing days, the Admiral chose his psychometric strategies and got to work.

The Johari Window

Before choosing his measures, the Admiral used his current knowledge about the problem to draw a Johari Window for Mammoth Insurance. According to his assessment, the window looked like this:

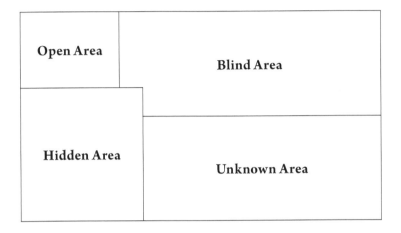

The MBTI

The Admiral decided to begin by finding out what Jane's profile looked like on the Myers-Briggs Type Indicator (MBTI). This measure is probably the best known personality metric available and has been widely applied in the workplace. The Admiral chose the MBTI because the tool lends itself well to helping people develop their leadership styles, improve communication, and manage change and stress.

I will detail the MBTI and its history in chapter 9. For now, I will say that the measure has a rather different background than other personality instruments. While based on the personality theories of the great psychologist Carl Jung, the model was developed by two non-psychologists: Katharine Briggs and Isabel Myers. Their goal was to translate Jung's powerful ideas into a form that as many people as possible could use. More than twenty years of research have gone into developing and updating the MBTI questionnaire.

The MBTI assesses people's *preferences* for how they process information and how they behave, and uses the preferences to identify a person's *type*. The measure identifies eight preferences; everyone exercises all eight but in different proportions. The preferences are not the same as abilities or skills. All preferences are equally valuable and important, and one personality type is not better or worse than another. Since Myers and Briggs believed people are the best judges of their own types, the MBTI is an *indicator*, not a *test*. It's meant to open up possibilities, not to limit individuals.

Upon completion of the MBTI, the Admiral learned that Jane's responses indicated the MBTI type known as **ENFP**. Thus her preferences were Extraversion (E) over Introversion; Intuition (N) over Sensing; Feeling (F) over Thinking; and Perceiving (P) over Judging.

ENFPs tend to be identity-seeking idealists. The Admiral's knowledge told him that a person of Jane's MBTI profile was likely to act as a facilitator, motivator, or energiser in her role as a manager. A person of this type would feel compelled to be personal in her relationships. She was likely to be uniquely capable to bring people together in cooperation, maintaining high morale and a positive outlook. But if difficult circumstances caused her to become estranged from herself or others, an ENFP might feel overwhelmed by negative feelings, which would paralyse her will.

An ENFP was likely to enjoy talking with others and prone to bubbly conversation. Her enthusiasm could be boundless when she was excited about a project. But if a task became routine, she was likely to lose interest. Painstaking detail and follow-through over time would make her restless. She might drop a project when she became excited about a new possibility and would remain oblivious to monotonous detail-oriented tasks.

The FIRO-B business profile

As always, the Admiral did not stop with his first measure. He wanted to achieve a balance of information to inform his solution. So he chose to complete a FIRO-B Business Leadership Report for Jane Sample.

The Fundamental Interpersonal Relations Orientation-Behaviour (FIRO-B) is a tool for improving workplace relationships and individual effectiveness. The FIRO-B was the 1958 brainchild of William Schutz, who based his theory on the work of three major psychoanalysts: Carl Jung, Alfred Adler, and Sigmund Freud. Schutz's work was based on the idea that people need people. He identified three ways in which people need each other, showing that everyone has interpersonal needs in the areas of Inclusion, Control, and Affection. Interpersonal needs are as fundamental to humans as the need for food, water, or shelter, but the amount of contact we need differs from person to person.

The Admiral chose this measure because he thought it might shed light on how Jane Sample was likely to behave in relation to her co-workers and might point up some development areas for her as a department leader which could help solve the problem at hand. Raising an individual's awareness of his or her own interpersonal needs can open up new choices and opportunities to develop new strategies.

The three areas of interpersonal need on the FIRO-B are explained thus:

- *Inclusion*: This need indicates how much you generally include other people in your life and how much attention, contact, and recognition you want from others.
- *Control*: This need indicates how much influence and responsibility you want and how much you want others to lead and influence you.
- *Affection*: This need indicates how close and warm you are with others and how close and warm you want others to be with you.

The FIRO-B further splits these three needs into two dimensions: expressed versus wanted Behaviour. *Expressed* behaviour is the extent to which a person prefers to initiate behaviour, how the person actually behaves, and how comfortable the person feels when engaging in behaviours associated with the three need areas. *Wanted* behaviour is the level of behaviour the person would like to receive from others.

Upon completion of the FIRO-B business profile, compilation of Jane Sample's scores on expressed needs looked like this:

Need	Category	Percentile Score
Expressed Involvement	High	85
Expressed Influence	High	84
Expressed Connection	High	89
Total Expressed Needs	High	93

And Jane's scores describing her wanted needs looked like this:

Need	Category	Percentile Score
Wanted Involvement	High	79
Wanted Influence	High	93
Wanted Connection	Low	10
Total Wanted Needs	High	65

After compiling the measures, the Admiral set up a meeting with Jane. He shared the results of her assessments and offered his evaluation.

"Jane," said the Admiral, "someone with a personality profile like yours is likely to have a lot of strengths when it comes to relating to colleagues. Your scores are consistent with someone who prides herself on being a team player and who does her best work when allowed the chance to collaborate with others. An ENFP usually feels comfortable communicating opinions and enjoys working in groups and taking a leadership role in public situations. Your colleagues have told me that you have a large network and that you spend more time and energy interacting with co-workers than working independently on your own projects. Does what I've described as an interpretation of your personality scores ring true for you?"

"Yes," replied Jane. "I do enjoy working with others, and I like to organise and plan meetings where we brainstorm ideas."

"You might also face some challenges in this area," continued the Admiral. "Someone with your scores may feel pulled in a lot of different directions and become overwhelmed at times. You might be likely to get excited about new possibilities but dislike mundane details. When an ENFP is faced with a task that seems monotonous, she might sometimes drop the ball. A person like you might spend a lot of time socializing and forget to focus on efficient, task-oriented work. You might tend to revisit issues over and over, continuing to talk about them without making a decision. Even when an ENFP *does* make a decision, it may not be clear to others. I believe that might be happening with your telecommunications upgrade.

"Let me ask you a question," the Admiral said. "What support do you need to make a final decision about the features of your telecomm system?"

"I need input from everyone who will be using the system," Jane responded.

"Who can give you that information?"

Jane thought briefly. "I guess I have it already," she said reluctantly.

"Jane, what do you think is really getting in the way of your decision?"

"I want to be absolutely sure everyone is happy," said Jane.

"That's an important realisation," said the Admiral. "First, your response indicates to me that you must care very deeply about the needs of others. You're intuitive and open to suggestion. But you may, in fact, be collecting *too much* input from your colleagues, which is distracting you from the issue at hand. Every new piece of information changes your whole perspective and sends you back to square one.

"Second, you're telling me that you're trying to make a perfect decision. Sometimes leaders who strive for perfection become so afraid of making a wrong choice that they don't make any decision at all.

"Your need to form strong connections in the workplace usually is a good thing because collaboration and teamwork are important tools for a good leader to employ. But that need can work against you too. Have you ever heard the phrase, 'It's lonely at the top'?"

"Yes," said Jane. "That means a manager can't expect to be friends with subordinates."

"To me, it also means that someone in a leadership role can't aim to please everyone. If you're too concerned about not making waves, nothing will ever get done. One stretch you could usefully make is to devote more private time towards reviewing tasks and making decisions. It might also help if you learned to facilitate meetings so they're more efficient both for yourself and for others.

"Do you think you could spend half an hour out of each workday alone in your office reviewing your workload and setting priorities?"

"Yes, I could do that," said Jane. "As long as I still have the chance to bounce ideas off my colleagues."

"It's productive for you to continue doing that," said the Admiral. "Here's another idea: how about if you took a seminar on how to plan and facilitate effective meetings?"

"I could probably improve in that area," Jane admitted. "Yes, I could take a class, and I might enjoy that."

This discussion resulted in the germ of a solution to the problems at Mammoth Insurance. With the Admiral's guidance, Jane went through the list of user features and classified each item as "must have", "preferred but not essential", or "desired but could do without". Together they listed Jane's decisions in order of priority. Jane agreed to spend at least half an hour per day in solitude prioritising tasks and to make at least one decision each day, no matter how small. She formed a plan to find a class in meeting facilitation that she could attend to improve those skills. She and the Admiral set a time two months in the future to review Jane's progress and accomplishments.

These two scenarios were meant to illustrate The Battle of Leadership and how psychometric personality measures can help wave the flag of truce and guide the involved parties towards alliance and peace. What role do you think the personality indicators played in helping the Admiral solve these issues? How well do you think their strategies will work, and what ideas have you formed for alternative solutions? Are you beginning to observe behaviours in these fictional characters that you recognise in yourself or your colleagues? I hope you're getting the idea that personality measurement might be able to aid you in solving your own workplace problems.

The leaders in these two scenarios are just people, each with their own foibles and facing their individual roadblocks. But all are working to develop the qualities that may eventually make them great leaders. And they're doing so by choice, not because they've been handed an edict. They have the potential to be great people contributing to the greatness of their organisations.

The Battle of Leadership is quite common; who among us has never had occasion to complain about his or her boss or supervisor? But such a fight is never insurmountable, and understanding the personalities involved can make a huge difference. Next I will turn to another battle that's widespread in our society: the Battle of Career.

CHAPTER II

What's the difference between a *job* and a *career*? Both involve getting up every day and going to a workplace, whether it be a corporate high-rise, laboratory, warehouse, soccer pitch, or computer in a home office.

The real difference lies in the mind of the worker: it's about how you perceive your work and how much you like doing it. A job holder is focused on the security of getting a steady pay cheque. All she needs to do is the minimum to keep that pay cheque coming: show up on time, complete assigned tasks, get along with boss and co-workers. One might take a job to earn money for a specific purpose, such as completing school, buying a car, travelling, or supporting a family. Once the original purpose is accomplished, the need for the job might even go away.

A career builder, on the other hand, is more concerned with doing work out of love, dedication, or devotion to a task or pursuit. One on a career path is more willing to take risks. He will build networks, create unique opportunities, and strategise innovatively to increase his sense of job satisfaction.

What happens when you end up in an unfulfilling job with no easy way out – the phenomenon known as the *dead-end job*? Most of us think of a dead-end job as one in which there is little or no chance of being promoted into a position with higher pay or increased responsibility. Implicitly the term calls up an image of menial tasks, long hours, and low pay. But with just a tweak of attitude, a Walmart greeter might have a rewarding career, or an internationally known psychiatrist might feel stuck in the drudgery of a job. Career satisfaction is not all about the pay.

When people feel no passion for their work – or the companies for which they work – and their personal goals are out of alignment with the company's mission, that's a good sign that they're in a dead-end job. It's easy to see how personality comes into play here. A job might not be a good fit for a given personality type, or a certain personality might not be a good fit for a position. Becoming satisfied in our jobs requires three things: (1) *ability* to complete the work successfully, (2) a *personality* reasonably well suited to the tasks, and (3) *motivation* to achieve success in the position. If one or more of these requirements is missing, we are likely to feel dissatisfied in our work.

Take a look at the following matrix, which illustrates the two dimensions that are important for achieving job success:

- **Suitability** describes how well the person fits within a given environment. Personality and motivation have a major impact on one's suitability, or fit.
- **Eligibility** describes the person's skills, abilities, and knowledge relevant to the position.

Figure 3 – Suitability/Eligibility Model
©Belbin, R. Meredith. Reproduced by kind
permission of Belbin Associates—www.belbin.com.

Where a person falls on the above matrix will help determine his or her level of job satisfaction. The following chart illustrates a typical person's satisfaction levels as that person progresses through time at a particular job. Having a "perfect" career doesn't mean that we will never find ourselves in a low satisfaction area, as illustrated by the low points on the chart.

Figure 4 – Career Satisfaction Chart

Think of a person's career moving through the above cycles. You start at A0 and move to B0; then go down to C0; then go up to A1 and into the next cycle. What is different for individuals is the slope and length of the lines. For example, for some people, moving from C0 to A1 happens very quickly; for others, the process might be very slow, even taking many years. It's important to accept that we all go through such cycles. What is essential to a successful career is that the overall trend should continue *upwards* over a period of time:

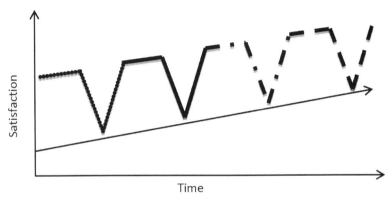

Figure 5 - Career Satisfaction Trending Up

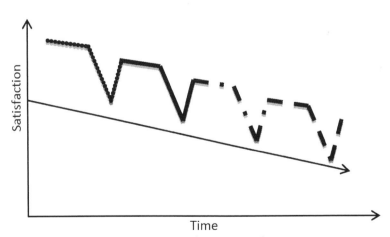

Figure 6 - Career Satisfaction Trending Down

It is important that we develop career strategies to help us rise up from a down cycle so we end up higher than when the fall began, as illustrated in the next figure:

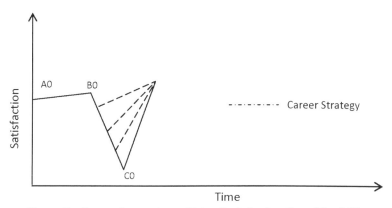

Figure 7 - Career Strategies to Bring Satisfaction Trend Back Up

This chapter deals with the Battle of Career, a battle often fought within a single person's psyche. Here I'll illustrate how to recognise one's suitability and eligibility for various careers using psychometric measures and how to translate that interpretation into career strategies that keep one's career satisfaction trending upwards over time.

Scenario: Breaking Out of the Box

Achievement seems to be connected with action. Successful men and women keep moving. They make mistakes, but they don't quit. ~**Conrad Hilton**

With ordinary talent and extraordinary perseverance, all things are attainable. ~**Thomas Foxwell Buxton**

Jacob Whiteside was sitting in his cubicle at Incisive Market Research Ltd., where he had been spending the majority of his waking hours for nearly three years. Wearing a hands-free phone headset, Jacob stared at the computer screen before him where his interviewing task of the day appeared. He sighed, got out a notepad, and prepared to make his first call.

At age twenty-four, Jacob felt his work life had screeched to a grinding halt. Just a few short years ago, he'd been a bright, freshly scrubbed, inquisitive university student, pursuing a business administration degree with big plans and high hopes. After completing his bachelor's, Jacob thought he would perhaps do a little global travelling before accepting a career-track position in some unspecified but gloriously successful cutting-edge international marketing firm. So how had his visionary career train gone off its rails?

Over time his business administration degree had lost its original appeal, and the glow wore off his imagined future. Some of the coursework held his interest, especially in marketing and communications, but the majority began to feel like sheer drudgery. Accounting. Quantitative Methods. Microeconomics. Business Finance. Principles of Management. Jacob had little aptitude for these topics which made up so much of his degree requirements; he lost interest. His optimism faded; his grades fell. With just one year left on the business administration degree, he chose to drop out, regroup, and re-examine his future prospects.

How had he ended up at Incisive? Stellar performance in a marketing class had landed Jacob a part-time job there as a market research interviewer. His task was to ask randomly selected people their opinions about various products, sometimes in person on location, but primarily over the telephone. At first, he'd quite enjoyed the position, which offered him a small but steady income while he worked towards his degree. And Incisive liked Jacob – he was lively, energetic, and responsible. When he dropped out of university, he had asked if Incisive would hire him full-time, to which they readily agreed.

That had been two and a half years before. Jacob could hardly believe how quickly the time had passed by. On a certain level he still liked the work. He got to talk with a lot of different people, and Jacob found varied human interaction very enjoyable. He'd received good reviews and a small pay raise each year at Incisive. After all, he was still young, and getting a steady pay cheque meant he could support himself and afford to do some of the things he loved, like an occasional snowboarding expedition with friends. But the money wasn't good enough to quell Jacob's nagging feeling that he was destined for something bigger. He had to be suited for something more challenging than reading scripts someone else had written, asking people mundane questions about things they didn't need – products he'd had no hand in developing.

Six months ago Jacob had learned that Incisive was advertising for an assistant to the finance manager. Jacob became excited. He had taken Accounting and Business Finance at university – maybe this was his big chance! The pay was much better, and there was room to advance. Jacob had applied for the position and was granted an interview.

Jacob's enthusiasm came across loud and clear during the interview, but the finance manager had found his experience lacking. Sure, he'd taken a few classes, but his grades were not that great. And when asked to describe hands-on financial experience, Jacob had come up short. After the interview,

Jacob suddenly remembered the summer he'd spent setting up an online accounting system for his father's small business. He tried to schedule a follow-up meeting, but by that time it was too late – the position had already been filled.

Jacob returned to his telephone interview position horribly disappointed. He had been so excited about the finance opportunity that he'd already mentally spent his pay increase on new snowboarding gear. Now he was back to square one. Frustrated and stonewalled, he resumed his work with diligence but no passion. What was Jacob to do? He could go back to school, he reasoned. But what should he study? If he finished his business administration degree, he'd be perfectly qualified for the assistant position in finance – but it might be twenty years before that promotion became available again. And university meant expense – he'd have to make do with a lot less money even than the pittance he brought home now.

The conservative part of Jacob said, "Stay where you are. You earn enough money to live on. You get to go snowboarding once in a while. There's plenty of time to figure out your career future tomorrow. For today, just do what you're doing. Don't rock the boat."

But another part of Jacob was saying, "Get out of there! You have talents and desires. This job isn't giving you what you need. What happened to your goals, your enthusiasm, your drive? You used to be happy and optimistic. Look what this job is doing to you!"

These two parts of Jacob's mind continued their fight over the coming months. Jacob became confused, unfulfilled, and miserable. The Battle of Career had begun.

Today Jacob was daydreaming. He went through the motions of his assigned telephone interviews, saying words he now felt he could repeat in his sleep. And as he spoke on the phone, dutifully entering participant responses into his computer, Jacob doodled on his notepad. And that's exactly how the Admiral found him as he walked past Jacob's desk on his way to the conference room.

"Jacob!" said the Admiral. "How wonderful it is to see you!"

Jacob looked up, startled. "Oh, Admiral!" he exclaimed. "I haven't seen you since university!"

The Admiral, a personal friend of Jacob's family, also taught a Conflict Resolution class at the university. Jacob had taken the course and received excellent marks. Now Incisive had asked the Admiral in to consult on the development of their employee grievance procedures.

"How long have you been working here?" the Admiral asked.

Jacob gave him a brief low-down on his history with Incisive Market Research. The insightful Admiral missed nothing – including the dissatisfaction and misery lurking just beneath Jacob's usually happy, positive exterior.

The Admiral looked down at Jacob's notepad, where Jacob had drawn three or four images of a snowboarder. Jacob's artistic talent shone clearly through his drawings – they were stylistic, graphically detailed, contemporary, and edgy.

"Nice," said the Admiral. "I didn't know you were an artist."

"Oh, thanks. I've always liked to draw."

"You're not completely happy at Incisive, are you, Jacob?" asked the Admiral.

"No," Jacob confessed. He explained his situation, recounting his failed attempt to get promoted. "I've been struggling to figure out what I should do next. I guess I should go back to university, but I really wasn't happy studying business admin. It seems kind of late in the game to start working on a new degree. But I feel stuck here in this job – there's nowhere to go. I just don't know what to do."

"Maybe you're approaching things from the wrong direction," said the Admiral. "I think I can help. Would you be willing to take a few psychometric evaluations?"

"Sure," said Jacob. "I'll do anything if it'll help me figure out what to do. But, wait – I can't afford your services, Admiral."

"No problem," the Admiral said, laughing. "How about this: I'm working on a university project that involves analysing some respondent data. You could do the data entry and cleaning for me in exchange for my help."

Jacob agreed, experiencing the first surge of enthusiasm he'd felt in months. The Admiral promised to leave a few questionnaires with Jacob the following day, and together they arranged a time to meet. The Admiral moved on to his consultation appointment confident that he could help Jacob make peace between the forces battling inside his brain.

What do *you* think?

Jacob is fighting a classic Battle of Career. He feels stuck in a position he fell into at a time when he just needed a job. Now he doesn't know how to find the job satisfaction that goes along with a career. What advice would you give Jacob at this point in his life?

The Admiral is a skilled career coach and has a specific approach to helping people resolve the Battle of Career. But before we move on to his analysis and recommendations, consider a few questions:

1. How would you describe Jacob's personality? As you think of a few descriptors, consider how Jacob's position at Incisive Market Research fits – and does not fit – his personality. By the same token, how eligible is Jacob for his job – that is, how well do Jacob's skills and qualifications fit the job he's in?
2. Does Jacob have a job or a career? Why?
3. Have you ever been in a situation like Jacob's? Were you able to get out of it? If so, what did it take?
4. Is there anything Jacob might do that would help him turn his position at Incisive Market Research into a rewarding career?
5. Where do you think Jacob falls in the Eligibility/Suitability Matrix?
6. How would you draw the career cycle chart for Jacob?

Eligibility/Suitability Matrix and Career Satisfaction Cycle

The Admiral's first step was to analyse where Jacob fell on the Eligibility/Suitability Matrix at his job with Incisive Market Research. Clearly Jacob had the knowledge, skills, and ability to complete the assigned work to maintain his position, and thus was *eligible* to serve in this role. But he did not feel happy and fulfilled, which the Admiral felt spoke to his *suitability* for the position. Refer again to the Eligibility/Suitability Matrix at the beginning of this chapter. The Admiral felt that Jacob lay in the top right corner of the Suitability/Eligibility Matrix (the "Poor Fit" box). That is, Jacob was able to complete his work adequately but had personality traits or other qualities that made him less than ideally suited to succeed in this particular position.

Next the Admiral drew a Career Satisfaction Chart to represent Jacob's situation. Following is the illustration he came up with:

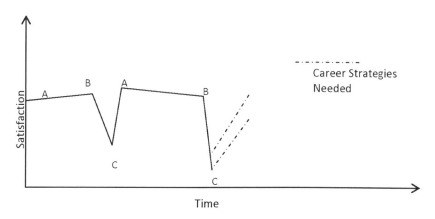

Jacob had been moderately satisfied with his position at Incisive while in school because he had other interests and activities to balance his work. Since he had begun working full-time at the job, Jacob's career satisfaction went into a slow decline and then had dropped off into a dramatic low over the past few months (after he was denied the promotion). Clearly, Jacob needed some career strategies to bring his satisfaction level back into an upwards slope.

MBTI Career Report

To help Jacob identify some useful career strategies, the Admiral's first choice of measure was the MBTI Career Report. Remember, the Admiral prefers to begin with a general measure, one that paints a picture of the person's overall personality. Then he turns to more specific measures relevant to the presenting problem. Moving from general to specific, the Admiral achieves the depth of understanding he needs to make positive recommendations for action.

The Admiral discovered that Jacob's MBTI responses fit the personality type **ENTP**. An ENTP tends towards Extraversion (E) rather than Introversion, prefers Intuition (N) over Sensing, Thinking (T) over Feeling, and Perceiving (P) over Judging.

The MBTI Career Report is designed to interpret a person's type indicator in a way that assists the person with career choice. This report identifies career families to which one is suited by showing the strengths and potential weaknesses of each personality type to guide a career search or study programme. The MBTI Career Report can help people increase job satisfaction within their current positions, ease a career transition or shift, or identify action steps towards positive change. The Admiral felt Jacob's profile on this measure would point out some possible career development strategies that could bring his career satisfaction chart back into an upwards trend.

The Admiral's expertise told him that an ENTP was likely to be good at scanning the environment for available opportunities, establishing an extensive network of contacts. He would probably be energetic and enthusiastic in an interview and at work. He most likely could adapt quickly and would be adroit at using the latest technology to solve problems or increase productivity. An ENTP often excels at developing creative solutions and thinking outside the box. He would probably feel most at home in a high-energy, fast-paced work environment with lots of interpersonal interaction, one that rewarded entrepreneurial initiative and offered autonomy to think differently and creatively.

Some of the challenges an ENTP might face include a tendency to enthusiastically chase every opportunity he sees, without careful consideration of his suitability for it or its risks. ENTPs sometimes have difficulty making concrete decisions or determining priorities among the many opportunities they perceive. A person with this profile might lack follow-through on decisions and might become overly excited about projects that would prove infeasible.

The Strong Interest Inventory

Having interpreted some of the implications of Jacob's ENTP personality type for his career, the Admiral next turned to the **Strong Interest Inventory (SII)**. This measure is a tool for making decisions towards a satisfying career. The SII provides a wealth of information that can benefit anyone, whether just starting out in a career, thinking about a career change, or considering education options to prepare for a future position. The SII measures interests rather than skills or abilities, making it an excellent complement to the MBTI Career Profile. The instrument informs not only career choices but also work tasks, educational programmes, and leisure activities. The SII encourages people to remember that managing a career is not a one-time decision but a series of decisions made across a lifetime.

The SII is designed to classify a person's "work personality" across six broad interest patterns called *General Occupational Themes (GOT)*. Work activities, potential skills, and values also can be classified into these themes. Jacob's GOT scores looked like this:

THEME	CODE	STANDARD SCORE & INTEREST LEVEL					STD SCORE
		<30	40	50	60	70>	
Artistic	A					VERY HIGH	73
Enterprising	E				MODERATE		58
Social	S				MODERATE		56
Investigative	I			MODERATE			49
Conventional	C			MODERATE			43
Realistic	R		LITTLE				37

Next the Admiral analysed Jacob's results and extrapolated what the Strong Interest Inventory classifies as the *Basic Interest Scales*. He found that Jacob's responses identified his top five interest areas:

1. Visual Arts & Design (A)
2. Performing Arts (A)
3. Marketing & Advertising (E)
4. Entrepreneurship (E)
5. Counselling & Helping (S)

Career Anchors Profile

The Admiral's third psychometric tool for Jacob was the Career Anchors profile, a measure developed by Edgar H. Schein. A person's self-analysis on this metric places that person into one of eight "career anchor" categories that increase understanding of one's talents, values, and motivations. Schein developed the Career Anchors assessment under the premise that, in an increasingly complex and global world, individuals must become more self-reliant; in order to do so, each individual needs to clarify an image of his or her particular competencies, motives, and values. Schein defines the eight Career Anchors as follows:

TF   Technical/Functional Competence
GM General/Managerial Competence
AU Autonomy/Independence
SE   Security/Stability
EC Entrepreneurial Creativity
SV Service/Dedication to a Cause
CH Pure Challenge
LS   Lifestyle

According to Schein's metrics, Jacob's self-analysis placed him in the Autonomy/Independence Career Anchor. That meant Jacob's career satisfaction would depend in large part on being able to define his own work in his own way. He would need to feel free and independent, even within an organisation. Jacob would probably thrive in a highly autonomous, nontraditional setting or self-employment. If he took a job within a traditional organisation, he should seek one that would allow flexibility in when and how he completed his work. Freedom and autonomy would be strong motivators for Jacob.

Identifying Jacob's dream job

The Admiral and Jacob met in the Incisive conference room on a Sunday afternoon, when only a couple of Interviewers were working near Jacob's cubicle. The Admiral had arranged to use this conference space because it contained several whiteboards that they could use for brainstorming. The Admiral also had brought and set up his computer so they could do online searches as needed.

The Admiral did not go over Jacob's psychometric results right away. Instead, he opened the conversation with a question.

"Jacob, what is your **dream job**?"

"My dream job?" repeated Jacob.

"Yes," said the Admiral. "Forget about your past history and your job here at Incisive. If you could have any job in the world, what would be the one you think would be the most fun, fulfilling, and satisfying to you?"

"Wow," said Jacob, a little overwhelmed. "I've never thought about it that way. I really don't have a dream job, per se."

"That's all right," the Admiral continued. "Then just think about the things you like to do. What's one thing you really love doing?"

"I love to snowboard," Jacob promptly replied. "But that's for fun. It's not a job."

"Are you sure?" said the Admiral. "Think about it for a minute. Aren't there jobs associated with snowboarding?"

"Hmmm." Jacob considered this. "Well, sure, you could be a professional snowboarder, like Shaun White. But that's kind of out of my league."

The Admiral went to the whiteboard. He wrote the word *JOBS* at the top of the board and underlined it. Beneath the heading, he wrote *professional snowboarder.*

"We're brainstorming now," he said, "so we'll write down everything we can think of, even if it seems far-fetched. We can narrow the list down later.

"How about being a snowboarding instructor?"

Jacob nodded. The Admiral wrote *snowboarding instructor* on the whiteboard.

They continued the process for about fifteen minutes, after which they had compiled the following list:

<u>**JOBS**</u>

Professional snowboarder
Snowboarding instructor

Snowboard team coach
Snowboard tester
Snowboard model
Snow resort manager
Snowboard company representative/salesperson/account executive
Snowboard shop owner
Snowboard shop manager
Snowboard repairperson
Snowboard design engineer
Boot and/or binding designer
Graphic artist for a snowboard company

As they got towards the end of this list, Jacob became excited. "Oh, I'd love to do artwork for a snowboard company!" he exclaimed. "That would be so much fun! I believe maybe that *is* my dream job."

"I think you would be good at it, too, Jacob," said the Admiral. "I saw your drawings the other day. They were great, and that was just doodling on a notepad.

"This is a good segue into an analysis of your psychometric assessments," the Admiral continued. "Let's take a look and see how your dream job fits with your measures."

The two of them went over Jacob's results. Their review indicated that a career as a graphic artist for a snowboarding company would fit Jacob's interests and aptitudes quite well.

"Someone with your profile is likely to have a very strong interest in artistic pursuits," said the Admiral, showing Jacob his SII scores. "And look at the **Most Attractive Job Families** section of your MBTI Career Report: your top score, at 100, is in the job family *Arts, Design, Entertainment, Sports, and Media*. That profile represents an excellent combination of the things you love to do – both graphic art and action sports.

"Now let's look at your Career Anchors Profile," continued the Admiral. "A person with scores like yours is likely to be strongly motivated by **Autonomy and Independence**. Since action sports is a nontraditional calling, it seems to me that the field might very well offer plenty of autonomy for you to work in your own way, setting your own hours and job parameters. A person with your profile often feels most satisfied in a position that offers such a high degree of freedom.

"You're an ENTP, Jacob, and the most popular occupations among people with your personality type cover a very broad range of career fields.

So as you pursue your dream job, keep your mind open to other possibilities. Don't be so stuck on a narrow vision of the career you want that you ignore good opportunities that arise. At the same time, ENTPs sometimes have a tendency to chase every opportunity that comes up, without carefully considering whether they're a good fit. I think that might be what happened to you with the finance position – you weren't a good fit for that job, which is why you didn't do well in the interview. As opportunities become available, I recommend that you prioritise them by how well they fit with your interests and skills.

"Next," the Admiral continued, "we're going to work backwards from your dream job and figure out how to get you there."

Working backwards

The Admiral led Jacob to the computer. "Okay, now I'd like you to surf the Internet looking for a couple of job descriptions for your dream job."

Jacob was surprised at the wealth of positions he found advertised. "I never knew there was this much opportunity for graphic designers in action sports," he said. "But then I guess I hadn't been thinking about looking for this type of job in the first place."

They found several promising ads that fit Jacob's job search. The following is an example of one of the job descriptions:

> **GRAPHIC DESIGNER/DEVELOPER**
> Alberta, Canada, snowboard company is in the middle of an unprecedented growth cycle. We are seeking a full-time, top-notch graphic designer with web development experience.
>
> **Skills and Experience:**
> Must be ready to hit the ground running and work at a very fast pace. After a part-time trial period of several projects, successful candidate will transition to full-time work. Relocation to Alberta, Canada, is required.
>
> Skills required, in order of importance:
> - Web design (including image optimisation)
> - Photo manipulation
> - Print design (including magazine advertising)
> - Vector artwork
> - Flash animation (including basic ActionScript, banner ads)
> - Apparel design (woven tags, screen prints, etc.)
> - 3D rendering
> - Ability to design/build sophisticated web pages using CSS,

HTML, MySQL, HTML5, etc., is preferred but not required, but you *must* have a working knowledge of web design and development.

Computer programs required:
- Photoshop (CS3 or 4)
- Illustrator
- Flash (mostly animation & some ActionScript)
- Dreamweaver or other web editor
- InDesign

To Apply:
Every applicant must provide a portfolio (PDF, links to online work, etc.). Applicants primarily will be judged on prior work. Please familiarise yourself with our brand and images on our website. Send portfolio, résumé, cover letter, and expected salary along with reasons why you want to live in Alberta, Canada, to: jobs@ albertasnowboard.com. No calls, please.

"Wow," said Jacob. "That's a lot of experience I don't have."

"Don't be discouraged," said the Admiral. "We're working backwards to get you there. Let's start by focusing on the skills you *do* have. Which of these requirements do you already have?"

"I know how to use Photoshop pretty well," said Jacob, "but that's about it."

"Okay, that's a good start. Now which of the other skills is most important to getting the job?"

"For this one, it looks like web design is the top requirement," said Jacob. "Maybe learning basic HTML skills would work."

"Yes, HTML and Flash," said the Admiral. "Where would you go to get those skills?"

"The university has a design school," said Jacob, "but I think it's pretty competitive to get admitted. Maybe the community college has some less expensive options."

"Good idea," the Admiral replied. "Keep your current position in mind, too. You don't always have to look outside your current situation to find new challenges. Doesn't Incisive Market Research have a Design Department?"

"Yes," said Jacob, becoming excited again. "Maybe I could find a mentor there."

"Finding a mentor is an excellent thought," said the Admiral. "Think about identifying someone you admire and respect in the Design Department.

Set a time for a brief informational interview. Ask that person if he or she would be willing to mentor you on your way to becoming a graphic designer. Be sure to offer something in exchange – help on a project, for example. If that person doesn't have the time to commit, ask if he or she could identify someone else who would be a good mentor."

Jacob and the Admiral continued to work on a list of action steps Jacob might take to move him closer to his goal: getting his dream job. Jacob found two evening web design classes in which he could enrol at the community college. He thought of a person in the Incisive Design Department whom he might approach as a mentor. He made a plan to collect his best drawings into the beginnings of a portfolio. Jacob also knew a snowboard shop in his own city. He decided to call the shop and ask if they would consider hiring him part-time on weekends to help out with any odd jobs they needed. "Gaining exposure to your field of interest is always helpful," suggested the Admiral. "Even if you don't start out in the job you want, you'll begin to understand how the industry functions."

Volunteering and entrepreneurship

"There's one more thing I want you to think about," the Admiral told Jacob. "Work experience doesn't necessarily have to be paid. Consider volunteer opportunities too. There may be volunteer organisations that would give you exposure to and experience with the skills you need."

"Someone who scores like you on the Strong Interest Inventory has high interests in the **Enterprising** area. Those people are likely to be good entrepreneurs. Also, people who fall into your position on the Career Anchors measure often find that self-employment offers the freedom and autonomy they most desire. What kind of a small business could you start that would help you move towards your dream job?"

They discussed the possibilities. Finally Jacob decided that he could combine volunteer and entrepreneurial pursuits. As he gained skill in web and graphic design, he could offer his services for free – designing websites for friends and family members who needed them. That would give him a chance to build his portfolio while helping out his network. After getting some experience under his belt, he could expand his business and begin charging for his services.

Set a timeline

The final step in Jacob's process was to set a timeline for following through with his action plan. He and the Admiral agreed that he would need to allow himself some time to make everything work. Jacob would need to remain in his position at Incisive Market Research, at least for the time being, and take most of his action steps outside of regular work hours.

The Admiral encouraged Jacob to be realistic. "Realism sometimes eludes ENTP types," he said. "So someone like you might tend to chase dreams without a specific plan in mind. Be sure to set clear priorities and make sure your goals are achievable. If you set the bar too high, you run the risk of failure and discouragement. Set small goals you know you can reach. Keep your final goal – having your dream job – in front of you all the time, but set smaller objectives along the way. Reward yourself and celebrate every accomplishment."

By the end of their session, Jacob had a specific plan and a realistic timeline for obtaining his dream job. He felt better than he'd felt in months – energised, optimistic, satisfied. Given the possibility of finding a mentor at Incisive, he even felt encouraged about staying in his job there for a little while. A new vision for his future gave Jacob the courage and motivation to stay the course.

Now what do you think?

How well do you think the Admiral was able to coach Jacob towards a rewarding career future? Can you think of other courses of action Jacob might have taken? Again, remember that a career is not a single decision but multiple decisions made along the course of an entire lifetime.

If Jacob succeeds in finding his dream job, where do you think he will fall on the Eligibility/Suitability Matrix in a role as a graphic artist for a snowboarding firm? Do you think the career strategies the Admiral helped Jacob identify will be adequate to bring the slope of his Career Satisfaction Cycle trending back upwards?

The Battle of Career is one that nearly everyone encounters at some point in life. While the battle often pits two factions of one's own mind against each other, the results of the battle can spill over into the workplace and into personal lives as well. When we're unhappy in our jobs, productivity and social interactions can suffer. A Career Satisfaction Cycle that continues along a downwards slope can send a person into a vortex of disappointment, suffering, and depression.

Jacob is a young person with a long future ahead of him. But that doesn't mean youth are the only ones who can resolve the Battle of Career. It's never too late to gain new skills, pursue entrepreneurial endeavours, or even get one's dream job. Psychometric measures can help you determine the most rewarding pursuits for your personality, and some creative thinking can turn up new ideas for following your dreams – not only in the workplace, but in your volunteer, social, and leisure activities too. The Admiral's process can help you work backwards towards reaping the rewards inherent in doing work you love.

CHAPTER III

The Battle of Communication

The simple meaning of *communication*, as defined by *Merriam-Webster*, is "an act … of transmitting" or "A process by which information is exchanged by individuals through a common system of symbols, signs, or behavior"[6]. So one might say that communication is the transfer of information from one person to another. Language – both spoken and written – is the communication mode to which we turn most frequently, particularly in the workplace. Most job descriptions will make at least some mention that oral or written communication skills are required for a given position.

But to promote positive communication in the workplace, we need to investigate communication in much broader form. The signs and symbols of language only paint a portion of the larger picture. Communication is the giving and receiving of information, signals, or messages. We use communication to persuade people, to seek information, and to deliver information. We can use a variety of media to give and receive information: speaking, writing, gestures, facial expressions, and other forms of body language all are modes of imparting information. Listening and watching are modes of receiving information.

To truly understand how communication works, we need to look at all its components. The behaviours by which we communicate are equally important as speaking and writing. To draw the entire picture, we need to consider not only *what* we say and *how* we say it but also *when* we speak and when we *choose* to remain silent, *how* we listen, *when* we listen, and when we *decide to stop* listening. The language we use, whether spoken, written, or physically expressed, must be understandable to the person with whom we're communicating. And the objectives of communication may be just as important as the communications themselves.

---

6   Merriam-Webster, *Merriam-Webster's Collegiate Dictionary, 11th ed.* (Springfield, MA: Merriam-Webster Inc., 2008).

Few people will argue with the statement that effective communication is essential to the success of any business. Consider an average employee's day: interactions with clients, customers, co-workers, bosses, consultants, or vendors are probably typical. Certainly the employee's personality will influence how each interaction turns out, as will the personalities of the others involved. Workplace communication affects sales, public image, community impact (both local and global), and employee satisfaction.

We've known for years that worker satisfaction is tied to productivity. More recently research has begun to show that interpersonal communication at work has a strong effect not only on productivity but also on an employee's personal health – both mental and physiological. Poor patterns of communication within a company have a negative impact that spreads much wider than company walls.

Some examples of communication patterns that cause workplace friction and its ensuing stress and distress include domination, avoiding issues, refusing responsibility for one's actions, shame and blame, misinterpretation, passive-aggression, expressed indifference, and hostility. While nasty or stressful interactions at work may be less frequent than positive interchanges, the negative communications have a much more powerful and lasting impact on a person's mood and health. A workplace communication war leaves deep scars.

Humans are inherently self-serving, and today's society encourages us to be more so: we're told we must look out for Number One because no one else is going to do it. But workplace communication could be instantly improved if people used more of their *spirits* than their *egos*. The most successful communicators are gracious; they focus on others more than they focus on themselves, listen to understand, and speak to be heard. Feeling valued is a deeply important human need, and believing that one's contributions in the workplace are valuable and appreciated are essential to a person's work satisfaction, happiness, contentment, and well-being.

When evaluating the quality of communication between people, it's helpful to do so from a conceptual framework that considers how trust is built in relationships. For example, study the following diagram:

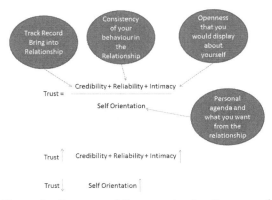

Figure 8 – Conceptual Communication Framework
Reproduced with kind permission from *The Trusted Advisor* by
David Maister, Charles Green, and Robert Galford (2000). Free Press.

This framework expresses trust as an equation where a person's credibility, reliability, and intimacy in a given relationship are offset by that person's level of self-orientation. Credibility represents the communication track record that the person brings into the relationship from his or her past. Reliability stems from one's consistency of behaviour within the relationship. Intimacy grows when the person becomes willing to open up and disclose information about him- or herself. These three features combine to build trust in the relationship. But that trust is undermined by the degree to which each individual is oriented to self – that is, people's focus on what they want to get for themselves out of the relationship. In a similar way to the Johari Window, this model points up the importance of communication and self-disclosure to building trust between people who work together. Too much focus on personal agendas rather than on openness and sharing destroys trust between people in any organisational structure.

Personality type has a tremendous impact on how people communicate. Consider how an extravert might communicate differently from an introvert, or how the interactions of serious, cautious types could differ from those of lively, animated, spontaneous people. An entire body of research has defined various communication styles. Psychometric measures can prove useful for identifying how personality types are likely to differ in the communication strategies they prefer and how the battle of communication can be resolved through understanding and accepting the personality types of one's associates. Personality theory also builds a framework within which thought processes can be communicated and understood, as will be clarified later in this chapter.

When people must work together in teams – which in most workplaces is difficult to avoid – it's best to have at least some personality differences among team members because variety offers a more perspectives from which to approach the job at hand. It's easy to see how problems arise when people of divergent personality types disagree on what to do, which methods to apply, or even whether the task should be done at all. But the solution to those problems can lie within the personality differences themselves. As Isabel Briggs Myers points out in her book *Gifts Differing: Understanding Personality Type*, knowing the various personality types of a work team can be extremely useful. She writes, "By considering the contributions of each member, the team or its executive head can make a more informed decision than would otherwise be possible. As a further aid to cooperation, these contributions demonstrate that each member is weak where another is strong but is also strong where another is weak. A healthy respect for one's opposite makes for peaceful and effective coexistence."[7]

To illustrate this point, let's revisit the Uncomfortable Zone of Debate (UZOD) for a moment. Remember, people stuck in Zone A agree on everything, avoiding any difficult topics in order to do so. In Zone B, people fail to agree at all – each individual in a group challenges the others' opinions to sustain that argumentative state.

Uncomfortable Zone of Debate (UZOD)

Figure 9 – The UZOD, Revisited
From Johnson G & Scholes K (1999). *Exploring Corporate Strategy: Fifth Edition.* Harlow, UK: Prentice-Hall.

The UZOD, as you may recall, is the zone where people have enough trust and self-awareness to agree and disagree appropriately. People in this zone keep emotional, personal, and political distractions to a minimum, leaving them free to raise questions and challenge ideas. At the same time, UZOD dwellers remain open to allowing their own ideas to be questioned and challenged. You can see how communication is the key to entering

---

7   Isabel Briggs Myers and Peter B. Myers, *Gifts Differing: Understanding Personality Type* (Palo Alto, CA: Consulting Psychologists Press, 1980).

– and remaining in – this optimal interactive zone. The UZOD in turn relates to the Johari Window model because interactions that foster sharing, discussion, challenge, and improvement of ideas are essential to widening that open Johari Window pane – the area where both awareness of self and understanding and acceptance of others are high. Finally, the conceptual framework presented above also helps clarify how people can move into the UZOD. By releasing personal agendas and employing credible, reliable, and increasingly intimate communication, people build trust that makes remaining in the productive UZOD possible.

Later in this chapter, the Admiral will present a theory describing how individuals live in a world of self-generating beliefs which largely remain untested. Our beliefs can lead us to conclusions about the communications of others that spur us to take destructive action. To illustrate this theory, let's explore a situation where opposite personality types are asked to work together on a set of tasks. As you read, try to identify the communication strengths and weaknesses of each individual, and consider how they might be balanced and synergised to work together effectively.

Scenario: Winning Over the Warehouse

> *To effectively communicate, we must realize that we are all different in the way we perceive the world and use this understanding as a guide to our communication with others.* ~**Anthony Robbins**

> *Kind words can be short and easy to speak, but their echoes are truly endless.* ~**Mother Teresa**

Ian Edwards got off the 7.30 a.m. train and walked towards Worldwide Widgets Inc. for his first day of work. He was looking forward to the position. He'd been unemployed for four months, scraping out an existence doing odd jobs for neighbours and friends, so the steady income had obvious appeal. But Ian was naturally cautious. He felt a bit nervous about having to learn a new job, even if it was just warehouse work. As he walked, Ian reaffirmed his determination to stay focused, learn quickly, and perform efficiently to keep this job in the long term. In time, maybe he could even get promoted.

At the reception desk, Ian was directed to the warehouse, where his new boss, Mark Matthews, was waiting for him. "Good morning, Ian," said Mark. "You're here early. Welcome to Worldwide Widgets." He gestured to the warehouse around them. Ian looked around at the massive expanse, which encompassed three loading platforms, a bank of standing computer stations, a large packing and shipping area, and rows and rows of ceiling-high metal shelving. Two forklifts manoeuvred busily about the concrete floor, moving wooden pallets full of boxes from the loading bay to the shelving areas. Other employees were taking smaller items from open boxes and carrying them up rolling extension ladders to their allotted shelf spots.

"This is the heart of Worldwide Widgets' operations," Mark continued. "At one point or another, everything we do filters through this warehouse. A lot of our success relies on warehouse employees doing their jobs right. From my point of view, yours is the most important position in the company."

Mark gave Ian a basic overview of warehouse responsibilities: receiving, unloading, and stocking materials and components; cataloguing completed widgets and storing them on the shelves; tracking available inventory; reordering and restocking as needed; packing, loading, and shipping widgets to customers. *It all sounds pretty simple*, Ian thought, *but a lot of work*. Mark guided Ian over to the bank of computer stations. "We use the WCS to make sure everything runs smoothly. WCS stands for Warehouse Control System. It's a computer programme that helps us manage our daily operations.

"One of your co-workers, Gordon Gilmour, is going to train you for the first few weeks. He's been here almost a year and knows the system inside and out. But let me warn you," Mark continued, "you'll have to make sure he stays on task – that Gordon is a real talker. Oh, here he is now."

The man moving towards them across the loading platform looked to be in his early thirties, tall but slight with short, dark, curly hair. He spoke to other warehouse workers as he sauntered by, waving, laughing – he had an easy greeting or good-hearted jab for each.

"Well hey there," said Gordon as he neared Mark and Ian. "This must be the new blood. He filling you in, buddy?" he said to Ian. "Gordon Gilmour." He shook Ian's hand vigorously. "Did the boss man give you the old spiel about the heart of the operation? How you have the most important job at Worldwide Widgets, blah, blah, blah?" Gordon chuckled, glancing sideways at Mark. "Well, don't worry; I'll set you straight. I'll have you moaning and groaning about management by lunchtime." He chuckled.

"That'll do," said Mark good-naturedly. "Ian, I've got a busy day. Gordon will start teaching you the ropes. About half an hour before lunch, come by my office and fill out all your paperwork."

"Thank you," said Ian. "I really appreciate your time this morning."

"Yeah, yeah," said Gordon as Mark walked off. "The old boss man is not so bad, at the end of the day." He rubbed his hands together. "Okay, let's get started. The number one job of the day is coffee. Am I right, or am I right?"

Gordon left Ian no room to respond as he steered him towards a small, brightly lit doorway in the corner near the computer banks. "We can't get going without that first cuppa joe," he said. "Now here's the *real* heart of the operation: the break room." He led Ian past a beat-up collection of folding tables and chairs to a small kitchen, where a full coffee maker sat on the Formica countertop. "Oh, and looky here," Gordon exclaimed. "Somebody brought doughnuts. It's just like Christmas."

Gordon poured two cups of coffee, and he and Ian stood sipping the hot liquid, Ian a bit self-conscious and Gordon munching a doughnut, as two or three others entered the room from the warehouse. Ian's trainer seemed friendly with all of them – talking, laughing, exchanging anecdotes – but throughout the entire fifteen-minute exchange, one voice clearly dominated: Gordon's. *Mark wasn't kidding*, Ian thought. *Gordon definitely is a talker. I just hope he teaches me the job right. I so want to make a good impression here at Worldwide.*

"Shouldn't we get to work?" Ian finally interjected, tentatively.

"Oh yeah," Gordon said. "Just a sec, let me polish off this doughnut. Hey, Sam, I'll finish telling you the story at lunch. We've got to bounce. All right, Mr Nose-to-the-Grindstone," he said to Ian. "Let's go."

"That's Sam McGill, the warehouse foreman," confided Gordon as they left the break room. "He's a pretty okay guy, but man, wait till you meet his wife. She's got him wrapped around her little finger so tight he can't even breathe, let alone get his pants off, ha ha." Ian smiled uncomfortably and remained silent.

They headed towards the computers. "Oh man, look what we got stuck with for our first assignment this morning," said Gordon. "We have to check in this shipment from Commercial Cogs." He pointed to a large pile of boxes on the loading platform nearest the computers.

Gordon continued a steady stream of conversation as he showed Ian their responsibilities. "The bills of lading are over here," he went on, "and this shipment is from Commercial oh yeah, here it is. Now we open the boxes," he handed Ian a box-cutter, "and check to make sure they've really got cogs in them, not marijuana, ha ha.

"Okay, let's see ten of these boxes should have 648 five-eighths-by-three-inch cogs per box." Gordon slit open a box and eyeballed the contents, Ian looking on. "That look like about 648 to you?" he asked Ian, winking.

"Aren't we supposed to count them?" Ian looked up, surprised.

"Wow, you really go by the book, don't you?" said Gordon, laughing easily. "All right, have it your way. It'll probably take us all day, but yeah, smart guy, let's count them."

Ian thought for a few moments. "We don't have to count each one," he offered cautiously. "We could just count the number in each layer, and then add up the number of layers to get a total."

"Sure, that's pretty bright," said Gordon. "I was just testing you, see? Okay, let's count them up and check them off this list."

They worked through the morning, Gordon talking non-stop and Ian soaking it in. Ian learned how to mark off each shipment on the bill of lading and then enter the inventory into the computerised WCS. He placed boxes on pallets to be moved out for shelving. He helped unpack boxes and learned how to use the WCS to locate the shelves where the items should be stored. The time passed by quickly. Gordon had a shortcut or a workaround for a lot of their tasks, Ian noticed. He also took frequent coffee and chatting breaks. But with Ian working slowly and steadily and Gordon working quickly in fits and bursts, they got the job done.

* * * * * * * * * *

Three months later, Ian and Gordon still worked side by side, but Ian was no longer a trainee. He'd passed his probationary period with flying colours. "Good job, Ian," Mark had told him. "You seem level-headed, and I'm glad to have you on board."

Over time, though, the striking personality differences between Gordon and Ian had become more noticeable. Their inherent differences appeared most evident in their communication styles. Gordon was enthusiastic and positive, and everywhere he went an atmosphere of fun and party followed. He thrived on personal relationships; small talk and humorous anecdotes filled his conversations. Gordon multitasked easily and often walked around the warehouse talking with others or directing a shipment load, eating his lunch at the same time. His communications were energetic and laced with joviality, his reactions quick. He was great at interpersonal interaction, teamwork, and negotiation, not so great at listening and remembering details, sticking to a timeline, or entering and extracting computer data.

In contrast, Ian appeared serious and deliberate, considering his responses carefully, often taking several minutes (even hours) to answer a question. He tended to process information internally, taking time to gain an in-depth understanding before reacting or changing gears. He had made a couple of friends at Worldwide Widgets but preferred to keep his personal life private. Ian was a good listener and caught on quickly; he had good ideas and could clearly present the pros and cons of a possible action plan. While grasping the larger picture, Ian found too many extraneous details – particularly personal details about people's lives – distracting and uncomfortable. Rather than punctuating his conversations with fun, jokes, and sarcasm, Ian tended towards targeted, efficient communication, getting right to the point and then shutting up and moving on. He had a competitive nature and wanted to stand out from the others; at the same time, he preferred working alone to being a team member.

Naturally, these widely variant styles were bound to generate some friction. One day Ian had arrived early, as was his habit. He consulted the WCS for his first assignment. "Move Washington Wheels stock delivery into warehouse via Platform C." Ian got right to work. By the time Gordon showed up and finished his regular morning coffee and chat period, Ian had already unloaded the delivery, checked it in, entered the data, and unpacked the boxes and was putting individual wheels onto shelves.

"What are you doing?" demanded Gordon.

"Shelving the Washington Wheels shipment," responded Ian.

"We don't have to unpack those," said Gordon. "All we had to do was bring the boxes in. You're tripling our workload."

"We always unpack and shelve them," Ian said. "That's the procedure."

"Yeah, but I talked to Mark and Sam about it last night when we all went out for a beer. Remember? I invited you to go, didn't I? You said no. I was telling them how much easier it would be if we just forklifted the whole box of wheels onto those wide shelves in the back. We all talked it over and decided we don't have to unpack big items like that – the production guys don't requisition the wheels one by one, anyway. They're always going to ask for a full box."

"I didn't have that information," said Ian defensively.

"Well, if you'd go out for a beer with us once in a while, maybe you'd stay up to speed. What do you do every night that you can't go out with us anyway – wash your hair or something? Plus, who told you to show up an hour early? Are you trying to make me look bad? You're just such an eager beaver, ha ha!" Gordon walked away, stopping to chat with another worker along his path. Ian saw Gordon gesture in his direction, laughing, and faintly heard the words "eager beaver" as he clambered down the ladder, red-faced and annoyed.

A whole string of ensuing incidents served to illustrate the communication differences between Ian and Gordon; I'll recount a couple to give you a sense of what was going on. One day Ian accidentally damaged some sensitive components while opening their shipping containers. Worldwide's procedure in such cases was to move the damaged items to a designated area and then enter them as "received but damaged" in the WCS – thus indicating that the Worldwide employee was responsible for the damage rather than the vendor or shipper. Upset with himself, Ian placed the damaged items into a single container and started carrying it over to the proper area.

"Hey, what's up? What're you doing?" asked Gordon, who had been working alongside Ian that morning.

"I accidentally broke these," said Ian. "I'm taking them over to the damaged area."

"Whoa, whoa, whoa!" said Gordon. "Not so fast! Keep your shirt on for a minute! That's a Combined Components shipment, isn't it? How many did you damage?"

"Six," Ian replied.

"How many boxes were affected?"

"Just two," said Ian.

"No problem!" said Gordon. "You leave this one to me, okay? I have a buddy over at Combined. Let me give him a call right now."

Gordon immediately picked up the warehouse phone and dialled. "Joe Johnson, please Hello, Joe? Gordy Gilmour." Ian followed the one-sided conversation intently. "Yeah, so's your mother, ha ha. Listen, Joe, we got this shipment of components from you guys today. Two of the boxes had damaged units in them, and we're pretty sure it wasn't our fault – we opened them according to fragile protocol and everything. Either they were damaged before packing, or maybe your shipper mishandled them. Anyway, you owe me a favour. What do you say, buddy? Can you help us out?"

Gordon listened for a time as his friend responded. "That's great, Joe," said Gordon. "You're really saving my backside here, dude. Send your guy over as soon as you can, okay? We'll be waiting at the loading dock. Thanks again!" He hung up the phone.

"Mission accomplished," Gordon said, turning to Ian. "Don't give up so easy! A little sweet-talking, a little negotiation works wonders. My buddy Joe is going to send his guy over with two replacement boxes. We exchange them, and then check them in like usual, and nobody's the wiser."

"But it's not true," protested Ian. "I *did* damage them."

"Shhhh," Gordon warned, looking around. "Nobody needs to know that. I took care of it for you, okay? Combined Components has insurance.

It won't cost them anything, and we end up smelling like roses. It's a win-win for everybody. So stop worrying, all right? Just say 'thank you, Gordon.'"

"Thanks, Gordon," Ian said grudgingly. But internally Ian was torn: on one hand, he resented how Gordon was always trying to one-up him and make him look stupid. On the other hand, Gordon had just saved him from a reprimand, maybe even a write-up in his employee file. He knew he should be grateful for the help, but it was hard to feel gratitude when he felt like Gordon was trying to undermine him at every turn. Sometimes Ian wished he were outgoing, talkative, and fun like Gordon. He liked the guy fairly well, but he could be so infuriating.

Another time, it was Gordon's antics that nearly resulted in a disaster that could have gotten both of them in trouble. Ian was working in the shipment area. Gordon and two other employees were retrieving items from the shelves and sending them down the conveyor belt to Ian's station, where Ian was responsible to pack them into the appropriate-sized boxes and ready them for shipment to customers. Ian had printed and carefully reviewed the packing slips prior to starting his shift and had prepared boxes of the correct size. Now he was just waiting for the widgets to come down the belt.

The conveyor started and widgets arrived. Most of the orders that day were for small widgets that packed eight to a box. Ian fit them into their individual containers, taped the containers, and packed them into the larger boxes. Then he checked the packing slip, placed a copy inside the box, sealed the whole thing up, and used the WCS to print the sticky label to affix to the top.

Everything was running along quite smoothly. Then without warning, instead of the small widgets arriving on the conveyor, a bunch of extra-large widgets showed up. Ian checked his packing slip. The first few numbers were right – he must have gotten them wrong, he thought, and he had to hurry. More widgets were already on their way. Ian ran to retrieve some bigger boxes, packed up the large widgets, and continued his process.

"Ha, ha, ha!" Ian heard Gordon's guffaw coming towards him from the shelving area, followed by Gordon himself. "Got you, didn't we? We sent you those big widgets to see if you were on your toes! I knew you wouldn't catch that, ha!" Gordon was still laughing, holding his sides as he turned to go back to his shelving post.

Ian was furious. "Hey, Gilmour," he said angrily. Gordon turned around. "I've just about had it with you," said Ian. "I'm trying to do a job here. I'm sick of your jokes. This is a warehouse, not Party City."

"C'mon, Ian," said Gordon good-naturedly. "Lighten up, will you? You're wound up tighter than a two-dollar watch. We were just having some fun with you. It doesn't hurt to have a little fun once in a while; that's what gets us through the day. Here, I'll help you unpack those bad boys and get you the right ones. C'mon, let go of it, okay?"

Without responding, Ian silently marched to the shelves, retrieved the correct widgets, and stomped back to his station. Gordon tried wheedling for a while in a futile attempt to reconcile, but Ian was having none of it. He refused to speak to Gordon for the remainder of the day. A little later on, Ian could hear Gordon recounting the story to a small group hanging around in the break room. "You should've seen his face!" Ian overheard. "He was as red as your shirt, Sam!" Still angry, Ian left the area and used his break period to walk briskly around the yard – taking some time to clear his head so he could get back to being productive.

*   *   *   *   *   *   *   *   *   *

The friction between Ian and Gordon grew, but it didn't reach the breaking point until a few months later, when Sam McGill was promoted to a position in the Production Department. Sam's departure left the position of warehouse foreman vacant. Replacing him would be Mark Matthews's call. There were two natural choices: Gordon and Ian.

As Mark pondered the decision, he considered the two men's strengths and weaknesses. Warehouse foreman was a position that required leadership combined with effective interpersonal interactions. Both men were productive workers. Gordon had seniority and certainly possessed interpersonal skills. But did he have the maturity and integrity to be a good leader? Ian was serious, level-headed, and fair-minded. But did he have the communication skills to make himself understood? Mark faced a quandary.

Both Gordon and Ian knew they were in line for the promotion, and each wanted it badly. Gordon perceived that the position would offer more opportunity for interaction, teamwork, and negotiation with outside parties, his favourite parts of his work. Ian desperately wanted to improve his position, standing, and income. Over the coming weeks, the two men locked horns more and more often, vying for recognition. The Battle of Communication was impeding productivity in the Worldwide Widgets warehouse.

Mark Matthews finally threw up his hands and explained the dilemma to his own supervisor. They decided a consultation with the Admiral was appropriate.

The Admiral met both Ian and Gordon and spent time talking with them and with their co-workers. Then he sat down with Mark to discuss the options. "Both these guys are qualified to be foreman," said Mark. "But they're such different people. To me, the question comes down to communication. A good foreman has to be able to set priorities and communicate them clearly to everyone in the warehouse. Ian can prioritise, but he doesn't interact with others that well. Gordon is a great communicator, but it's all about personal stuff – I'm not sure how well he'll do communicating systems and priorities professionally. I couldn't resolve this to my own satisfaction, so that's why I called you."

"I have a few ideas," the Admiral told Mark. "But I'd like to start with some psychometric measures. Communication seems to lie at the heart of the matter, and I'd like to learn more about these two men's personalities. Once I've got a handle on their possible communication styles, you and I can talk through a solution to your hiring problem."

Gordon and Ian were only too happy to complete the measures; anything that would help resolve their issues and clarify who should fill the warehouse foreman position was fine with them. Each man secretly believed that his own qualities would make him stand out as the unmistakeable best choice.

What do *you* think?

It's time for you to take a moment to assess the situation in the Worldwide Widgets warehouse. Here are some questions to guide your thought process:

1. How would you describe Ian's personality? How do you think his personality affects his communication with others?
2. How would you describe Gordon's personality, and how does his type colour his communication patterns?
3. Where do you think Ian and Gordon fall on the UZOD scale? What does the Johari Window look like between the two men?
4. How much trust do you think exists between Ian and Gordon? What could they do to increase trust in their work relationship?
5. Have you encountered a situation like this one, where two distinct personalities struggled to communicate? What did you do, and how well did it work?
6. If you were Mark Matthews, which of the two men would you choose to fill the warehouse foreman position? Why would you choose that one over the other?

The MBTI

As anticipated, the personality metrics told the Admiral that the two men had widely differing personality types. On the Myers-Briggs Type Indicator, Ian's responses were consistent with an **INTJ** (Introversion, Intuition, Thinking, and Judging). Gordon's profile was closely identified with an **ESFP** (Extraversion, Sensing, Feeling, and Perceiving). In fact, these two personality types are almost polar opposites.

As discussed earlier in this chapter, communication refers not only to what we say but also to how we say it, when we choose to speak up or remain silent, when we listen and when we tune out. An Extravert can spread his focus across a wide range of topics, while an Introvert prefers to focus on problems one at a time. Those who prefer Sensing seek practical, realistic messages, while those who prefer Intuition want messages that are imaginative and creative. Thinkers trend away from having a lot of significant relationships, while Feelers place significant relationships in high regard. Judgers prefer not to be surprised – they want to see things coming. On the other hand, Perceivers enjoy spontaneity. In terms of communication style, an ESFP is likely to speak, listen, speak, speak, and listen, and then possibly reflect on what was said. In other words, he would be likely to speak much more than he would listen or reflect. An INTJ would probably listen, reflect, listen, and reflect, and then maybe speak – if he felt it necessary. The Admiral had perceived some effects of this difference in communication style as these two men had struggled to interact during the preceding events.

ESFPs are likely to be natural performers, to enjoy being the centre of attention, and to view the world as a stage upon which they are the stars of a one-person show. They usually prefer the company of others over solitude; often they are lively, witty conversationalists. ESFPs are also jovial and fun to be around. They always have a wisecrack or play on words at hand; nothing is so sacred or serious that it can't be poked fun at. An ESFP might have trouble holding his tongue or hiding his feelings in appropriate situations. People of this type tend to look on the bright side of things, sidestepping controversy and avoiding anxiety, exhibiting skills in diplomacy and negotiation.

INTJ types often are rational and plan oriented. They usually trust intellect and reason over emotion and maintain a calm demeanour. INTJs are likely to take a utilitarian approach to achieving goals, tending towards abstract thinking and communication. They tend to appear reserved around others, preferring time alone over group interactions. INTJs are likely to adopt only those ideas that prove useful in moving him towards the accomplishment of a well-defined goal. They are serious and approach decisions with caution.

The Admiral could certainly see how these dichotomous personalities might have difficulty communicating with each other. He also perceived how hard it would be to choose a foreman between two people with such wildly divergent MBTI scores. Since Mark was convinced that communication lay at the heart of the issue, the Admiral decided to delve a little deeper into the communication realm.

The MBTI Communication Style Report

We've seen how MBTI results can apply to interactions between leaders and followers and how they can influence a job search. Any personality indicator can be interpreted more specifically to solve a given problem. Now the Admiral was going to employ the MBTI to provide insight into preferred styles of communication. The MBTI Communication Style Report takes personality type a step further to help people recognise their natural communication styles and discover how they differ from the styles of others, thus pointing up strategies for communicating more effectively.

The MBTI Communication Style Report says that an INTJ's communication strengths might lie in his calm, quiet presence. He would probably be thoughtful and careful in responding to questions and a good listener. He would likely be able to anticipate possibilities and recognise trends; he could use available information to analyse and evaluate strategies. Ian could provide feedback honestly and frankly, but his feedback would likely be corrective as opposed to positive. Ian was probably motivated by well-defined goals and would communicate in an organised and efficient fashion. He would be independent, keeping ideas to himself at first and sharing them only when they were fully thought out and ready to translate into action. He would be direct and to the point, serious and straightforward.

ESFPs tend to be enthusiastic and positive, preferring others with the same qualities; they enjoy interactions with many different people, dislike being alone, and often seek to be the centre of attention. Gordon probably formed personal relationships first, expanding those relationships later to include the workplace. Fun and laughter are often essential components of a conversation with an ESFP. Gordon was likely to tend towards direct action with immediate results, as opposed to long-range or time-driven planning. An ESFP frequently communicates through storytelling punctuated with wit and banter, using personal experience to drive his point home. Gordon probably responded quickly to questions and was adept at thinking on his feet.

The Admiral believed that Ian and Gordon might find each other's personality types to be the most challenging to communicate with. The Intuitive function is the least used, least energised, and least preferred function of an ESFP. In an INTJ, Intuition is dominant. The challenge for an INTJ in communicating with an ESFP is to bring abstract ideas down to earth, providing concrete examples of specific realities and details that can be immediately applied. ESFPs tend not to like people who are so serious or focused on responsibilities that they forget how to have fun.

Steps towards a solution

The Admiral explained his analysis to Mark Matthews.

"But this doesn't move me any closer to a decision," exclaimed Mark. "It's just like I thought: they're completely different. If I choose Gordon, people will be happy and morale will be high, but processes might be neglected and productivity might suffer. If I choose Ian, he'll have great ideas for systems that can take us into the future, but the staff might feel criticised and underappreciated. And whichever one I choose, the other one is going to be disappointed and angry."

"I like the way you're thinking about the problem," said the Admiral. "I can see that you recognise and appreciate Gordon's and Ian's individual strengths. One of the most important things to remember about personality measures, and especially the MBTI, is that personality types point out people's strengths. Each person has unique gifts and contributions. You recognise those in your employees, which helps make you a good manager. Can you think of some way you might combine the strengths of the two men to address your problem?"

Mark thought carefully. "I think I have something," he said. "What if I gave the foreman position to *both* Ian and Gordon? We could divide the salary increase between them and have them work together to split up the workload."

"I think that's an excellent idea," said the Admiral. "You've hit on a possible solution.

"There may be some issues that arise, though," he warned. "Gordon and Ian need to learn how to work together effectively before your plan will work. I think there's more we can do to help them break out of the negative communication patterns that have developed between them over time. I'd like to do a couple of afternoon workshops with both of them, and I'd like you and Sam McGill to join us."

Mark agreed, and they set an agenda. First Mark would tell Ian and Gordon that he wanted to conduct two communication workshops to help decide which of them would be the best fit for the foreman job. "I don't want to let them in on your idea of co-foremen just yet," said the Admiral. "I want to leave their communication patterns in place so we can show them how they might break out of the negative cycle." The workshops would set the stage for a trial period in which the two men would work in tandem in the foreman spot.

The Ladder of Inference

The Admiral opened the first workshop by explaining that he, Mark, and Sam wanted a chance to observe Ian's and Gordon's communication styles closely to help them decide which man would be the best fit as warehouse foreman. The Admiral knew this would pit Ian and Gordon against each other in a competition. He had a strategy in mind based on a communication concept developed by Chris Argyris called the **Ladder of Inference**.[8]

"Today I want to do a little demonstration about how we communicate," began the Admiral. "We live in a world of self-generating beliefs – beliefs that we use to make fundamental assumptions about, how we understand and interpret our communications and those of others. Communication is not only about talking; it's also about listening and watching body language.

"All right," the Admiral continued. "Now we're going to try something. Ian and Gordon, I would like each of you to go into another room – each into a separate room, not the same one. We're going to give you twenty minutes to think about a single simple way in which you could change warehouse operations to make a process work more smoothly. You may jot down some notes if you like. Then I'd like you to come back in here and each give us a ten-minute presentation about your idea."

Ian and Gordon agreed and left the room. During the allotted twenty, the Admiral turned to Mark and Sam. "While they're doing their presentations, I want you to be equally attentive to each of them. Nod approval, show interest, and write down a few notes while they're talking. Then ask each of them a couple of questions about their ideas. Make sure the questions are relevant to show that you were interested and listening. As much as possible,

---

8   Chris Argyris, Robert W. Putnam, and Diana McLean Smith, *Action Science: Concepts, methods, and skills for research and intervention* (San Francisco: Jossey-Bass, 1985).

I want you to react exactly the same way to both of the presentations, no matter what I do. Okay?"

"Okay," said Mark. "Sure," said Sam.

When the twenty minutes were up, Ian and Gordon returned to the conference room. The Admiral had both men sit facing their three-man audience so each could observe audience reactions while the other was talking. "Gordon, why don't you go first?" said the Admiral.

Gordon's idea was to divide the warehouse staff into functional teams and have each team meet every other week to brainstorm ideas for streamlining operations. He proposed that, as foreman, he would attend all the meetings at the beginning and then phase out as the teams became self-sufficient. As instructed, Mark and Sam listened intently, taking notes, and asked Gordon a few pointed follow-up questions. The Admiral mimicked their behaviour. He appeared clearly engaged as Gordon spoke, nodding approvingly from time to time and maintaining eye contact and a bright, pleasant demeanour. He also posed a couple of questions, listening carefully and showing interest as Gordon responded. As usual, Gordon was animated and talkative; his presentation was laced with humour and personal anecdotes. When it was finished, he sat down evidently quite pleased with his performance and the audience's reaction.

Then it was Ian's turn. His idea involved adding an available upgrade to the WCS that would allow them to call up historical data regarding vendor shipments. Comparing the history of prior shipments to new shipments coming in would help ensure accuracy, and the software upgrade could raise an alert whenever there was an anomaly. Ian presented clearly and concisely, sticking to the facts and providing concrete examples.

Mark and Sam responded just as they had done with Gordon. They stayed engaged, showed approval, jotted down notes, and asked relevant questions. But the Admiral made a 180-degree turn in his behaviour. He remained silent. He looked off to the side or at the floor while Ian spoke, propped his elbows on the table, and sometimes put his hands over his mouth. Several times he glanced at the clock, and once he yawned widely and audibly. When Ian had finished and Mark and Sam were asking questions, the Admiral interrupted Ian mid-sentence. "Let's have Ian put his idea in writing," he said abruptly. "I think we're done here."

Ian flushed and sat down, clearly flustered and upset. "Okay," said the Admiral, "that's it for today. We'll meet again tomorrow and discuss the two presentations."

Ian left with a sinking heart. *Wow*, he thought. *That guy does not like me.*

Mark and Sam seemed genuinely interested in my idea, but that Admiral wasn't even listening. I could tell he liked Gordon's presentation, but when I was talking, he was bored and distracted – he even yawned! *I'll bet he thinks I'm stupid – he believes I'm incompetent. He's just like Gordon – a self-centred power-hungry jerk. I'm definitely not going to get the foreman job now because the Admiral's already decided he wants Gordon. It's a shame, because my ideas are exactly what this warehouse needs. I wonder if I should just quit now that I know I've got an enemy on the team.*

The next day just the Admiral and Mark met with Ian and Gordon for the communication workshop.

"I'd like to debrief on what happened yesterday," said the Admiral. "Gordon, how did you feel about your presentation? Were you happy with it?"

"I think so," said Gordon. "I thought I came up with a pretty good idea, and everyone seemed to agree with me. And you all had some great questions, which made me think about ways I could make my idea even better."

"Thanks," said the Admiral. "Ian? How about you?"

Ian looked down at the table. "I guess I must not have presented my idea very well," he said reservedly. "Or else you would have been more interested. Maybe I should just withdraw my name from consideration for warehouse foreman."

"Ian, I'm going to let you off the hook now," said the Admiral. "I reacted to your presentation the way I did in order to prove a point." He got up and went to the whiteboard.

"Yesterday I mentioned that we use self-generating beliefs to make fundamental assumptions about how we understand and interpret communications, and how others interpret what we say. People tend to understand communication based on these four ideas."

On the whiteboard, the Admiral wrote:

- Our beliefs are *the* truth.
- The truth is obvious.
- Our beliefs are based on real data.
- The data that we select are the real data.

"For example," continued the Admiral, "yesterday while Ian was talking, I didn't look him in the eye. I looked away, checked the clock, put my hands over my face, and yawned. Then I interrupted Ian and cut the presentation short. Ian, you probably made several assumptions about what I was thinking about you. Am I right?"

"Well," said Ian hesitantly, "I figured you didn't like my presentation. Maybe even that you didn't like me."

"Of course you did," said the Admiral. "And then you started believing that I think you're incapable and that I'm opposed to choosing you as the warehouse foreman. After that you decided you should withdraw your application, and maybe even quit your job. Is that correct?"

"Yes," admitted Ian.

The Admiral put a large poster of the following diagram up on an easel.

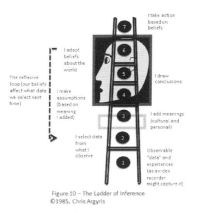

Figure 10 – The Ladder of Inference
©1985, Chris Argyris

Figure 10 – The Ladder of Inference
©1985, Chris Argyris

"This is an illustration of what Chris Argyris calls the **Ladder of Inference**," the Admiral explained. "Start at the bottom rung. Here's the sequence of events Ian went through yesterday after I was rude during his presentation."

The Admiral pointed to the bottom rung on the ladder. "Ian started with observable data, that is, when I cut his presentation short by saying 'Let's have Ian put his idea in writing.' Along with my looking at the clock and yawning, those were data to which all of you were privy: observable actions so evident that they would have showed up on a video recording." He pointed to the second rung. "Next Ian selected some details from my behaviour. He remembered that I avoided eye contact, checked the clock several times, and yawned. Now, Ian, were you looking at me every minute while you were talking?"

"No," said Ian, "I was looking around at each person, trying to engage everyone in my presentation."

"Of course," said the Admiral. "So consider this: for all you knew, there were other times when I was looking at you and listening intently – moments that you missed because you were looking elsewhere. Remember that you choose which data you select.

"At the third rung on the ladder," he continued, "Ian added some meaning of his own based on cultural or environmental factors. In this case, the added meaning was that I wanted his presentation to be over. Then he moved on to the fourth rung, where he made assumptions about my current state – he assumed that I was bored.

"At the fifth step on the ladder, Ian drew conclusions about what I was thinking. He concluded that I didn't like his presentation and that possibly I didn't even like him. In fact, Ian, you concluded that I think you're incompetent for the foreman job. Is that right?"

"Yes," said Ian.

"Okay," said the Admiral. "Then you moved on to taking action – the top rung. You decided to withdraw your name from consideration for the position, and you considered the possibility of quitting your job altogether.

"The rungs on this ladder represent steps that all of us take. Notice that most of the steps are hidden and take place inside our heads. The only rungs visible to others are the first one, the observable data, and the last one, the action. The rest of the trip up the ladder, which is where we spend most of our time, is unseen and unquestioned – it's enormously abstract and generally considered unfit for discussion. And the whole process takes place so fast that we're not even aware it's happening.

"Each time we communicate, we move up the ladder many times. Over time, if Ian observes more data from me that leads him to conclude that I'm an evil guy who has it in for him, he would be more likely to notice any malevolent behaviour on my part later. This is called a 'reflexive loop': our beliefs influence which data we select next time. Thus the conclusions we reach are not always correct. For example, Ian, I might have been eager to see how your report looked on paper. Maybe I'm shy, or perhaps I was afraid a question or comment might embarrass you.

"Ian and Gordon, your communication styles are very different. I'd like you to think about how the Ladder of Inference might influence your opinions of each other and how you treat each other."

"I think I get what you're talking about, but I have a question," said Gordon. "It's all fine and dandy to paint a picture of how we jump to conclusions. But how do we figure out whether our conclusions are right or wrong?"

"That's a good question," said the Admiral. "We can't know until we find a way to check. Now, assumptions and conclusions are difficult to test. In this example, Ian could have pulled me aside and asked, 'Admiral, do you think I'm an idiot? Did my presentation bore you silly?' But he'd be very unlikely to do that, and even if he did, he probably wouldn't be able to trust my answer, because we have not built a foundation of trust between us yet.

"We can't live our lives without assumptions or conclusions; our world would be tedious and inefficient. But what we *can* do is use the Ladder of Inference to improve our communications in three ways."

The Admiral went to the whiteboard and wrote down three concepts:

1. **Reflection**
2. **Advocacy**
3. **Enquiry**

"First," he said, "We can use the diagram to become more aware of our own thinking and reasoning, through *reflection* about the data we choose to observe and the conclusions we draw from it." The Admiral drew a picture of the Johari Window and explained how communication works to increase the open windowpane. Then he showed the relationship framework diagram and discussed how open communication, self-disclosure, and letting go of one's personal agenda helps build trust.

"Second," he went on, "we can work towards making our thinking and reasoning process – the middle rungs on the ladder – more visible to others." The Admiral drew the UZOD chart on the whiteboard. He explained that the UZOD was the place where people felt enough trust and self-awareness to introduce ideas even when they knew those ideas would be challenged. "If you enter the UZOD, you're willing to *advocate* for your ideas, which essentially makes your travel up the ladder visible to others. That's the advocacy step.

"Finally," said the Admiral, "within the UZOD, we feel free to *enquire* into other people's thinking and reasoning processes. This facilitates self-disclosure and may help expose the steps others are making up the Ladder of Inference. And the more information we have about those thought progressions, the better we communicate with one another and the more trust we build, so the more productive we become at solving problems and working effectively as a group."

"How would we go about that?" asked Ian. "I mean the enquiry step?"

"Another good question," the Admiral responded. "When someone makes an abstract or controversial statement, you could literally stop a conversation in its tracks and ask a few questions." He wrote the following questions on the whiteboard:

1. What are the observable data behind that statement?
2. Does everyone agree on what the observable data are?
3. Can you run me through your reasoning?
4. How did we get from the data to these abstract assumptions?
5. When you said "your implication", did you mean "my inference about it"?

Ian and Gordon listened carefully to the Admiral's words. Each of them was thinking about times when he'd drawn conclusions about the other by climbing up the Ladder of Inference.

"I think this is a good time to make your announcement, Mark," said the Admiral. Mark went on to explain his decision to promote both men to warehouse foreman, splitting the pay increase between them and leaving them with the task of dividing up the duties.

"Although you may separate the workload in whatever way makes sense to you, I also want you to work together on some projects," said Mark. "Your first assignment is to create a training programme to teach new staff how to use the WCS. That will require you to develop viable systems that can take us into the future, which is one of Ian's strengths. It also will require hands-on interaction with a lot of people, which is one of Gordon's strong points."

"Congratulations, Ian and Gordon," said the Admiral. "Mark, I think you've hit on a winning combination."

Following up

In the coming weeks, Mark watched the progress of his two newly appointed warehouse foremen. Over time, Mark witnessed important changes in the two men. They had appreciated the fairness and faith Mark had demonstrated by offering them the foremanship jointly. Instead of being pitted against each other in a constant battle to communicate, they started to strike a more harmonious balance. They dropped some of their desires for personal achievement and built trust in their working relationship.

At the beginning, Mark made time every two weeks to meet with Ian and Gordon. He asked them to summarise what they were working on and to identify challenges or barriers to production. Then he facilitated a problem-solving discussion. Mark kept the Ladder of Inference diagram up for all these meetings. Whenever Gordon or Ian made a statement that sounded like an abstract and negative conclusion, Mark would halt the conversation and go back to the Admiral's five questions. Eventually Mark was able to attend fewer of the meetings and allow his two foremen to work out their own discussions. Although the two men still differed widely in communication style, they began to trust one another enough to spend more time in the UZOD and less time in Zone B, the space of constant disagreement.

As each man became more willing to make his mental processes more visible to the other, bring his ideas up to be challenged, and strive for new solutions with the other, they synergised – forming a work unit greater than the sum of its two parts. Worldwide Widgets was one step further along its way towards achieving global presence and success.

Now what do you think?

This time the Admiral did not pose a solution to the problem. Instead, he gave all the parties some tools to help them discover solutions for themselves. How well do you think Ian and Gordon will continue to trust each other and move towards synergy? Do you believe their communication problems may crop up again in the future? Think of a time when you had a difficult communication issue. How did the Ladder of Inference figure into your problem? Were you hanging on to a personal agenda, and were you making assumptions? What might have happened if you had used reflection, advocacy, and enquiry to make the steps up the ladder more visible to yourself and to others?

The Battle of Communication is perhaps the most prevalent of the workplace wars. Using psychometrics to reveal the various personality and communication styles involved can help an organisation with the *reflection* step – that is, learning to understand people's psychometric differences can increase awareness of the thinking and reasoning behind their behaviour. Psychometric evaluation also offers a vocabulary to help make one's own thinking and reasoning more visible and a framework for assessing others' thinking and reasoning processes. Recognising the differences between personalities as strengths rather than weaknesses and combining those personality attributes in ways that move individuals into the UZOD not only eliminates the Battle of Communication, it can help guarantee company success.

CHAPTER IV

The Battle of Decision-making

Every day we face choices. Fried eggs or scrambled for breakfast? Should we take surface streets or the expressway for our morning commute? Which item on our to-do list should we tackle first? Should we vote Conservative or Liberal? When we select a course of action that we perceive to have the highest value compared to its alternatives, that process is called *decision-making*. Decision-making is distinctly human; our large brains are built for such activity. We choose actions using complex mental processes influenced by reason, bias, analysis, emotion, judgement, and memories of past success and failure.

At work we must make decisions daily, especially if we are workplace leaders: decision-making is what a manager is paid to do. Workplace decisions often carry even more weight than personal ones. We make some decisions quickly, even subconsciously; over others we agonise and fret. The difference between a good decision and a horrible one is far from random. Decision-making is a skill – one that can be learned and perfected. And while mastering the skill of critical decision-making has clear benefits to one's work life, those benefits extend to the home and community as well. A smart decision is informed by a set of psychological, social, and emotional components. Understanding those components allows us to grasp the consequences of past mistakes and avoid repeating them.

Bad decisions are usually the result of a poorly defined thought process. Good decision-makers place heavy emphasis on *how* they make each decision, following a series of logical steps. Once a problem is recognised and clearly stated, the decision-maker must gather information and obtain input from other interested parties, identify and evaluate the alternatives, choose the best alternative based on available data, and put methods in place to evaluate how well the choice works. Decision-making should be dynamic: if one choice proves unsatisfactory, the decision-maker should have backup choices ready to implement. Equal attention to each of these constructive steps can greatly strengthen the decision-making process and ensure successful outcomes.

What you've read so far in this book should show you some ways personality might affect decision-making. For example, whether a person leans towards Thinking or Feeling, Perceiving or Judging on the MBTI will influence how they define problems or how (and from whom) they seek information. Consider how a Serious versus Lively score on the 16PF might colour personal biases, or how Tradition versus Openness to Change might alter one's identification and evaluation of various alternatives.

Those whose MBTI scores show a preference for Thinking might be considered "left-brained," or analytical, while those whose scores indicate that they prefer Feeling might be considered "right-brained," or intuitive. A balance between left-brain analysis and right-brain intuition is critical to making a good decision. And while everyone's personality has dominant functions, we all should strive to understand our non-dominant functions as well in order to strike the balance needed to make an informed decision.

In today's rapidly changing business world, employees must be encouraged to think creatively to find innovative solutions. Companies have to meet customers' needs through an effective problem-solving process that identifies both novel and traditional alternatives and then helps them choose the best alternative – or combination of alternatives – from the array. Decisions are guided not only by the personality characteristics of the individuals making them but also by the guiding principles, or *values*, of the individuals, of the organisation, and of society as a whole.

In his book **Building a Values-driven Organisation**, personal transformation and leadership expert Richard Barrett offers a conceptual framework by stating that decisions are made in four stages:[9]

1. *Data gathering*: We gather data from the outside world using our five senses: visual, auditory, kinaesthetic, olfactory, and gustatory.
2. *Information processing*: We use our brains to integrate the data we gathered through our five senses into information packages.
3. *Meaning-making*: Our minds compare the information packages with information stored in our memories to locate a match.
4. *Decision-making*: When the brain finds a match, it releases the instructions attached to the memory along with any associated emotional charges, resulting in actions and behaviours. If the brain does not find a match, it uses logic to formulate a response to the

---

9   Richard Barrett, *Building a Values-Driven Organization: A Whole System Approach to Cultural Transformation* (Oxford: Butterworth-Heinemann, 2006).

situation. In other words, we choose a decision-making mode with which to respond.

Six modes of decision-making

According to Barrett, the difference between each decision-making mode is the source of and emphasis we give to the meaning-making stage. There are six progressive sources of meaning: instincts, subconscious beliefs, conscious beliefs, values, intuition, and inspiration.

1. ***Instinct-based decision-making***. The main features of the instinct mode are as follows:
   - Actions always precede thoughts; there is no pause for reflection between meaning-making and decision-making.
   - Decisions are always based on previous experience.
   - We are not in control of our actions and behaviours.

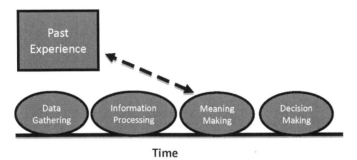

Time

Figure 11 – Instinct-based decision-making
Reproduced with kind permission from Barrett, Richard
(2011). *The New Leadership Paradigm*. Lulu.com.

2. ***Subconscious belief–based decision-making.*** The main features of this mode are the same as in the instinct model. The only difference is that during instinct-driven decision-making, we refer to actions that are not taught – like crying when our needs are not being met or smiling when we get attention. During subconscious decision-making, we refer to personal history – i.e. we draw the decision from our personal memories.

3. ***Conscious belief–based decision-making***. Here we pause between meaning-making and the decision. The pause allows time for reflection and thought; we use logic to understand what is

happening and attach appropriate meaning out of the situation. Like subconscious decision-making, conscious decision-making uses information from past experiences.

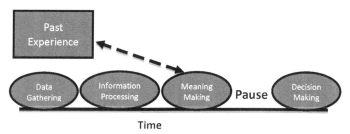

Figure 12 – Conscious belief-based decision-making
Reproduced with kind permission from Barrett, Richard (2011). *The New Leadership Paradigm.* Lulu.com.

4. ***Value-based decision-making.*** In this mode we shift from making decisions based on beliefs to making decisions based on values. That is, we ask, "Is this decision rational, and does it align with my values?" "How can I respond to this situation in a way that expresses my most deeply held values?" In this mode, our values rather than our beliefs guide the decision.

5. ***Intuition-based decision-making.*** The shift from values-based to intuition-based decision-making develops over time as one's centre of gravity of consciousness shifts from the ego to the soul. There is no focus on past or future, and one simply accepts what is without judgement. Barrett suggests that here we tap into a mind space that is collective rather than individual.

6. ***Inspiration-based decision-making.*** Inspiration refers to the way our minds receive soul-based prompts. Inspiration is personal and directive and is about the things we need to do. Inspiration will continue prompting us to take action until we actually do.

The scenarios I present in this book allow you to compare and contrast various methods for how people (including you) go about making decisions. Thus you refine your ability to distinguish between decision-making strategies. Every scenario in this book includes some element of decision-making. In the scenario that follows, consider which decision-making modes the characters use. Do you perceive that any of their decisions are instinctive or subconscious? Are the characters conscious of the beliefs behind their decisions, and do they allow time to pause for logical consideration? Do they consider the values behind their decisions before proceeding? As you read, try to identify the process *you* would follow to reach a solution.

Scenario: Healing Healthwell

> *The time to take counsel of your fears is before you make an important battle decision. That's the time to listen to every fear you can imagine! When you have collected all the facts and fears and made your decision, turn off all your fears and go ahead!* ~George S. Patton

MegaPharm Sales Manager Sarah Strong sat at her desk that afternoon writing content for a promotional brochure to distribute at the upcoming hospital and health-care expo. She was feeling confident and energetic. As manager of a Pharmaceutical Sales Department, Sarah knew her team of ten skilled, dedicated, and professional employees was out there backing her up.

Sarah had moved into management two years prior, taking full responsibility both to manage existing clients and to create new business for MegaPharm product distribution. Half of her sales team was an inherited group of people who had once been her peers; the other half she had carefully screened and selected herself. Sarah had complete faith in all of them. MegaPharm used a functional system to assign its primary customers – the hospitals and large clinics – to a dedicated sales representative who handled all their pharmaceutical orders. Four of Sarah's staff members filled those roles. The remaining six were responsible for obtaining new customers and building and maintaining individual client bases comprised of private-practice physicians and small clinics. The system worked well.

Sarah had just finished writing her copy and was preparing to contact the layout designer when her desk phone rang. She picked up the receiver. "Sarah Strong," she answered briskly.

"Sarah, this is Ann Baker at Healthwell."

"Oh, hello, Ann," said Sarah. "It's wonderful to hear from you. How was your trip to the mainland last month?" The two women spent a few moments exchanging small talk about children, families, trips, professional pursuits. Healthwell Hospital was the largest health-care facility in the city and MegaPharm's most important client; Ann was hospital administrator.

At one time, Sarah had served as the hospital's dedicated representative – a spot considered rather a plum by the MegaPharm sales staff. Since she had taken over department management, Sarah did everything possible within the scope of her position to keep the hospital happy. She had assigned her top sales rep, Winifred Wilson, to the account. Winifred was the best liked, hardest working, most experienced person Sarah had on staff.

In time the conversation turned to business. "So what can I do for you today, Ann?" asked Sarah. "I trust Winifred is treating you well?"

"Actually," said Ann, "that's just what I'm calling about. Sarah, we're really not satisfied with Winifred's service."

Sarah was stunned. She had placed absolute trust in Winifred's ability to handle the Healthwell account, and this was her first inkling of any problems. "I'm so sorry to hear that," she said. "Please fill me in. What are the issues? If you can tell me specifically what's going wrong, maybe I can help."

"We don't have an issue with MegaPharm per se," Ann responded. "It's really all about Winifred. She's quite slow to acquaint us with new products when they become available, and she's unresponsive to specific requests. And she behaved quite unprofessionally at one of our recent meetings. Sarah, we were so spoiled when you were our MegaPharm rep. Winifred doesn't have your style, your competence. She doesn't respect us or understand our needs. I'm afraid I must ask you to remove her from our account."

"Again, Ann, I do apologise," said Sarah. "Winifred has always been so responsible; I can't imagine what's gone wrong. You know we want to make sure Healthwell Hospital's needs are met. Isn't there something we can do to reconcile the situation?"

"I'm afraid not," Ann responded. "Please just assign us a new representative. Winifred simply won't do. I'd hate to have to take our business to Pharmaceutical Wonders."

Sarah sighed. Pharmaceutical Wonders was MegaPharm's biggest competitor. "Of course. I certainly will look into it." *I need to buy some time,* she thought. "All our sales staff will be focused on preparing for the expo for the next several days," she continued. "If you need anything in the meantime, please call me directly, and I'll make sure you're served. I'll be back to you with our decision about your sales rep by the end of next week."

As Sarah hung up the phone, a bit of the shine had worn off her usually bright exterior. This was a sticky situation indeed. Healthwell was a client MegaPharm could little afford to lose. But Sarah could hardly yank Winifred abruptly off the account. Winifred was an exemplary employee who was very well liked and respected within the MegaPharm ranks. Sarah simply didn't understand it. How could the hospital find Winifred incompetent when Sarah herself had hand-picked her? Sarah had observed Winifred's work carefully. She'd wanted to make absolutely certain that she had chosen the best qualified rep to succeed her in serving Healthwell. How could she have been so wrong?

I can't make this decision on the spot, and I don't want to make it alone, Sarah thought. *If I don't handle it right and Healthwell pulls their business, I may lose my job.* Something in Ann Baker's manner nagged at Sarah – like there was more to the problem than Ann was disclosing. She determined to make a few subtle enquiries. Maybe she could get to the bottom of the real situation.

Over the next few days, Sarah enquired discreetly among her own staff and Winifred's contacts at Healthwell. Just as she'd suspected, she learned there was more to the issue than Ann Baker had expressed over the phone. In fact, the information she uncovered hinted that Ann herself played a major role in the situation. Winifred had told someone that Ann didn't like her. Ann had criticised Winifred publicly at least twice. Ann and Winifred had been seen arguing in the Healthwell cafeteria. But it wasn't until Sarah spoke with Winifred's closest friend on the MegaPharm sales team that she felt she hit the root of the problem. "Winifred and Ann have a personal conflict," Sarah was told. "They're both very active members of the Urban Women's League, and a few months ago they got into a big disagreement about the club's leadership. They haven't gotten along since."

Aha, thought Sarah. *That puts things in better perspective.* She had been sure Winifred's work ethic was not at fault. But if Winifred and Ann were unable to solve their personal differences and work together effectively, the professional issue still had to be addressed. Sarah needed backup to help her identify the possibilities and make a good choice. She called in Irene Isaacs, MegaPharm's human resources manager, to serve as a sounding board.

Together Irene and Sarah talked through the problem and listed four possible options:

1. Dismiss Winifred.
2. Transfer Winifred to another account or to client development, and assign a new rep to Healthwell.
3. Leave Winifred on the Healthwell account and suffer the consequences; maybe Ann was bluffing.
4. Do nothing. Dodge Healthwell's calls and hope the problem resolves itself in time.

Neither Sarah nor Irene was in favour of the first option. "Winifred is a good employee," Sarah said. "She's a respected team member, and I want to keep her."

Irene concurred, adding, "We haven't gone through the company's due process for termination, anyway. You would have to put Winifred on notice and give her a chance to make improvements before you could make a case for letting her go.

"It's your decision, Sarah, but I'd like to advocate strongly for option number two," continued Irene. "That seems like your best bet for keeping everyone happy."

"Not really," said Sarah. "The Healthwell account is recognised as the best position in the MegaPharm Sales Department, the one with the most benefits and perks. Winifred will be devastated if she's transferred, she will view it as a demotion. Not to mention how it would affect morale in my department. The rest of my team will be living in constant fear of being transferred any time a client complains.

"And on top of all that," Sarah mused, "there's no way to be certain that Ann Baker can get along with the new rep I assign to the account. No, I really don't like that option either."

"I don't see how you can maintain the status quo, however," Irene responded. "Option three or four could mean losing the Healthwell account entirely."

"And perhaps my job as well." Sarah sighed. "Well, thank you, Irene. I need to wrestle with these alternatives a bit longer. I'll let you know what I decide." She concluded the meeting.

Sarah was stymied. She felt squeezed between a rock and a hard place. None of the options appeared likely to yield a positive outcome. After struggling a while longer with her problem, she decided she needed an objective opinion. So she called the Admiral.

What do *you* think?

Sarah is struggling with the Battle of Decision-making. None of her perceived options stands out as a clear best choice. Consider these questions:

1. Has Sarah engaged in a good decision-making process?
2. What more could Sarah do to inform her decision?
3. Which alternative do you think she should choose? Why?

4. Have you ever had to make a decision like the one Sarah faces? What did you decide, and how well did it work?

5. How would you describe Sarah's personality? What aspects of her personality are affecting this decision?

6. If you were the Admiral, with access to his entire psychometric toolkit, which measures might you use to help Sarah decide? From which people in the situation would you want to obtain personality measures?

7. Can you think of any alternatives Sarah and Irene have not yet imagined?

Decision-making Guide

Sarah was able to arrange a meeting with the Admiral on short notice, pleading that her decision was time sensitive so she needed immediate help. The Admiral sent over a copy of the MBTI and asked Sarah to complete it prior to the meeting. "I can compile an MBTI Decision-making Style Report that will guide our discussion," the Admiral told her.

At the meeting, the Admiral listened to Sarah's story and reviewed her notes and the options list she and Irene had generated. "Before we examine the options, Sarah, I want to review with you what goes into making a good decision," he said. "We should start there, because if we can identify a step in the process that was left out, we might turn up some new ideas."

The Admiral showed Sarah the following decision diagram:

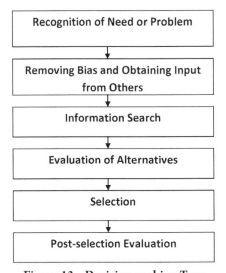

Figure 13 – Decision-making Tree

"This is a decision tree that illustrates the steps in a good decision-making process," said the Admiral. "Based on what you've told me, I'm convinced that you've followed most of the first four steps. First you learned from Healthwell that there was a problem, and then you gathered information from several people. You obtained input from Irene about possible solutions, and you came up with a set of alternatives. But I'd like to go back to the second step for a moment and talk about *bias* in decision-making. Removing our personal biases from a decision is important because it changes the way we think. It forces us to move from intuition into reasoning."

Next the Admiral explained Barrett's four modes of decision-making to Sarah: instinctive, subconscious, conscious, and values. "You seem to have developed some beliefs about what's going on behind the scenes," he continued, "and you've taken time to pause for reflection before making your choice. So your decision will be conscious. But you also may receive some guidance if you consider the values behind your decision – your own values, of course, but also the values of the other individuals involved and the organisational values of the two companies."

Two-system thinking

Next the Admiral showed Sarah another picture:

SYSTEM 1	SYSTEM 2
Unconscious	Conscious
Intuition	Reasoning
Effortless	Effortful
Fast	Slow
Process-automatic	Deliberate
Emotional	Rule-following
Decisive	Possibilities and probabilities
	Indecisive

Ficure 15 – Two-system Thinking Model

"This diagram depicts something psychologists call *dual-process thinking*," he explained. "The idea has been around for quite a long time; William James introduced the concept back in the early 1900s. Some people call it the rationality debate. It's possible for human beings to make rational decisions, but most of us find it very difficult, for three reasons. First, our minds don't work that way; second, the world is too complex; and third, we hurry because we're busy and stressed.

"Dual-process theory says that our minds are both rational and irrational at the same time. Think of your mind as a computer. Now, a computer can show one programme up on the screen while another programme is running in the background. Our minds work the same way. We have one programme running up on our mental screen, the programme of which we're conscious. But other things are being processed in the background, thoughts of which we're not aware – they're unconscious. You can see how this theory ties in with the four modes of decision-making, where decision processes are influenced by different levels of consciousness.

"In 2000, two researchers named Stanovich and West named the dual processes **System 1 and System 2.** Here, look at the diagram. System 2 is the conscious, rational process. That's the system you're aware of when you think, listen, or read. It's the programme up on your mental screen. System 2 is controllable; it follows rules; it's slow and deliberate.

"System 1 is what you might call your gut feeling or intuition. That's the system running in the background. It's those thoughts and feelings that pop into our minds, the ones whose origin we can't pinpoint. They're effortless and familiar, and we usually don't even consider where they came from – they just show up unbidden. System 1 thinking is fast and automatic and is based in our emotions.

"Let me try to illustrate the systems for you," said the Admiral. "Look at the following problem:

"**A bat and a ball together cost €1.10.**
"**The bat costs €1.00 more than the ball.**
"**How much does the ball cost?**"

"Ten cents," Sarah responded promptly.

"That's an intuitive answer, a System 1 answer," said the Admiral. "That's the answer that will pop into most people's heads immediately. Unfortunately, that answer is also wrong."

Sarah considered the problem for a few moments. "Oh, of course," she said. "The ball costs five cents, not ten. I wasn't thinking it through carefully enough."

"You had to use your System 2 functions to come up with the correct answer," the Admiral said. "Can you see how we might be influenced to make a quick System 1 judgement before we've completed the rational steps necessary to make a good decision?"

"Yes, I certainly can," mused Sarah. "Are you saying that my intuition is colouring my decision about Winifred?"

"Not at all," said the Admiral. "I'm just suggesting that you enter the rational System 2 zone and remove all your personal biases from the decision-making process before you evaluate the options. That way you can be sure you've followed the decision tree and that you'll make a choice with a higher probability of success.

"The world is too complex, and there's too much going on around us – we're incapable of consciously evaluating all those stimuli using System 2 thinking. System 2 is good for evaluating probabilities and possibilities, but it's slow and indecisive. We need System 1 to perceive stimuli in the environment, assess their significance, and react as needed. System 1 gets System 2's attention when it perceives danger; System 2 is a primitive function. But we need both systems to make decisions."

The Admiral got out Sarah's MBTI Decision-making Style Report. "Let's go over this report now," he said. "Looking at your decision-making strengths and challenges might help you to identify the important values driving your decision and to identify the balance that will guide your selection."

MBTI Decision-making Style Report

"Sarah, your scores are consistent with those of an **ENFJ** on the Myers-Briggs Type Indicator," the Admiral stated. "ENFJs lean towards Extraversion over Introversion; they prefer Intuition over Sensing, Feeling over Thinking, and Judgement over Perception. Now remember that one personality type is not better or worse than any other. They're simply different. And of course, you may relate at different levels to what the measures indicate. The psychometrics can aid decision-making because they point up areas we might find challenging. If we rationally bring our non-dominant functions into clearer focus, we can strike a balance, and better decisions come from that balance.

"When you're making a decision," the Admiral continued, "The importance you assign to each function makes a difference too. For example, look at this diagram.

ENFJ

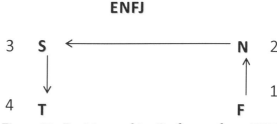

Figure 15 – Decision-making Preference for an ENFJ

"A person whose scores are consistent with an ENFJ will usually first strive to make sure the subject is aligned with his or her values (point 1), then she will look at the big picture (point 2), followed by detail (point 3), and will finally use some logic (point 4).

"Now let's look at a different type for comparison. Here's what the same diagram looks like for an ISTP:

Figure 16 – Decision-making Preference for an ISTP

"In other words, many ISTPs turn first to reasoning and logic (point 1), then to details and data (point 2), followed by big picture (point 3), and finally the value alignment (point 4)."

The Admiral went on to explain in more detail how someone of type ENFJ might prefer to make decisions. An ENFJ would be most likely to want to talk a situation through, starting with external data and considering the impact on her environment first. She would seek to involve others in the process, sharing her thoughts and feelings. Her preference for intuition would lead to a desire for conceptual data, as she wants to consider the possibilities first, looking for meanings and associations and seeking novel options. Since ENFJs lean more towards feeling than towards thinking, she would probably want to receive motivation from an external source, and her decisions would be value based. She probably would be caring and would therefore seek solutions with positive consequences for the other people and relationships involved. A tendency towards judging would lead her to want certainty, progress, and timely closure.

The decision-making strengths of ENFJs lie in their preference to involve and consider other people. They often seek solutions that empower others, and they exhibit enthusiasm, warmth, and optimism while motivating others to take action. ENFJs often raise concerns about how a potential decision would affect people's feelings. Their decisions are likely aligned with values and with the company's mission and long-term goals. An ENFJ tends to persevere and remain dedicated in the face of obstacles.

"How well do you feel this personality assessment relates to you?" the Admiral asked Sarah.

"Quite well," Sarah responded. "I see many of those qualities in myself. In particular, I consider possibilities carefully and look for solutions that generate positive outcomes for everyone involved."

The Admiral nodded agreement. "Now let's take a look at the potential challenges you might face as a decision-maker," he said. "The desire of ENFJs to make a quick decision sometimes makes them impatient with prolonged debate; it also might cause them to cut short the exploration of possible options or to overlook important details. ENFJs sometimes shy away from decisions that have potential to generate conflict. When they imagine outcomes, they are sometimes too idealistic about what can be achieved or might neglect their own ideals in favour of others'.

"Here are some suggestions meant to enhance an ENFJ's decision-making," he said. He handed Sarah the following list.

- Remember that it takes time to find the most caring and responsible goals.
- Understand that some people may feel satisfied with only a peripheral role.
- Consider investigating what is utilitarian or practical in addition to what is possible.
- Recognise that allowing more spontaneous discussion can yield new insights.
- Realise that discussing differences can be a means for deepening relationships.
- Practice speaking up – others may share the same concerns.
- Recognise that even when things don't go exactly as desired, it doesn't mean things are going wrong.
- Realise that enjoying each step in the process may yield a better result than skipping to a quick decision.
- Consider the cons of outcomes as well as the benefits for people.
- Remember that achieving a vision involves missteps and temporary setbacks.

Sarah read the list carefully. "These are good suggestions," she said. "I can see how I sometimes avoid looking at the more practical side of things because I'm considering the possibilities and have a grand vision for the future."

"That relates to System 1 versus System 2 thinking," said the Admiral.

"If you consider the issues rationally using System 2 first and then move into System 1 to make your decision, that's part of the balance."

"The idea that discussing differences can be a means for deepening relationships strikes me as particularly relevant to the issue at hand," said Sarah.

The Admiral agreed. "Does that bring any new options to mind?" he asked.

"Yes, it does," said Sarah. "I wonder if we might be able to bring Ann and Winifred together to discuss *their* differences."

"I think that's a good idea," said the Admiral. "Although we would probably be better equipped to mediate their conflict if we had personality measures for both of them as well, we can still apply what we've learned about your decision-making style. If they agree to mediation, we might stimulate the spontaneous discussion that will uncover new insights."

Thus Sarah and the Admiral formed the seeds of a plan. The following Monday, Sarah proposed mediation to both Winifred and Ann. Winifred agreed readily. She realised the alternative might be transfer or even dismissal. Ann was reluctant at first, but she finally consented after Sarah explained that mediation demonstrated a good faith that would enhance the hospital's reputation. Sarah's persuasive skills and warm, caring approach were convincing and the mediation was scheduled. The Admiral agreed to facilitate the meeting.

The steps involved in a good mediation process will be more fully described in chapter 5, "The Battle of Conflict". For my purposes here, suffice it to say that the mediation succeeded. The Admiral facilitated a discussion between Ann and Winifred that exposed the root of the problem. Both women had been nominated to chair the Urban Women's League, a powerful professional women's network in the city. Eventually their campaigns had turned to ugly accusations, and as a result, neither Ann nor Winifred had won the election. Each blamed the other for her loss. The Admiral moved the conversation into a more productive arena, appealing to the professional qualities for which the two women had been nominated in the first place. Somewhat sheepishly, Winifred and Ann agreed to set their personal differences aside and focus on the professional aspects of their relationship. Sarah committed to holding a follow-up meeting in a month to evaluate how well the solution was working and to address any new issues that might arise between Ann and Winifred.

Sarah Strong learned a great deal from her consultation with the Admiral. Understanding and accepting her natural tendency to empower others and seek solutions that improved their lives strengthened her relations with employees, colleagues, and clients alike. She also discovered a budding interest in the mediation process. In the months that followed, she enrolled in seminars and began working towards certification as a conflict resolution mediator.

Now what do you think?

The Admiral helped Sarah engage her less preferred decision-making functions to generate a new alternative better aligned with her personal and professional values. How well do you think the option worked, and do you think the mediation will have lasting positive effects? Do you believe Sarah followed a good decision-making process? Can you think of other ways she might have achieved the same or even better outcomes?

The Battle of Decision-making is a critical process for managers, clearly. But all employees face decisions daily about how to complete their work, how to pace efforts and prioritise tasks, and how to interact with co-workers and supervisors. Some decisions may be made quickly on the spot; others require careful deliberation and consideration. Some choices are yours alone, while others merit input from extensive data and from associates who have a stake in the outcome.

A good decision-maker must be a risk taker. There is never a guarantee that any decision is the correct one. The key is to follow the steps in due process. Remove your personal biases and use rational thinking to gather data from multiple sources, generate several viable options, and then weigh the pros and cons of each option to select the most attractive one. Understand and examine the values behind each decision you undertake. Remember that your gut reaction is often wrong and that sometimes the best option is a combination of choices. Set a follow-up procedure to monitor results. Then use your mistakes as opportunities. If you make a bad decision, what didn't work and why? Don't second-guess yourself; decide and then let the chips fall. Lessons you learn from poor decisions only drive you to make better decisions down the road.

CHAPTER V

It would be an unusual workplace that never produced differences of opinion. After all, workplaces are social environments where we interact with a variety of people, and different people affect us in different ways. No matter how hard we try, we will never agree with everyone all the time.

Merriam-Webster's New World Dictionary defines **conflict** as "a fight, battle, or war." In that context the title of this chapter, "The Battle of Conflict," may appear redundant, but it is an appropriate extension of the book's central metaphor. Conflict underlies every scenario in these pages; how each battle is resolved changes based on the reasons behind that conflict. The root of **workplace conflict** can be a difference of wants, needs, or expectations between employees. Certainly the workplace is filled with people whose wants, needs, and expectations are likely to differ at any given moment. The myriad aspects of personality alone practically guarantee that conflict among colleagues will occur.

What causes conflict at work? Communication – or lack thereof – forms the basis of most disagreements. How information is shared (or *not* shared), how colleagues relate, and how tolerant workers are of differing communication styles easily can generate conflict. Poor organisational systems place strain on employees, especially when decisions are made out of hand without employee input or buy-in. Other sources of conflict include differences in values and priorities (perceptions of what's important), how and when things get done (scheduling and procedures), and assignment of responsibilities (work distribution, workload, and structure). Unfair hierarchies, quotas, incentives, or promotional policies can breed unhealthy competition and turf battles among co-workers. And while some amount of stress in the workplace is normal and necessary, when added to stress from employees' personal lives, the overload may cause frustration and blow-ups on the job.

Workplace conflict can be costly to an organisation. Conflict can have devastating impact on the parties directly involved, on surrounding colleagues and teams, on clients – in short, conflict affects the entire business. Conflicts at work produce stress and anxiety, which translate to absenteeism, lost productivity, client complaints, and employee turnover – even to injuries, accidents, or sabotage. In 2008 CPP Inc. (the organisation that publishes and distributes many of the psychometric instruments guiding this book) conducted research which indicated that employees in the United States spend an average of 2.8 hours per week dealing with conflict, which cost more than $359 billion in lost time that year.[10]

But, as I hope earlier chapters in this book have conveyed, workplace conflict is not all bad; its effects also can be positive. In relation to the Uncomfortable Zone of Debate (UZOD), stepping outside one's comfort zone to enter an area where difficult problems can be brought to light and productively discussed is the key to maximum workplace performance. A work environment with no competing ideas or viewpoints would be a dull one, and such a business would likely end up stuck in an unproductive past. Creative conflict within the UZOD is desirable, as it leads to positive change and development. So perhaps the trouble with workplace conflict lies not in the conflict itself but in how we deal with it. Just as disagreements come in different shapes and sizes, so do methods of conflict resolution.

Conflicts at work escalate, but their results have a narrowing effect. That is, as conflicts grow, employees' focus and productivity shrink. One thing leads to another, relationships deteriorate, and positions harden into battle formations; the situation gets sucked into a downward spiral something like this:

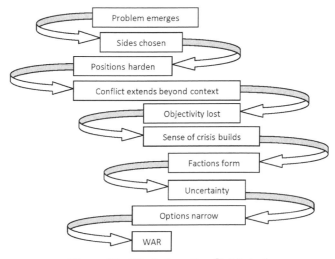

Figure 17 – Workplace Conflict Spiral

10   CPP Inc., *CPP Global Human Capital Report: Workplace Conflict and How Businesses can Harness it to Thrive* (Mountainview, CA: CPP Inc., 2008).

As war ensues, working relationships are the primary casualties. At that point, it's important that a workplace have a clear plan for dealing with disputes.

Picture dealing with conflict as points along a scale. At one end of the scale, you just turn your back on the problem. You say, "Forget about it," and try to move on – you ignore the issue. But how often does that strategy work? At the other end of the scale is full-on war, and war's inevitable casualties should deter you from resorting to that option.

In between "ignore" and "war" lies a progression of steps you, a manager, or an employer might take to resolve a conflict, as described by this diagram:

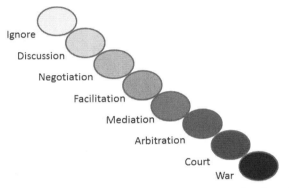

Figure 18 – Conflict Progression from "Ignore" to "War"

Note that each process along the scale demands some communication. Since conflict often results from a communication breakdown between two people, seeking support from an objective third party – someone like the Admiral – has clear merits for fostering resolution.

Continued growth within an organisation inevitably means adding staff. As the number of employees working alongside each other increases, the potential for conflict increases as well. Personality conflicts are more likely as more personalities gather. And burgeoning growth often calls for creative allocation of space, putting people closer together and limiting their chances for solitude. There's no workplace battle more classic than a fight over office space. This chapter's scenario addresses a typical office-space conflict and a possible strategy for its resolution.

To set up a conceptual framework for this chapter's story, study the following three-point diagram:

Figure 19 – The Drama Triangle*

*The drama triangle is a psychological and social model of human interaction used in transactional analysis (TA); first described by Stephen Karpman in his article Fairy Tales and Script Drama Analysis (1968).

Each point in the triangle represents an extreme position from which an individual might approach a conflict. In reality, few people would sit at any of these three extremes in a given interaction; most would be likely to fall someplace along the triangle's lines, using a combination of approaches. Someone sitting at dead centre would represent an ideal balance, successfully avoiding all three extremes. As you read this chapter's story, think about where the characters fall on this conceptual triangle. Are they staying safe by playing the victim and avoiding blame? Are they seizing power through persecution, claiming their position is the only right one? Or are they seeking acceptance by assuming the role of rescuer? Finally, consider whether the characters are combining their modes of approaching the conflict and whether any one of them has achieved that balance in the centre. This conceptual framework can apply to any conflict situation, whether in the workplace or elsewhere.

Scenario: Moving Up at Fine Restaurant Design

Character ... is a habit, the daily choice of right over wrong; it is a moral quality which grows to maturity in peace and is not suddenly developed on the outbreak of war. ~**Charles Wilson**

To jaw-jaw is always better than to war-war. ~**Winston Churchill**

As Pat Price made his way back from the client meeting to his cubicle, he stopped briefly at the closed door of the empty office at the building's northwest corner. The office had been vacated ten days before when Jared Jones had been kicked upstairs with a handsome promotion. Pat moved closer to the hallway window, cupping hands around his eyes to view the interior. It was a spacious office, close to 14 feet square, neatly and professionally furnished. A good-sized exterior window looked onto the courtyard below. He pictured himself sitting at the desk, imagining how he would arrange photos of his wife and kids on the glossy surface. He fantasised about sitting opposite important clients in the comfy guest chairs instead of entertaining them in the conference room he'd just left. It was a great office. He wanted it.

As Pat reluctantly resumed his walk down the hall, he looked up as Keith Kaiser passed him carrying an armload of blueprints. "Afternoon, Keith," said Pat.

"Price," Keith said with a brusque nod. "Checking out the vacant office, I see."

"Just looking," said Pat wistfully. "It sure would be nice to have all that private space. But it's just a pipe dream, I suppose."

Keith looked down at the floor and went on without another word. Pat headed back to his cubicle and called up the CAD software on his computer. He had two designs with deadlines that day, so he'd better get started if he wanted to finish before midnight. But as he worked, he stopped briefly from time to time, daydreaming about that vacant office in the corner.

Pat Price and Keith Kaiser had started working at Fine Restaurant Design within a month of one another. Both were restaurant planners – the idea men who helped budding restaurateurs design kitchen and dining-facility layouts to suit visionary clienteles, chef teams, and waitstaff. Sometimes they drew plans for seasoned restaurant owners to remodel an existing facility; sometimes they designed a new eatery from the ground up. Both were pros at using computer-aided design (CAD) systems, which placed them just south of being drafters and just north of being architects. While the two men brought different strengths and perspectives to their work, both enjoyed their positions immensely and were near equals in both talent and skill.

Fine Restaurant Design had suffered somewhat from the recent downturn in the global economy, but imminent recovery meant business once again was booming. Pat and Keith had come on board during one of FRD's growth spurts the previous year, and they'd witnessed a steady influx of new employees ever since. Growth had made space allocation an ongoing challenge – the office was bursting at the seams. Pat's and Keith's cubicles lay in an open centre area on the second floor, bordered by hallways containing offices occupied by managers, administrators, and designers with seniority. Although the cubicles were large and well equipped, an office was a badge of respect. Jared's promotion to vice president of design had earned him an even larger space in the executive suite. Either Pat or Keith could be in line to fill the office now sitting empty on the design floor; they were equally deserving of the recognition.

Finally Pat gave in. He wouldn't be able to finish his designs as long as he was distracted by dreams of that beautiful office. He was going to do something about it.

Resolutely, he strode down the west hallway to Art Carroll's office. Art was the design manager, administrator in charge of Fine Restaurant Design's large design team. A designer of considerable skill himself, Art had been in their position for many years before being chosen to fill the shoes Jared Jones had so recently vacated. Now he was Pat and Keith's new boss.

As Pat approached Art's open door, he was surprised to see Keith already sitting inside. Although Pat and Keith were peers of similar perceived value to the firm, Keith was the far less outspoken of the two. Pat couldn't imagine that Keith would be there to ask for the corner office. As it turned out, he was right.

"Come on in, Pat," said Art. "Keith and I were just discussing some of the finer details of his design for that new Bean Stop on Eighty-Fifth Street."

"Thanks," said Pat, entering and taking the empty seat at Keith's right. "Actually, I'm glad Keith's here. I'd like to run something by you, Art, and I think it would be a good idea for Keith to hear it too."

Out of the corner of his eye, Pat could just see Keith's face – did he look shocked and upset, or was that Pat's imagination?

"Okay, shoot," said Art. Keith remained quiet, so Pat forged ahead.

"It's about that corner office, Jared's old space," Pat said. "Now, I know Keith and I both have our eyes on it, and I want to be upfront about this. Keith here is an excellent designer. I really respect him and his work. I know making a decision about who gets the office won't be easy for you. But I want to make a case for why I should get that space, and just to keep things fair and above board, I want Keith to hear it too.

"The other designers with private offices have lots of seniority," continued Pat. "But Keith and I are next in line to get one. And while we both started our tenure at close to the same time, I did start working for FRD three weeks before Keith. That's my first justification."

"Go on," said Art.

"Second, I want to say again that Keith is a great designer, and I know the company values his work. But I've brought in at least 20 per cent more clients than he has over the past year because of my connections at the Restaurateurs'

Guild." Pat's father was a restaurant owner and member of the guild; he regularly referred members of his network to Pat when they needed new designs. Pat's connections in that organisation were well known at FRD.

"And finally," Pat concluded, "I'm taking the certification test for the latest version of AutoCAD next week. Once I pass, I'll be the first designer at FRD with the new credential. I really think that should give me the edge for that corner office."

Art considered silently for a moment. Then he turned to Keith. "Do you have anything to say about this?" he asked.

Keith demurred. "It's really up to you," he said. "I trust you to make the best decision."

"Okay," said Art, turning back to Pat. "Thanks for giving me your perspective, Pat. You've made a good case, but I'll have to think it over, and it's not my decision alone. I'll let you know when the management team has had a chance to discuss it."

"I couldn't ask for more," said Pat. "Thanks, Art. Keith." He nodded to Keith on the way out. Keith did not respond, but as their eyes met, Pat thought he detected a hint of malice in Keith's.

Pat returned to his design work. Satisfied that he'd done all he could do towards acquiring his dream office, he was better able to concentrate and worked productively through the rest of the afternoon. Across the maze of cubicles, he could see Keith's head bent over his own tasks. A little before five o'clock he heard Keith packing up his briefcase and then saw him walk to the elevator and get on. *Quitting time for some people*, thought Pat. He still had another hour or so of work to meet his deadline. Just then his computer pinged to alert him that an email had been delivered. He opened the programme and saw the new message. It was from Keith.

> To: Pat Price
> From: Keith Kaiser
> Subject: Discussion in Art Carroll's office today
> Dear Price,
>
> I feel compelled to comment on your behaviour in Art's office this afternoon. Your plug to be assigned the northwest corner office was selfish, premature, and inappropriate. Art has been design manager for no more than ten days before you started bothering him about office space. I'm sure he has more important decisions on his plate than satisfying your petty desire for status and prestige.
>
> Further, your case for getting the office was lame at best. First of

all, three weeks hardly constitutes seniority. Second, while you may exploit your father's position to attract clients, I've brought in as much or more business than you have, if you look at the bottom line. My Bean Stop contract alone is worth three of yours in terms of earned revenue. And finally, for your information, I am taking the AutoCAD certification course a day ahead of you next week, so that argument doesn't hold water either.

I guess I shouldn't be surprised at your behaviour. I tend to agree with others who have suggested that your work and your communication style are inappropriate and unprofessional. I've also observed that you spend a good deal of company time and resources conducting your own personal business. In the future, you might think twice before making such a self-serving request in front of your colleagues.

Sincerely,
Keith Kaiser

Wow. That was a zinger of an email, all right. *Keith Kaiser is a piece of work*, Pat thought. *He doesn't say a word in Art's office, and then he gets all passive-aggressive on me.* In three short paragraphs, Keith had managed to disparage Pat's talent, professionalism, and work ethic, and even to imply that a lot of other people agreed with his negative opinion and were talking about him behind his back. Pat ran his hands over his face. What should he do? He could forward the message to Art, but that might make him look as petty as Keith said he was. He could ignore it, but that would give Keith license to continue undermining his reputation behind his back.

Pat decided he wasn't going to let this one go. He was going to confront Keith first thing tomorrow.

And that was exactly what he did. The moment the elevator doors opened on the design floor, he strode directly to Keith Kaiser's cubicle. "What's the idea?" he demanded. "That was some email you sent me last night."

"If the shoe fits," said Keith curtly.

"It doesn't," Pat responded. "Listen, Kaiser, if you have a bone to pick with me, at least have the courtesy to do it in person. What's this about my work being substandard? You've certainly been more than willing to take my suggestions on *your* projects. Now you're putting me down behind my back? That's pretty cowardly, if you ask me."

"I have a lot of work to do," said Keith, turning to his computer and pointedly away from Pat.

"I'm not done yet," rejoined Pat. "I'd like to know how you can accuse me of wasting company time when you leave at four-thirty every night. Don't think I can't hear you talking to your wife ten or twelve times a day. And what did you mean by saying my communication is inappropriate?"

"I think I was quite clear," Keith said. "I really have nothing more to say."

Pat gave up for now. "Fine; have it your way," he said. He marched to his own cubicle and slammed his briefcase down.

In the days that followed, the schism between Keith and Pat grew. The two men had been used to eating lunch together in the employee lounge, relaxing in comfortable camaraderie. Now Pat left the building at lunchtime while Keith took to brown-bagging in the courtyard. Art observed the two men avoiding each other in the hallways and that Pat would not enter Art's office if Keith was inside, and vice versa. Factions formed around them. Pat's supporters were the social, outgoing employees who leaned towards vocal expression, group interaction, and innovation. Keith's group comprised quieter, more private people who usually kept to themselves and strictly adhered to rules and policy. Art perceived that although the conflict had arisen over office space, the battle had extended far beyond the context of that empty corner office. The Battle of Conflict had begun, and he realised that he was facing his first major challenge as design manager.

Art considered his options. The office had remained empty too long; he knew he had to make a decision soon. But the conflict between Pat and Keith made it more difficult. Art was disappointed with how they were handling the situation and felt disinclined to give either of them the office in view of the circumstances. Their divisive behaviour was disrupting the office and narrowing Art's alternatives. He believed the conflict, which had spilled outside the boundaries of the original issue, needed to be addressed before the office assignment could be made.

After consulting with Jared Jones, Art called the Admiral.

What do *you* think?

The battle at Fine Restaurant Design arose over a single issue. Like so many conflicts, this one has escalated; the two men are attacking each other's value and integrity as they seek to gain the upper hand. Consider the following questions to help clarify your own thoughts about the situation.

1. How would you describe Pat Price's personality?
2. How would you describe Keith Kaiser's personality?

3. Recall the Johari Window, where the size of the open windowpane is based on what people know and share about themselves and what others know about them. What do you think the Johari Window looks like between Keith and Pat?
4. Where do each of the two men fall on the UZOD scale?
5. Is this conflict really about office space? If not, what do you think it's about?
6. Have you encountered a conflict like this one? What did you do, and how well did it work?
7. If you were Art Carroll, what decision would you make about the empty office?

The 3rd Alternative

When the Admiral arrived at Fine Restaurant Design, he met first with Art Carroll, who brought him up to speed on what had occurred. "As I see it, I have to choose whether Pat or Keith gets the corner office. And whichever one I choose, the other one is going to believe I think he's less valuable to the company. It seems like the whole design floor has chosen sides in the conflict. My decision has implications for how people think they're going to be treated now that I'm manager."

"You seem to be thinking carefully about the problem instead of making snap judgements," said the Admiral. "That's a quality of a good manager. Keep in mind that each of your employees has unique gifts and contributes to your company in a unique way. If you recognise those special qualities and help them mesh, that'll build your management skills.

"But you've been approaching the issue as if it has only two sides. Maybe you could try a different approach," he continued. "Recently I've been reading some work by Stephen R. Covey. You may know a book he wrote in the late eighties called *The 7 Habits of Highly Effective People*."

"I've heard of it," said Art, "but I haven't read it."

"It's got some great principles, and it's worth a read," said the Admiral. "But his newer work is what I'd like to bring up to you today. In his book *The 3rd Alternative*, Covey presents an idea that can help people resolve problems when they feel faced with two choices, each of which seems to lead to equally negative consequences.

"Instead of getting stuck in what Covey calls '2-Alternative Thinking'," the Admiral went on, "he suggests that there may be a third alternative, something no one has thought of yet, a solution that can only be reached by achieving synergy between the two opposing sides."

"Hmm," said Art. He thought for a little while. "I guess another choice might be not to give the office to either of them."

"That may not be what Covey intends when he describes finding the third alternative," said the Admiral. "He talks about achieving synergy between two sides in a battle – and by *synergy* he means a combination of the strengths of two factions that think completely differently. Once the two synergise, together they may create new alternatives that no one has yet discovered."

"I like that way of thinking," mused Art. "Maybe I should read the book."

"I have a copy right here," said the Admiral. "Please read it at your convenience. I believe Covey's principles can guide the process I have in mind to help you resolve the conflict here at Fine Restaurant Design."

"What do you propose we should do?" asked Art.

"I would like to do a personality assessment first," said the Admiral. "When I've had a chance to characterise Keith's and Pat's personality traits, I have another measure that's designed to describe how people handle conflict. I think that will give us a good foundation from which to proceed to conflict resolution."

Both Pat and Keith were quite amenable to completing the personality tests. They were tired of the conflict, which was draining their creative energies and making the workplace tense and unhappy. Their work quality was suffering, as were their personal lives. Besides, each of them secretly believed that the results of the personality measures would point him up as the clear winner of the empty office.

The OPQ

For his initial personality assessment, the Admiral chose the Occupational Personality Questionnaire (OPQ). This measure is similar to the 16PF in that it scores the individual across multiple dimensions, but it lends itself particularly well to settling conflict for two reasons. First, the OPQ examines more dimensions than the 16PF, and second, the OPQ is targeted to an occupational point of view.

First launched in the UK in 1984, the OPQ was developed by Peter Saville – an occupational psychologist who standardised the British version of the 16PF instrument in the 1970s – in collaboration with Roger Holdsworth and a small group of colleagues.[11] The OPQ is designed to describe a person's

---

11   Peter Saville et al., "A Demonstration of the Validity of the Occupational Personality Questionnaire (OPQ) in the Measurement of Job Competencies over Time", *Applied Psychology*, 45/3(1996): 243–262.

preferred or typical style specifically as presented within the world of work. The OPQ yields in-depth information describing how individuals are likely to fit into their work environments, how they work in combination with others, and how they are likely to perform across specified job competencies.

The Admiral compiled the OPQ results for the two men into the chart that follows this section.

From these results, the Admiral could clearly perceive that Pat and Keith probably had very different workplace personalities. Most relevant to the matter at hand, they were likely to handle interactions with their colleagues very differently. A person with scores like Keith's would probably prefer to avoid blatant conflict and confrontation. He might hold back his opinions publicly and bend to the needs and wishes of others; he was probably happy to let others take charge and would generally accept consensus rather than put forth his own ideas. Someone consistent with Keith's results would lean towards emotional detachment and seriousness and would value spending time alone more than he was likely to seek out the company of others. His interactions with his co-workers were probably tentative and subdued. A person who scored this way might be uncomfortable meeting new people and thus might avoid social situations. He would probably be detail oriented and practical minded and would strive to adhere strictly to rules and policies. Someone with Keith's profile was unlikely to trust his colleagues and instead would probably question their motives and intentions and internally analyse their behaviour as it related to himself.

In comparison, Pat's profile described someone who was likely to be social, comfortable and confident expressing opinions, negotiating, and persuading others. A person with these scores would probably be able to lead a project comfortably, taking charge and maintaining control. More of an open book, a person with this profile was likely to appear attentive and interested in others, to prefer time in groups over time alone, and to consult with a variety of other people before making an important decision. Someone consistent with Pat's scores probably felt comfortable meeting new people and was lively, animated, and talkative in group settings. He probably liked to approach problems from new angles, adopted a big-picture perspective, and sought unusual or creative solutions to issues. Less likely to follow strict rules or be deadline driven, a person with this profile preferred change and variety and might become bored with repetitive tasks. He was probably more trusting of his co-workers than someone with Keith's profile would be. He was likely to be energetic, optimistic, and exuberant in his interactions.

In two areas Pat and Keith fell very close together in their OPQ scores, which the Admiral found quite interesting: both men were likely to make their success and achievements known to others, and both were quite competitive by nature. The Admiral believed these similarities were just as informative to the presenting conflict as were the areas where Keith's and Pat's personalities differed.

RELATIONSHIPS WITH PEOPLE	1	2	3	4	5	6	7	8	9	10	
Rarely pressures others to change their views, dislikes selling, less comfortable using negotiation					**Persuasive**						Enjoys selling, comfortable using negotiation, likes to change other people's view
Happy to let others take charge, dislikes telling people what to do, unlikely to take the lead					**Controlling**						Likes to be in charge, takes the lead, tells others what to do, takes control
Holds back from criticising others, may not express own views, unprepared to put forward own opinions					**Outspoken**						Freely expresses opinions, makes disagreement clear, prepared to criticise others
Accepts majority decisions, prepared to follow the consensus					**Independent Minded**						Prefers to follow own approach, prepared to disregard majority decisions
Quiet and reserved in groups, dislikes being centre of attention					**Outgoing**						Lively and animated in groups, talkative, enjoys attention
Comfortable spending time away from people, values time spent alone, seldom misses company of others					**Affiliative**						Enjoys others' company, likes to be around people, can miss the company of others
Feels more comfortable in less formal situations, can feel awkward when first meeting people					**Socially Confident**						Feels comfortable when first meeting people, at ease in formal situations
Makes strengths and achievements known, talks about personal success					**Modest**						Dislikes discussing achievements, keeps quiet about personal success
Prepared to make decisions without consultation, prefers to make decisions alone					**Democratic**						Consults widely, involves others in decision making, less likely to make decisions alone
Selective with sympathy and support, remains detached from others' personal problems					**Caring**						Sympathetic and considerate towards others, helpful and supportive, gets involved in others' problems

THINKING STYLE	1	2	3	4	5	6	7	8	9	10	
Prefers dealing with opinions and feelings rather than facts and figures, likely to avoid using statistics			**Data Rational**								Likes working with numbers, enjoys analysing statistical info, bases decisions on facts and figures
Does not focus on potential limitations, dislikes critical analysis, rarely looks for errors			**Evaluative**								Critically evaluates information, looks for potential limitations, focuses upon errors
Does not question the reasons for people's behaviour, tends not to analyse people			**Behavioural**								Tries to understand motives and behaviours, enjoys analysing people
Favours changes to work methods, prefers new approaches, less conventional		**Conceptual**									Prefers well-established methods, favours a more conventional approach
Prefers to deal with practical rather than theoretical issues, dislikes dealing with abstract concepts			**Conventional**								Interested in theories, enjoys discussing abstract concepts
More likely to build on than generate ideas, less inclined to be creative and inventive			**Innovative**								Generates new ideas, enjoys being creative, thinks of original solutions
Prefers routine, is prepared to do repetitive work, does not seek variety			**Variety Seeking**								Prefers variety, tries out new things, likes changes to regular routine, can become bored by repetition
Behaves consistently across situations, unlikely to behave differently with different people			**Adaptable**								Changes behaviour to suit the situation, adapts approach to different people
More likely to focus upon immediate than long-term issues, less likely to take strategic perspective			**Forward Thinking**								Takes a long-term view, sets goals for the future, more likely to take strategic perspective
Unlikely to become preoccupied with detail, less organised and systematic, dislikes detailed tasks			**Detail Conscious**								Focuses on detail, likes to be methodical, organised and systematic, may become preoccupied with detail
Sees deadlines as flexible, prepared to leave some tasks unfinished			**Conscientious**								Focuses on getting things finished, persists until the job is done
Not restricted by rules and procedures, prepared to break rules, tends to dislike bureaucracy		**Rule Following**									Follows rules and regulations, prefers clear guidelines, finds it difficult to break rules

FEELINGS AND EMOTIONS	1 2 3 4 5 6 7 8 9 10	
Tends to feel tense, finds it difficult to relax, can find it hard to unwind after work	**Relaxed**	Finds it easy to relax, rarely feels tense, generally calm and untroubled
Feels calm before important occasions, less affected by key events, free from worry	**Worrying**	Feels nervous before important occasions, worries about things going wrong
Sensitive, easily hurt by criticism, upset by unfair comments or insults	**Tough Minded**	Not easily offended, can ignore insults, may be insensitive to personal criticism
Concerned about the future, expects things to go wrong, focuses on negative aspects of a situation	**Optimistic**	Expects things will turn out well, looks to the positive aspects of a situation, has optimistic view of future
Wary of others' intentions, finds it difficult to trust others, unlikely to be fooled by people	**Trusting**	Trusts people, sees others as reliable and honest, believes what others say
Openly expresses feelings, finds it difficult to conceal feelings, displays emotional clarity	**Emotionally Controlled**	Can conceal feelings from others, rarely displays emotion
Likes to take things at a steady pace, dislikes excessive work demands	**Vigorous**	Thrives on activity, likes to keep busy, enjoys having a lot to do
Dislikes competing with others, feels that taking part is more important than winning	**Competitive**	Has a need to win, enjoys competitive activities, dislikes losing
Sees career progression as less important, looks for achievable rather than highly ambitious targets	**Achieving**	Ambitious and career-centred, likes to work to demanding goals and targets
Tends to be cautious when making decisions, likes to take time to reach conclusions	**Decisive**	Makes fast decisions, reaches conclusions quickly, less cautious
Has responded less consistently across the questionnaire	**Consistency**	Has responded more consistently across the questionnaire

■ PAT   ▢ KEITH

The TKI

Although the Admiral found the OPQ scores of the two men revealing, he wanted more information to guide them towards conflict resolution. The second measure he employed was the **Thomas-Kilmann Conflict Mode Instrument (TKI)**. The TKI was designed by Kenneth W. Thomas and Ralph H. Kilmann to assess individuals' behaviour in the context of conflict. In situations where the concerns of two people appear incompatible, Thomas and Kilmann hypothesised that a person's behaviour can be described across two dimensions: **assertiveness**, or the extent to which an individual seeks to satisfy his or her own concerns; and **cooperativeness**, or the extent to which the individual seeks to accommodate the concerns of others. The degree of presence (or absence) of these two behavioural dimensions is then used to define five modes of handling conflict:

> *Competing* is assertive and uncooperative. In this mode, the individual pursues his or her own concerns at the other person's expense, using whatever means possible.

> *Collaborating* is both assertive and cooperative. In this mode the individual tries to work with the other person to find a solution that completely satisfies the concerns of both parties.

> *Compromising* has elements of both assertiveness and cooperation. Here the objective is to find an expedient, mutually acceptable solution that partly satisfies the concerns of both parties.

> *Avoiding* is unassertive and uncooperative. An individual in the avoiding mode simply does not address the conflict at all.

> *Accommodating* is unassertive and cooperative; it is the opposite of competing. The accommodating individual neglects his or her own concerns to satisfy those of the other person.

Everyone is capable of using all five conflict-handling modes; a person cannot be characterized as having a single, rigid style of dealing with conflict. But most people use some modes more readily than others and develop more skill in those modes and therefore tend to rely on them more heavily. Many people have a clear favourite. The conflict behaviours individuals choose are the result of both personal predispositions and the requirements of the presenting situation.

When a person takes the TKI, he or she chooses from a series of statements that assess the preferred modes of behaviour along the two dimensions. Then the person's scores are compared to a representative sample of 8,000 employed adults in the United States who also took the TKI to determine the person's percentile, indicating the percentage of people in the sample who scored the same or lower on each mode than the person being tested.

The Admiral compiled Keith's and Pat's TKI scores into the following charts.

Pat Price's TKI Profile

MODE	RAW SCORE	LOW	MEDIUM	HIGH
		0	25%	75%
ACCOMMODATING	5			
COMPROMISING	8			
AVOIDING	4			
COMPETING	6			
COLLABORATING	7			

Keith Kaiser's TKI Profile

MODE	RAW SCORE	LOW	MEDIUM	HIGH
		0	25%	75%
ACCOMMODATING	7			
COMPROMISING	8			
AVOIDING	6			
COMPETING	4			
COLLABORATING	5			

Again, the Admiral found these results quite telling in the face of the current situation. Someone who scored like Pat on the TKI would usually prefer the *compromising* mode of handling conflict. This conflict-handling mode is suited for time-pressured situations that call for the most expedient solution. It is useful when two people with equal power must negotiate between mutually exclusive goals and settle on a temporary solution to get the conflict out of the way – at least for the time being. "Let's split the difference" might be the mantra of a compromiser. But compromise has drawbacks. Over-reliance on compromise can lead parties to unintentionally sacrifice principles or long-term objectives, and it may create a cynical climate that undermines trust.

In contrast, someone with a TKI profile like Keith's leaned towards *accommodating* as a preferred conflict-handling mode. Accommodators often seek to preserve harmony and avoid disruption, "killing enemies with kindness," so to speak. The accommodating mode is useful when people recognise they're wrong and want to demonstrate how reasonable and generous they can be. But the Admiral didn't believe this was happening in the situation at hand. Accommodating has value when an issue is more important to one person than to the other; people sometimes accommodate to earn credit that can be used towards a more important issue down the road.

Of equal interest to the Admiral was the closeness of the two men's scores on the *competing* function – consistent with their scores in Competition on the OPQ. The competing mode, founded on the concept of "might makes right," becomes useful in an emergency situation when quick, decisive action is called for. But in less vital scenarios, too much competition can get in the way of constructive communication. An overly competitive climate may cause people to project more certainty and confidence than they actually feel, making it less likely that they'll ask one another for opinions and information. Competitors can become isolated and work at cross purposes.

The Admiral believed competition lay at the heart of the conflict between Keith and Pat. He also noted that neither man would be likely to choose avoiding as a preferred mode of handling conflict. Now he felt ready to bring the two men together to resolve their differences.

Game theory

The Admiral met with Pat and Keith in the FRD conference room, where he had several visual aids ready to guide them. First he presented them with the combined OPQ chart and their TKI scores.

"Pat," said the Admiral, "someone with a profile like yours on the OPQ is generally self-assured, relaxed, forthright, and trusting of others. When faced with a conflict, people with this profile often like to strike a bargain quickly and move on. They often are willing to negotiate and make concessions. But sometimes their need for compromise can undermine their trust in colleagues. In a conflict, when such people feel that they're in the right, they're likely to take a firm stand. How well do you relate to that profile description?"

"Fairly well," responded Pat. "I think I've made a pretty good case for what I believe I deserve. I'm willing to talk it over, but I've lost trust in Keith because of the nasty remarks he's made behind my back."

"Let's save that for later," said the Admiral. "Keith, your scores are consistent with a profile that usually describes a private person, someone who is conventional and grounded in approach who often likes to follow a solid set of rules. In a conflict situation, these people tend to accommodate others rather than fight to ensure that their own needs are served. However, in a conflict, when such people feel that they're in the right, they might take a more competitive stance. Does anything I've described about this TKI profile resonate with your ideas about your own personality?"

"I guess so," said Keith. "I feel like Pat dragged me into a competition for the empty corner office, and now I need to do whatever I can to win."

"I'm glad you brought up winning," said the Admiral. "That's a good segue into what I want to talk about next.

"Conflict can be a healthy thing," he continued. "If people manage conflict well, it can lead to better decisions, creativity, and high-quality work. But if conflict is handled badly, it impedes both teamwork and individual goal accomplishment." The Admiral showed Pat and Keith the UZOD chart and explained the concept.

"Where do you think you fall right now on the UZOD chart?" he asked.

"Zone B," said Pat. Keith nodded.

"I agree," said the Admiral. "You've both become focused on scoring points over the other; winning has become the most important goal. As a result, both your relationship and your work are suffering."

"The most widely used conflict-resolution methods apply something called **game theory**," he continued. "Game theory is a complex science, but it's based on simple principles that we can apply in our everyday interactions.

"Everyone is trying to achieve some kind of payoff, or benefit. But the perceived payoff will be different for different people. Each of us is motivated by a different incentive. For example, one person might be highly motivated to obtain financial reward, while another might gain a sense of achievement from feeling that his job is worthwhile or his work is of high quality.

"In game theory, getting your payoff is called a 'win', and not getting your payoff is called a 'loss'."

Next the Admiral wrote the following on the whiteboard:

	I don't win	**I win**
You win	Submission	Collaboration
	Acquiescence	Assertiveness
	Compromise	
	Withdrawal	Aggression
You don't win	Blocking/Sabotage	Dominance

"We play different types of games to get our payoffs," he went on. "In a *competitive* game, for you to get your payoff, someone else has to lose his, like in a tennis match at Wimbledon. In order for one player to win and advance to the next round, the other player has to lose and be eliminated from the tournament.

"In a *cooperative* game, your maximum payoff relies on the other players getting their payoffs as well. For example, say you're out driving your car. Your payoff is reaching your destination safely and on time. You're most likely to get your payoff if all the other drivers on the road get their payoffs too – that is, they all reach their destinations on time. If other drivers crash, they might cause you to lose your payoff as well as their own.

"The cooperative game, in which both parties win their payoffs, is preferable. As we've just been discussing, you two have been playing a competitive game, and it's not working. What I'd like to do is help you find a solution in which you both win – that's what you've heard called a 'win-win' situation."

The Admiral walked to a flip chart and revealed the following diagram.

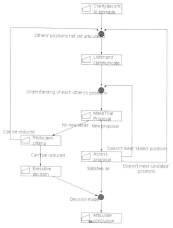

Figure 20 – Decision-making Process
Reproduced from Steve Myers, Team Technology, Conflict Resolution
Process: http://www.teamtechnology.co.uk/conflictresolution.html

"This is the process we're going to follow to help resolve your conflict," he told Keith and Pat. "First we need to clarify what the conflict is about. Then we'll agree on the decision that needs to be made."

"Who gets the corner office," said Pat promptly.

"Are you sure?" said the Admiral. "I'd like you to consider the situation carefully. Clearly defining what the conflict is about will keep our discussion from going around in circles while we only dance around the real issue."

Pat and Keith pondered for a few minutes; both drew a blank.

"Maybe it would help to think through your win positions. Remember that each person's payoff might look different. Although you both want the corner office, try thinking outside the box – or in this case, outside the office." They all laughed, slightly easing the tension in the room. "Instead, consider what getting that office represents to you."

"It would make me feel good about myself," said Pat at length. "I'd feel like I was really worth something to the company."

"Yes," Keith agreed. "I've worked so hard for Fine Restaurant Design. Getting that office would feel like recognition for all my hard work."

"Now we're getting somewhere," said the Admiral. He walked to another whiteboard and wrote **Decision: Recognition** at the top. "Okay, next I'd like you each to express your win positions. Just listen to each other; don't judge or criticise."

"Getting the office is my win position." Pat looked confused.

"Mine too," said Keith.

"Sure," said the Admiral. On the board, he wrote **Win Positions**. Underneath he wrote **Pat** and **Keith** as separate headings. Under **Pat,** he wrote **Pat gets the office.** Under **Keith,** he wrote **Keith gets the office.** "Okay, that's obvious," he said. "But what else can you think of?"

They thought. "I guess we could share it," Keith said finally, a bit grudgingly.

The Admiral wrote **both get the office** under each heading. "We're brainstorming, so say everything that pops into your head," he said.

"Or neither of us could get the office," said Pat, "but that's really a lose-lose."

The Admiral wrote **status quo** under each heading. "Think of it this way," he said. "You both envision that getting the office will serve as recognition for your contributions to the company. But how else could the company recognise you for your contributions?"

"Oh, I see," said Keith. "You know, actually, I wasn't all that interested in the office at first. But when Pat started telling Art all the reasons why he should get it, it got me thinking that I deserved recognition just as much as Pat does."

"Ah," said the Admiral. "That's good, and it's very astute of you to bring it up, Keith. So do you have any other ideas for how the company might reward your efforts?"

The three of them hashed out a few ideas – new equipment, change in title, a designated parking space. None of them seemed to quite fit. Then Keith had an idea.

"I know," he said. "Pat and I just received certification in the latest AutoCAD features. Both existing and new designers are going to need training in those features so they can pass the test and get the credential as well. If the company put me in charge of that training, I would feel rewarded."

"Excellent," said the Admiral. "Does that feel like a win position you could live with?"

"Well," Keith added, "I wouldn't mind a little extra money to go along with it."

"Okay, let's say you become the designated trainer and you get paid an extra €1.50 an hour during the time you spend training," said the Admiral. "Would that do the trick?"

"Hey," said Pat. "That doesn't seem entirely fair. I'd like extra money, too."

"We're presenting win positions, Pat," the Admiral said. "Keith's idea might constitute an opportunity to settle your conflict with a win-win. If the empty office is the only win position for both of you, we're at a standstill at the 'Reduce Win Criteria' spot on the chart. From there we would have to let Art make an executive decision, and there's no way that can end in a win-win. It'll be a lose-win at best.

"You've challenged the fairness of Keith's win position," he went on. "Can you think of a way to make it fair so you can come up with a trial proposal?"

The two men mused. "Well," said Pat, "If I get the office all to myself, I guess I could live with Keith making a little extra while he's training. But I've got the certification too – maybe we both could do training."

"How about this," suggested the Admiral. "For now, Pat gets the office and Keith gets the training designation and a pay increase. The next time an office becomes available, each of you gets the inverse, and everything is even. How does that sound?"

This proposal became the springboard for conflict resolution. Both Pat and Keith left the meeting feeling relieved and satisfied, even liberated. Having achieved deeper understanding of the reasons behind their mutual desire for the same office space, each man became more accepting of the other's perspective and needs. Together with the Admiral, they proposed their solution to Art Carroll.

"Congratulations," said Art. "You two have figured out a way to synergise. I thought you both were bigger than the way you've been behaving over the past couple of weeks. Now I'm convinced of it, and I'm impressed. You've succeeded in finding a third alternative in a spot where only two choices seemed possible.

"I'll have to propose your idea to my superiors, but I think they'll approve," he concluded. "Admiral, I appreciate your role in this solution, and I hope we can continue to consult with you as we try out this new idea."

"Of course," said the Admiral.

Now what do you think?

Pat and Keith found a solution that, at least for the moment, appears to be a win-win. How well do you think it will work? Did you have any other ideas about ways to achieve win-win balance at Fine Restaurant Design? What kind of follow-up do you think the Admiral should do to ensure continued harmony in the Design Department?

Healthy competition can be a good motivator, but too much competition – or a contest with unfair advantages – can inspire anti-productive behaviour. Balancing assertiveness (to address one's own needs) with a spirit of collaboration (to consider the needs of others) forms the key to finding a win-win path out of conflict. Understanding how one's emotions come into play during conflict and managing them productively can improve the results of conflict resolution as well. Learn when to fight and when to let go; avoid falling into the extremes of playing the victim, the rescuer, or the persecutor. Focus on competing with yourself rather than with others. One person's success is good for the whole company; try to accept and honour the achievements of others as you do your own. Remember that encountering some conflict during your career is highly likely. Conflict can be managed either well or poorly. If you learn to manage it well, success will follow.

CHAPTER VI

Teamwork has become a buzzword in today's work world. People talk about team players, working on a team, building a team to accomplish a task. But what exactly is a team, and how do we go about building an effective one?

Stated broadly, teamwork is made possible when you feel part of something larger than yourself. One's entire company or work organisation is a single team working towards a common goal – meeting customer requirements. Regardless of who a company's customers are or whether one works in management, on the front line, or behind the scenes, everyone's efforts contribute to the end result. Smaller teams also form naturally based on a company's structure. Each department or work unit with its own specific goals or assignments may be a separate team.

We need teams because groups are often stronger than the sum of their parts. Teams working together can identify problems not previously recognised, locate their root causes, and develop and implement innovative solutions combining the unique skills of each team member. Teams can determine employee assignments, improve scheduling systems, and conduct organisation-wide communication more effectively than individuals. And employees often will accept and respect a decision made by a group more readily than one handed down by a single dictator.

Executives, managers, and human resources professionals universally explore methods to improve organisational results and profitability. In recent years many have touted a horizontal, team-based design (over more traditional hierarchical systems) as the best structure for profitable business. Certainly, involving all employees in business decisions, spreading responsibility for success, and sharing profits or rewards has clear potential to increase employee buy-in and long-term commitment.

But putting a group of people together and assigning them a task does not automatically make them a team. Quality teamwork requires development of team skills, time for individual differences to mesh, and patience. A good team does not form overnight. To be most effective, workplace teams need to develop standards, identify and obtain necessary skills, and then undergo ongoing coaching and monitoring to ensure that the skills are appropriately employed and the standards are upheld.

Regardless of what they call the process – team building, total quality management, lean manufacturing, continuous improvement, or self-directed workgroups – few organisations are completely satisfied with the results of their team efforts. If teams are not working as they should, an organisation can take steps to diagnose the problems. Successful teamwork requires attention to each of the following steps, known as the *Twelve Cs of Team Building*.[12]

Twelve Cs of Team Building

1. *Commitment*. Team members should want to serve on the team, and they should believe in the importance of its mission. They should buy into the team approach.
2. *Clear expectations*. A good team needs clearly defined goals for performance and outcomes.
3. *Context*. Team members must understand the team's role within the organisational framework and in relation to the organisation's overall mission.
4. *Communication*. Team members should be clear about task priorities and effectively provide and accept performance feedback.
5. *Competence*. Team members must have appropriate skills, knowledge, and capability to tackle the task at hand.
6. *Charter*. In addition to the goals provided by organisational leaders, the team should create its own mission statement, including a timeline, statements of outcomes and respective contributions, and a plan for evaluation.
7. *Control*. A team must be afforded adequate freedom and power to accomplish its goals.
8. *Collaboration*. Team members must understand and employ effective group processes.
9. *Creativity*. If the organisation does not value innovation, accept change, and reward new ideas, team progress may founder.

---

12 Susan M. Heathfield, "Twelve Tips for Team Building: How to Build Successful Work Teams", *About.com* [website], <http://humanresources.about.com/od/involvementteams/a/twelve_tip_team.htm> accessed 12 Feb. 2012.

10. **Consequences**. Teams must be held responsible for accomplishments towards the recognised goals.
11. **Coordination**. The team should be centrally coordinated to provide the tools and resources necessary to achieve success.
12. **Culture**. The organisation must embrace and support the differences between a team-oriented structure and a hierarchy.

Personality plays a major role in team dynamics. As I've discussed in earlier chapters, teams are most successful when team members complement each other and are willing to respect and accept each other's differences. A good team generally will comprise a variety of personality types, each with a unique perspective for understanding the problem and developing innovative solutions. An organisation should emphasise the value of different personality traits and support the integration of multiple viewpoints. If team members cannot respect each other's differences, such lack of respect is likely to extend to an organisation's customers as well.

To truly succeed, teamwork must be incorporated at all organisational levels, including the top. Teamwork principles produce similar benefits when employed at the lower levels and when adopted among executive leadership. The value of working as a team should be instituted organisation-wide as a management philosophy – if everyone practises good team skills internally, those skills will transfer externally to improved customer relations.

In a perfect world, teamwork is creative, effective, value driven, and holistic. But teams have potential for negative by-products as well, especially in the early phases of the team approach. Team building is a complex task with its own set of risks. A team can be ineffective, inflexible, idealistic, or unreasonable. Team members might devalue one another and perceive responsibilities differently. Miscommunication or miscomprehension, lack of clarity or focus, poorly defined policies, or even group pathology might arise. Anticipating and controlling negative team dynamics requires skilful leadership and stellar interpersonal and communication skills among all the team members. In other words, building and maintaining a high-quality team – paradoxically – takes teamwork.

To help develop a conceptual frame within which to understand the scenario for this chapter, consider the following.

Distraction is caused by:

- Lack of identity – low self-worth, low self-confidence, lack of clarity of one's own values and behaviours, need for career advancement.

- Remuneration and other financial issues.
- Perceived fairness in the work environment.

In other words, a team becomes dysfunctional when team members get sidetracked by any of these extraneous distractions: personal egos, individual desire for advancement, budget and money issues, or clashes between representatives of different departments. And when teams become distracted from their tasks and exhibit dysfunctional tendencies, the Battle of Team will probably ensue. Client disappointment is likely to follow; conflicts between teams or team members all too often create client conflict as well. The team structure erodes, and the organisation regresses into its traditional hierarchical mould. Modern organisations striving towards a more democratic style of leadership must learn how to avoid or deal with the Battle of Team. The following scenario depicts just such a battle and describes some possible pathways to resolution.

Scenario: Meshing at Massive-Mart

Coming together is a beginning, staying together is progress, and working together is success. ~**Henry Ford**

Miranda Mason returned to her office from an informational interview to find an email from Ed Hathaway, the executive director: "Stop by my office at your convenience," it read. Miranda was prompt to respond. Her boss never issued such a request unless it was important.

As Miranda walked down the hallway, she looked around appreciatively at Massive-Mart's understated yet elegant executive offices. Miranda was proud to be senior manager of human resources at this successful, forward-thinking retail giant. In the three years since Miranda had accepted their offer, Massive-Mart had made huge strides towards leaving behind the traditional executive hierarchy, looking for ways to involve employees at all levels in decisions, structuring teams around key tasks. Miranda was pleased to play a part in improving company culture and encouraging positive change.

Ed's office door was open. "Miranda," he greeted her warmly. "Thanks for stopping by. Please sit down; I have something I want to discuss with you."

Miranda sat down in the plush chair before the director's desk, alert and eager. Her boss was a youthful, vigorous forty-something, the major impetus behind Massive-Mart's recent cultural changes. Miranda greatly admired and respected him.

"Miranda, I'm putting together a team to create our professional development programme," Ed went on, "And I want you to head it up."

"Wonderful!" exclaimed Miranda. "I'm quite excited to be part of that process." Massive-Mart had more than a thousand retail outlets spread across the nation. The firm placed high value on employee development, promoting from within at every opportunity. The professional development programme would demonstrate that value. Miranda had been privy to several discussions about the programme over the past few months and had been hoping to take a major role in its development.

"That's fantastic," said Ed. "I had hoped you'd be eager to take this on. The executive committee had a meeting to select the rest of your team as well. First, of course, you'll have Carrie Collins."

Miranda nodded. Carrie was the newly hired training and development coordinator, a position created for the very purpose of getting Massive-Mart's employee training programmes in place and implementing them in the future.

"We decided Douglas Jones could represent the regional interests," Ed continued.

Miranda nodded again. "Douglas is an excellent choice," she said. Douglas Jones was one of Massive-Mart's twelve regional managers of operations. He'd worked his way up through the ranks from entry-level, starting his career as a retail clerk making minimum wage. Twenty years and five promotions later, Douglas would know just what was involved in gaining the professional skills to get ahead. Miranda approved wholeheartedly.

"And finally," said Ed, "Richard Reasoner."

Miranda's face fell. *Oh no*, she thought, as emergency sirens went off in her head. Richard Reasoner, senior manager of operations, was an older gentleman who represented everything Massive-Mart was trying to leave behind. To Miranda he embodied the very principles of classism and hierarchy. In his heyday he'd been one of the highest powered executives in Massive-Mart history. Now Richard was nearing retirement. The search committee, to which Miranda had been an advisor, had passed him over for the executive director position in favour of Ed's more vital, cutting-edge style. Consequently, he had a chip on his shoulder the size of a house. Miranda and Richard had locked horns before; he treated her like an incompetent schoolgirl.

"I know you and Richard have had your differences in the past," said

Ed, "but I'm counting on you both to put those behind you. Richard's been around a long time and will be retiring inside of two years. I think his perspectives on professional training will offer a good balance to the rest of you. Don't worry; I'll make it very clear to him that you're the team leader.

"You're a talented, dedicated, and enthusiastic manager, Miranda. I know you can find a way to work with Richard and build a positive team."

Miranda had no choice but to acquiesce. She knew Ed had included Richard more for political than for practical reasons. He wanted to placate Richard for being overlooked as executive director, and Richard's experience would lend credibility to the team's accomplishments – especially among older long-term employees. Yet although she and Richard were peers, Miranda knew Richard would never be satisfied with a role he perceived as subordinate to hers, no matter what Ed told him. She couldn't argue with the logic of Ed's decision to include Richard on her team. That didn't mean she liked it.

*　*　*　*　*　*　*　*　*　*

The team's first meeting took place the following week. Miranda opened by suggesting that their first task was to reach consensus about their mission, goals, and timeline.

"As I see it," she stated, "we're charged to come up with a comprehensive professional development programme that facilitates employee retention and rewards long-term service. Promoting from within is part of Massive-Mart's employment philosophy. We need to ensure that our stores can fill general manager and regional operations manager positions seamlessly with existing employees once those positions come open through promotion or retirement."

"First we need to think about top-level positions," objected Richard. "My position is a prime example. I'm going to be retiring in less than two years. I want to be sure the people in line to take my place have the skills to fill my shoes. And I'm not so sure Massive makes such a big deal about promoting from within. We've sure hired a lot of outsiders lately."

Is that a thinly veiled reference to Ed? Miranda wondered. *Or is he talking about me?*

"Certainly," she responded, stiffly but politely. "Top-level positions are part of the mix; Massive-Mart makes no distinction between executive, regional, or store-level promotions. We're committed to hiring from within whenever there's someone qualified. It's part of our mission statement."

"We could start with the overall Massive-Mart mission statement and go from there," chimed in Carrie. "The company states its commitment to rewarding long-term service in its mission. And as I understand our task, we're supposed to come up with a programme that's aligned with the company goal to become more socially responsible."

Richard snorted. "Social responsibility is just one of those popular buzzwords companies think they have to use now. It doesn't really mean anything. Here," he said, brusquely handing out pieces of paper. "I took the liberty of drawing up an organisational chart mapping out the lines of authority. We'll start at the top and work down. We should just look at the position descriptions at each level and list out the formal education and training required for each position. That will inform our training programme."

"I'd like to back up a bit," said Miranda. She could feel her energy level sagging. She'd been sure Richard would balk at team process and try to undermine her leadership, and she hated being so right. This was not going to be easy. "Let's reach agreement on exactly what we need to accomplish, and in what timeframe.

"Thank you for the organisational chart, Richard," she added. "It may prove useful later on. But we also should remember that an organisation is more than just boxes and lines on a piece of paper. An organisation is people, and Massive-Mart's goal for the future is to become more people oriented. That's what we're here to support."

"Well put, Miranda," offered Douglas. "I'm living proof that Massive-Mart treats its people well. I've been promoted five times in the twenty years I've worked here, and I for one believe that promoting from within is the best way to go. It's great for morale and makes the company look good in the community."

Richard rolled his eyes. "Can we get back on task?" he said to Miranda. Turning his chair sideways, he muttered to no one in particular, "You'd think he was the only person who'd ever gotten a promotion."

"Let's brainstorm for a bit," said Miranda, rising and going to the whiteboard. "Why don't we take the next ten minutes to identify everything we can think of that our training programme might be designed to achieve?"

The group agreed, Richard somewhat reluctantly. But he was the first to jump into the brainstorming session.

"Excellence," said Richard. "Increased profits, and new customers – those are very important."

"Okay," said Miranda, writing them on the board. "Those are indirect products of training. What are some of the direct outcomes?"

"Leadership," said Richard promptly, "direction, and authority."

Miranda wrote them on the board. "I'd like to hear from the rest of the group too," she said. "Carrie?"

"Employee development?" said Carrie hesitantly, "And perhaps employee equity. And well, I think social responsibility *is* important." Richard rolled his eyes again.

"Good," said Miranda. "Douglas, what do you think?"

Richard interrupted, "We need to make sure we don't promote people prematurely," he said. "When I retire, I want to know my replacement really has the guts and know-how to do my job."

"Thanks, Richard," said Miranda abruptly. "But I'd like to hear what Douglas has to say."

"To be honest," said Douglas, "I'm not really sure why we need this new training programme at all. Take me, for example. I learned my job by doing it, not by sitting in a classroom. I don't see why we have to make people jump through a lot of hoops. We just need to get supervisors to teach their subordinates different parts of what's required to be a supervisor."

"So I'm hearing there's an aspect of mentorship involved," said Miranda, "and empowerment." She wrote the terms on the board.

Richard snorted again. "More buzzwords," he said. "They should call us the buzzword team."

The meeting continued along this vein. Miranda strove to keep discussion on track, and Richard fought to take over the lead. Carrie and Douglas offered tentative suggestions, and Richard met each with a brusqueness approaching hostility, interrupting frequently, punctuating his terse communication with body language that left his contempt for Miranda in little doubt. Then whenever the group seemed close to a decision, Carrie would inevitably stall the process by introducing an aspect they had failed to consider. Although Douglas didn't take a firm stand, he clearly doubted the training programme's chances for success and felt little stake in its development.

When their scheduled hour was up, Richard simply got up and marched out the door without a word. Douglas rose and followed him, looking somewhat baffled; Carrie looked at Miranda hesitantly. She started to say something but apparently thought better of it; she left too. Miranda packed up her materials with resignation. They were no further along than when they'd begun. Somehow she would have to figure out how to bring these very different personalities into a unified mindset or the team would get nowhere.

Over the next month, nowhere was exactly where the team *did* get. Miranda was a skilful professional and an energetic leader. She was enthusiastic about the team's project. But placed in the same room with Richard, she had to fight to maintain any energy at all. Richard was a knowledgeable executive and brought a wealth of experience to the table – he'd seen Massive-Mart through its entire cycle of new-business growth, downturn, and back into burgeoning growth. But his foundations were old school; used to making snap decisions and watching subordinates jump to carry them out, he lacked respect for the team process. He insisted on arguing the tiniest details and interpreted every suggestion as personal criticism.

Carrie continued to inhibit progress by questioning whether they had considered all the possibilities before making a decision final. Without fail, she would bring up something new that threw a wrench in the works, always right when a decision was imminent. Douglas was uncommitted to the process and indifferent to the outcomes. The meetings grew increasingly tense and uncomfortable. Miranda and Richard wasted a good deal of time trying to define and control the boundaries of leadership, making team progress impossible. The Battle of Team was well under way.

Ed Hathaway had asked Miranda to provide regular progress updates. When none were forthcoming, he pressed her, only to receive vague answers and sidesteps. Finally he decided to drop in on one of the team meetings to get a sense of what was going on.

Right away Ed could feel the tension in the room. Group discussion was clipped and formal. Ed could see Miranda struggling to maintain effective leadership. Carrie and Douglas spoke rarely and chose their words carefully. Richard was sullen and close-lipped; although his resentment towards Ed and Miranda was nearly palpable, he avoided expressing any except the most banal and uncontroversial ideas. Ed left the meeting with the realisation that putting Miranda and Richard on the same team had effectively created a toxic work environment. The two people cancelled each other out – they were less productive together than they were on their own, defeating the whole purpose. And the other two members brought additional challenges to the team. These four people – although they possessed individual talents that were widely observed and well documented – had failed to gel into an effective team.

After reflecting a while, Ed decided he'd received his cue to take action.

Massive-Mart really needed to get moving on its employee development programme. The team was dysfunctional, but Ed wasn't ready to give up on it yet. He picked up the phone and called the Admiral.

What do *you* think?

In this Battle of Team, the various personalities are working against each other instead of merging to create a unified voice that amplifies and focuses each individual's strengths. What do you think might be done to fix the problems and move forward? Consider a few questions:

1. Based on what you know, how would you describe Miranda's personality? How about Richard's, Carrie's, and Douglas's?
2. What communication patterns may be getting in the way of this team's progress?
3. Reviewing the conceptual framework diagram shown earlier to depict a dysfunctional team, do you think any of these team members are being distracted by ego, desire for advancement, money, or departmental issues?
4. What do you think the Johari Window looks like for this group?
5. Where does this team reside on the UZOD scale?
6. Have you ever found yourself on a dysfunctional team like this one? What did the group do to solve its problems? How well did your solutions work?

Diagnosing the problem

The Admiral appointed himself an ad hoc member of the team so he could observe group dynamics and assess the problem. At the first meeting the Admiral attended, he perceived the same tension, hostility, and forced formality that Ed had observed. Discussion was confined to mundane topics to avoid any conflict. The process hit constant snags and the team would just spin its wheels. Afterwards the Admiral drew the following Johari Window to illustrate the team's communication for Ed:

Open Area	Blind Area
Hidden Area	Unknown Area

Then the Admiral showed Ed the Uncomfortable Zone of Debate (UZOD) scale and explained its meaning. "Where do you think the team usually stays on the UZOD scale?" asked the Admiral.

"In Zone A," said Ed after brief consideration.

"I agree with you," said the Admiral. "They tread carefully and refuse to bring up anything that might be perceived as controversial by any of the others. They avoid confrontation that way, but they're also stalling progress towards any of their goals."

"What do you recommend?" asked Ed.

"I'd like to ask each team member to complete a Myers-Briggs Type Indicator assessment," the Admiral responded. "I can use their individual profiles to develop an MBTI Team Profile Report. That report is designed to characterise a team as a whole and can guide team-building discussion. Then I have another psychometric measure in mind, one that describes how different personalities fill different roles in a group. These strategies should offer some solutions for helping your team move forward."

The MBTI Team Profile Report

Each team member was asked to fill out an MBTI assessment. To help you understand how the Admiral comprehended each of the types, recall the four preference areas on the MBTI:

E = Extraversion	vs.	I = Introversion
N = Intuition	vs.	S = Sensing
F = Feeling	vs.	T = Thinking
J = Judging	vs.	P = Perceiving

The Admiral learned that Miranda most closely fit the MBTI profile for an **ESFJ**. ESFJs are likely to bring the skills of a provider to the group concerned with meeting the needs of others and leaning towards logistics and diplomacy. Richard's scores were consistent with an **ENTJ**, the personality type Isabel Myers called "leaders of leaders". The strength of an ENTJ often lies in marshalling effective forces towards externally imposed goals. Carrie's profile fit that of an **INTP**, whose primary aim might be to design systems and strategies, seeking underlying structure and cohesion. Douglas's MBTI scores were most like those of an **ISTP**, a master of tools and artisanship, someone likely to value workplace autonomy to the exclusion of regulations or hierarchical boundaries.

Next the Admiral merged the four team members' MBTI profiles into an **MBTI Team Profile Report.** According to his calculations, the team as a whole fit the **ESTJ** team profile. ESTJ teams are generally well equipped to handle situations calling for tough decisions and decisive action. Such teams are usually good at organising and directing others to accomplish clear objectives. But this team had failed to unify and focus its energies, so the Admiral identified a few potential blind spots that a team fitting this profile might encounter. These spots fit into the blind area in the Johari Window. The blind spots were also related to the conceptual factors by which team members may have been distracted (ego, advancement, money, or departmental concerns).

A typical ESTJ team might be prone to making decisions too quickly and having to repeat work later. This clearly was not happening with the Massive-Mart team; they'd stalled all decision-making in favour of remaining in Zone A on the UZOD scale. An ESTJ team might be likely to reject new ideas as impractical before giving them a fair chance. Thus this team might lack the spark of innovation. They might fail to envision the big picture or recognise trends, focusing exclusively on short-term results. Such a team might steamroll obstacles without careful consideration. Or an ESTJ team might fail to observe and celebrate its successes.

The Admiral shared these results with Ed Hathaway. "You've taken one good step towards resolving the issues," he said. "Bringing me in as an observer to suggest alternative procedures is one good way to help an ESTJ team get past its challenges. I may be able to help them brainstorm ways to overcome the blind spots.

"With its preferences for Sensing and Thinking, an ESTJ team may be neglecting the processes of Intuition and Feeling, which can get in the way of progress," the Admiral told Ed. "I propose helping them work on intuitive behaviour, such as considering the future and identifying patterns and trends. They may also need help with feeling processes, such as involving all parties in the discussion, keeping harmony, and evaluating options based on values.

"There's also more measurement I'd like to do," he continued. "I'd like to conduct a Belbin Team Role assessment."

Belbin Team Role theory

The Admiral explained to Ed that Dr Meredith Belbin and his team at Henley Management College had done extensive research during the 1970s on how teams work (and *don't* work). Belbin's group discovered that a team's success or failure was not derived from inherent conditions like its members' intellect but instead was derived more from team members' *behaviour*. That was good news because behaviour can be measured, characterised, and – most importantly – changed.

Belbin Team Role theory defines a Team Role as: "A tendency to behave, contribute and interrelate with others in a particular way." Belbin's research group identified the following nine Team Roles:[13]

The *Plant* tends to be highly creative, good at solving problems unconventionally.

The *Monitor Evaluator* provides a logical eye, makes impartial judgments, and dispassionately evaluates options.

Coordinators focus on team objectives, draw team members out, and effectively delegate assignments.

Resource Investigators provide inside knowledge about opposition, making sure team ideas carry to the outside world, and help avoid isolation and inward focus.

Implementers plan practical, workable strategies and carry them out efficiently.

Completer Finishers are most effective at the end of a task, to "polish" and scrutinise work for errors, employing high quality control standards.

Teamworkers help teams to gel, using their natural versatility to identify required work and complete it on behalf of the team.

Shapers are challenging individuals who provide necessary drive to ensure that the team keeps moving and doesn't lose focus or momentum.

The *Specialist* has in-depth knowledge of a key area. His weakness might manifest as a narrow focus on his subject of choice, prioritising it over team progress.

Figure 21 – Belbin Team Roles
©2010, R. Meredith Belbin. Reproduced by kind
permission of Belbin Associates—www.belbin.com.

Belbin believed that balancing Team Roles was the key to building a high-quality team. Although some roles might tend to maintain higher profiles during group interaction, each was essential to success. For example, a team with no Plant might struggle to identify an initial spark of an idea, but too many Plants on a team could cause bad ideas to override good ones. Or a team without a Shaper might lack direction and energy.

The Admiral's next step was to have the four team members complete the Belbin Team Role assessment, which would determine the Team Role

---

13   R. Meredith Belbin, *Management Teams: Why They Succeed or Fail*, 3rd ed. (Boston: Butterworth Heinemann, 2010).

that each filled. The results were quite telling, and the Admiral began to understand the difficulties the Massive-Mart team was encountering.

Richard seemed to serve the team as a **Shaper**. He was blunt and to the point; he wanted to get things moving and get out; "just do it" was his mantra. Carrie fit the role of an **Implementer** with her focus on structure and practical strategy. Douglas most closely resembled a **Specialist** with emphasis on hands-on learning. Miranda's Team Role seemed to be a composite. While she exhibited many characteristics of a **Coordinator**, she also had the drive and energy of a **Shaper**; unfortunately for team dynamics, her energy was driven in a different direction from Richard's.

The Admiral knew that too many Shapers on a team, especially Shapers with differing agendas, would lead to infighting and decreased morale. In addition to that problem, the Massive-Mart team lacked optimal Team Role balance for moving forward.

The Admiral presented his findings to Ed. "It's unusual for me to say this," he commented, "but I believe this team would benefit from having *more* members rather than fewer. In particular, the team needs someone to fill the Plant role. An effective Plant might help them get past their roadblocks and offer the innovative spark they need to get started. You need a highly creative person, someone good at innovative problem-solving.

"Next, this team really needs a Teamworker. This should be a highly versatile employee. You need someone who can help the different personalities in this group to gel and unify. In your perfect scenario, this person also might possess some Completer Finisher traits – the ability to see the project through to completion."

Ed pondered these recommendations. "I think I know just the two people to fill these roles," he said. "This assessment is amazingly helpful. It points up exactly what the team is lacking and defines the qualities needed from the team members I should add. It's also interesting that the measure helps qualify and build upon the roles the current team members play. Would you be willing to share this information with the team so they understand how their behaviour affects team performance?"

"That's exactly what I was going to propose," said the Admiral.

The beginnings of a solution

Ed selected two new members to supplement the roles of the current team: Arlene Akin and Sydney Simpson. Arlene was Massive-Mart's marketing director and known for her creative spark. Her reputation for innovation and unconventional solutions recommended her to fill the **Plant** role. Sydney Simpson was a regional manager, one of Douglas's peers – in fact, he had been partly responsible for training Douglas to fill that position. He was a strong supporter of the promote-from-within policy. Sydney was very active in his community and well known for undertaking projects that required organising large teams of volunteers. Ed believed Sydney would be an excellent *Teamworker* on the Massive-Mart training programme team.

The Admiral continued to sit in on the meetings for the next month. He shared the psychometric measures with the team members and helped them to understand their possible strengths and to appreciate the strengths of their fellow team members. The Admiral also partially served the team in the *Monitor Evaluator* role. He became their sounding board – offering logical, unbiased judgements and helping the group weigh various options objectively.

The first week saw the team agree upon their goals and desired outcomes; in the second week, the Admiral observed much greater balance and accord among team members. By the third week, the team had made significant progress towards their first goal – normalising the standards for hands-on management training and writing the outline of a training curriculum. The team completed this task by the end of the Admiral's month of consultation, and he joined them to celebrate their success.

Now what do you think?

The Massive-Mart training programme group fought the Battle of Team caused by competing personality features and a lack of balance both of their behavioural preferences and of their team roles. The Admiral helped them understand how their differences could become strengths and how to strike an adequate balance in roles. How well do you think his strategies worked?

Consider the Johari Window for the team now. What does it look like? How did the Admiral help them widen the open windowpane?

Where has the team gotten on the UZOD scale? Do you think they can maintain what they've achieved, or will they revert to infighting after the Admiral has left?

The Battle of Team is likely when a company decides to instil a new management philosophy – any move from traditional hierarchical systems to more democratic ones is likely to meet with resistance and apprehension. But team problems can be pre-empted when we strive to build balance and harmony among team members and help them reduce or eliminate individual distractions. Involving people in the decisions that affect them builds trust, and trust among employees paints a trustworthy image for your customers. Give teams the power to create change, balanced with responsibility and accountability to meet goals and deadlines, and they will move mountains.

CHAPTER VII

The Battle of Learning

Every job comes with a built-in learning curve. All employees must learn not only at the beginning of their jobs – when the task is to gain understanding of the expectations and requirements of the position – but throughout them, as they seek career development, work towards promotions, or acquire new skills to keep up with changing technology. Today's organisations want employees to learn important interpersonal skills in addition to their job functions and place a premium on skills like leadership, communication, and problem-solving. Regardless of our formal education or experiential background, when we take a position with a new organisation, we will be asked to learn new job requirements, company policies, or procedures.

Job training takes many forms; the nature of the position will drive how training is conducted. Many positions require specific educational coursework, degrees, or certification. Once we accept a job, we might be asked to undergo intensive training in a formal programme. Or we might learn through time focused on observing another employee or learning hands-on under the tutelage of a colleague or supervisor. Only rarely will we be thrown into a new task without some type of learning beforehand.

One of the best ways to get ahead in a career is to pursue additional learning during tenure. You might learn more about your current company, discovering what goes on in other departments and exploring future plans for diversification or expansion. Learning how your job fits into the larger picture helps build self-worth and might put you in line for advancement. Making the effort to learn additional skills can increase your value to the organisation and bolster your résumé. And every step you take towards acquiring knowledge teaches you a little more about yourself.

Personality strongly affects how you prefer to learn and thus may influence the kind of work you choose. People's preferences for learning methods are widely referred to as *learning styles*. A whole body of research surrounds the identification of various learning styles and how educational tools can reach people across the range of learning preferences. Recognising and understanding your learning style can help you identify techniques best suited to you. Employers can improve the speed and quality of job training by incorporating multiple learning techniques.

The Battle of Learning might arise in a workplace when co-workers with different learning preferences are asked to learn the same skills using the same training methods. A given training technique might work very well for one employee yet cause another employee to struggle. Or conflict might ensue when an organisation adopts a new system or procedure, forcing employees to drop an existing mode of working in favour of a new one. As an employee, taking time to understand your learning style and the learning styles of your colleagues can prevent conflict and encourage teamwork. For an organisation, recognising, accepting, and accommodating the range of learning styles among employees can build high-quality teams that achieve success and promote job satisfaction.

As you read the scenario for this chapter, think about how learning style might have an impact on different employees' apparent job capabilities. Training failure might cause problems in employee interactions to snowball. Something that may seem small, like an inattention to results, can build into fear, conflict, and distrust if not addressed at the outset. And addressing problems at the outset requires that they be handled during the training process. That's why this chapter's scenario brings the Admiral into the mix while the employees are still in training. If you consider learning styles from the beginning and adapt training materials to suit individual preferences, your results may improve immediately, and you can avoid serious issues later on.

Scenario: Clearing Up at Clean Home Solutions

Ancora Imparo (I am still learning). ~**Michelangelo**

You don't understand anything until you learn it in more than one way. ~**Marvin Minsky**

It had been a long day at Clean Home Solutions. Julie Johnson placed her caddy in the storeroom and carried her briefcase back to her workstation, heaving a sigh of relief as she sank down in her chair. Only three weeks had passed since Julie had been named Clean Home Solutions' new training manager, but it seemed like a century.

Julie had accepted the new position, along with all its extra work and responsibility, with enthusiasm and zeal. She had been a cleaning technician for the company – a large residential cleaning service – for five years, and she loved it. Her friends had trouble believing she could really *enjoy* cleaning homes, but she felt a sense of satisfaction and accomplishment every time she left a spotless house behind her. Just knowing she offered the solution to someone else's problem carried its own reward.

The promotion to training manager had been part of a reorganisation process at Clean Home Solutions. The owner had adopted a new cleaning system as the company standard, a method she wanted all the cleaning techs to employ going forwards. Julie had been using the Swift Cleaning Method herself for two years and had recommended it to the CHS owner. The method was designed to provide professional, efficient, consistent cleaning service in minimal time. It left nothing to chance – and technicians who used the method wholeheartedly became expert, nearly complaint-free service providers. Recognising that both existing staff and new hires would need to be trained in the system, the owner placed Julie in the newly created training manager role.

Julie had spent the last three weeks training the current technicians in the method and using their input to design a training programme for new hires. She was quite proud of her efforts. She'd combined the Swift Method book, paper handouts, videotaped instruction, in-person demonstration showing the proper usage of each tool and solution, and a question-and-answer period into a neat day-and-a-half programme. Then she'd written a quiz to measure how well new employees had absorbed the training. Julie was satisfied that it all was going to work very well.

Next week she would have a chance to find out. Three new employees were coming on board, providing her an opportunity to test the programme and find out how quickly (and how well) new staff could reach optimum competency levels in the field. Julie would conduct the training with the three newbies, and then they would tag along with her as cleaning helpers for the rest of the week, applying what they'd learned to serving actual homes.

* * * * * * * * *

Management had certainly selected a diverse group of trainees, Julie observed very quickly as training began Monday morning at nine o'clock sharp. The three new hires had very different demographics, backgrounds, and capabilities. Katie was in her mid twenties, bright, attractive, and eager to please; she'd worked for a large janitorial firm. Katie paid attention well

– particularly to the video and visual demonstrations – and asked a lot of good questions. Brad was even younger, and he was quieter and more reserved; he read the written materials carefully and took copious notes in a notebook. His only prior work was in fast food, and he'd taken this job part-time while he completed college courses. Sharon looked to be in her late forties and was married with kids. She had a good deal of residential cleaning experience under her belt already, so perhaps she viewed cleaning as a career. Julie was unsure whether Sharon was absorbing the material; she neither asked questions nor took notes, and Julie thought she might be giving off a faint vibe of impatience. *Well*, thought Julie, *the quiz will tell us how much they've learned.*

When Tuesday's half-day training session had wrapped up, Julie administered the quiz. She gave the trainees an hour to complete it, bringing a few of her own paperwork tasks into the room to complete as she proctored. She had asked the three new employees to remain in the room the full hour so she could give them their instructions for the following day. Sharon finished first, fifteen minutes before the hour was up, and spent the remaining time looking at the clock, drumming her fingers on the table, and fidgeting. Katie was next, followed by Brad, who used up the entire hour. Julie collected their exams. "Please be here tomorrow at 8.30 a.m.," she instructed. "I'll have your quiz scores then, and we can talk about addressing any areas where you might need a little more training. We'll start the hands-on portion of training tomorrow. You get to apply what you've learned to cleaning a real house!"

When the trainees had left, Julie sat down to take a look at their tests. As she had expected, Katie's test outshone the others'. She had answered the questions completely and enthusiastically, clearly grasping the concepts behind the cleaning technique they'd been asked to learn. Her writing was tidy, her answers precise and accurate. Julie scored her quiz at 95 per cent. Brad had done a fairly good job as well. His answers tended to be lengthy but were well thought out and covered the material comprehensively. Many of his answers showed that he had memorised sections of the book and repeated them on his test. Julie calculated Brad's score at 86 per cent.

Sharon's test was a bit disappointing. While she'd answered all the questions, her responses were brief; she often abbreviated words, and in certain areas, it seemed as though she had picked up a portion – but not all – of the technique in which she'd been instructed. All in all, she'd answered well enough to pass, but Julie perceived a lack of motivation. She gave Sharon a score of 74 per cent. *Well, we'll see how it goes tomorrow,* she thought. *There's nothing like hands-on training to flush out the problem areas.*

* * * * * * * * * *

Brad and Katie arrived promptly at 8.30 the next morning, as directed. Sharon arrived a few minutes late; Julie's watch read 8.39 when she strolled in. "Good morning," Julie addressed them. "Before we go out to our first house, I want to go over the sheet I'm going to use to grade you every day for the rest of this training week.

"I'm going to give you a letter grade – A through F – in eight areas: attitude, job knowledge, quality, speed, punctuality, enthusiasm, system, and cooperation. Most of those are pretty self-explanatory. By "system" I mean that you're following the Swift Cleaning System that you learned during the training programme. By the end of the week, you'll need to have passing grades – B or higher – in every one of those areas. Now, in quality and speed, I'm going to cut you some slack, because I don't expect you to achieve top results in such a short time. If you use the Swift System to a T, you'll get faster, but it might take a little while. On all the rest of the areas, I'm going to hold you to the highest standard."

Julie turned to Sharon. "Sharon, that means today you get a D in punctuality because you were late this morning."

Sharon bristled. "Only a couple of minutes," she said defensively.

"It was nine minutes. Our appointments are very tight, and I expect you to keep an exact schedule. Our customers count on us to be on time." Julie went to the supply closet and had the trainees pull out their cleaning caddies. She gave them each an apron and reviewed how to store tools, sponges, and spare cloths in their apron pockets. At nine o'clock, they were ready to go.

Arriving at the first client's home, Julie said, "Remember, in this first house you are just going to watch me. Watch and learn. In the second house, I'll give you a chance to do some actual cleaning."

Julie reviewed the Swift System as she cleaned and the three trainees watched. "Pick your starting point, and then work right to left, top to bottom, back to front, all the way around the room. Finish cleaning everything in front of you before you move on to the next location." She went over the cleaning rules, describing each action as she completed it, explaining why she chose each tool or spray solution, her motions quick and efficient. Yet even as she worked, Julie's sharp eyes observed the attitudes and attentiveness of her trainees.

Their first home was a fairly small single-story; Julie took two and a half hours to finish. Then they stopped for a quick luncheon break. "How long have you worked at Clean Home Solutions?" Katie asked Julie.

"Five years," Julie said, "but I've only been training manager for three weeks. In fact, you're my first group of trainees."

"Hmmph," snorted Sharon. Julie looked sideways at her. She thought she might have caught Sharon rolling her eyes as though she knew it all.

"You're very good," said Katie. "I love watching you work. You're so efficient and thorough!"

"I don't know if I'll ever be able to clean as fast as you do," offered Brad.

"It doesn't matter," said Julie. "If you follow the system, you'll be fast enough. Since the system defines all the steps, you don't have to second-guess anything. You know exactly what to do, and eventually your speed picks up."

Katie nodded. "I can see that. I'm looking forward to trying out the system. I've never done anything like it before."

Their second assignment was a bigger house with two storeys, several bedrooms, and two large baths. "This time, I'm going to let each of you help me clean a room," Julie explained. The plan was for each trainee to assist while the other two watched, giving Julie a chance to see how well they followed direction. Katie went first, in the master bedroom. Julie showed her how to choose the starting point. "Now you work clockwise from here, and I'll start on the opposite side," she said.

Katie had clearly picked up the concepts of the cleaning system. She kept a steady pace and copied Julie's movements. "Okay, Katie, we leave the vacuuming for last, and I'll let you do it," said Julie. "Use a tidy pattern, and vacuum your way out of the room so you don't leave footprints." *Katie's going to get high marks today,* Julie thought. *She's quick and pays attention.* But Julie had noticed that Katie talked a lot, too. She seemed incapable of working in silence – instead, she would fill every moment with conversation.

Brad was next and helped Julie clean the master bath. He worked methodically and followed directions pretty well; he had stashed his notebook in his apron pocket and referred to it from time to time to remind himself what to do next. He was slow, and Julie wasn't surprised. "Like I said, don't worry about going too fast," she encouraged him. "You've picked up the idea behind the system. Just be sure to do it correctly, the same way each time. It won't be long before you get used to it and speed up." *At least he's concerned about doing things the right way,* she thought.

Now it was Sharon's turn. Julie put her to work in the kitchen. "I'd like you to help me in here because I know you have a lot of experience," Julie told Sharon. "The kitchen is the room where we're most likely to get complaints."

Julie observed Sharon carefully while they worked. Sharon worked quickly enough and obviously was no stranger to cleaning. But she wasn't completely following the system; Julie had to keep reminding her. "Top to bottom," she said. "No, don't move around the corner yet, you missed the backsplash." And a little later, "Wait, use the special spray on the granite, remember?" Sharon might have been a good cleaner, but Julie would have to watch her like a hawk to make sure she stuck with the system.

*   *   *   *   *   *   *   *   *

The next day Julie's training strategy was to get two new employees started in a room while the third assisted her in a separate room. At their first house, she put Katie and Sharon in the kitchen while she and Brad tackled the living room. Since the rooms were adjacent, Julie could keep an eye on what all three of them were doing.

"Okay, everybody, stop what you're doing," she said after a while. "Sharon, it looks like you're going all the way around the kitchen just wiping the counters. Remember what you learned about the Swift System? You're supposed to clean everything in front of you in a given area before you move on."

"I just thought it would work better to clean everything I needed to use the all-purpose spray on first," said Sharon.

"But that's not the system," said Julie. "At Clean Home Solutions, we've adopted the Swift System, and I want you to follow it completely."

Sharon shrugged. "This is the way I've always done it, and it's going to come out just the same," she said.

"I don't care," said Julie patiently. "We want every Clean Home employee to work the same way. That means using the system."

"Okay." Sharon shrugged again. "Whatever."

They went back to work. Julie observed that Katie – as predicted – was following instructions well. As the cleaning system became instilled in her muscle memory, Katie's speed was improving. But she continued to fill every quiet space with chit-chat. Brad still worked slowly but referred to his rule card and his notes less often. Julie thought he was starting to get the hang of it. He applied himself well and clearly wanted to do a good job. But he seemed to rely heavily on the printed words to cue his next task.

Katie and Sharon were still working in the kitchen when the living room was clean, so Julie took Brad to help her in the master bedroom. When Katie and Sharon finished, Katie came to the bedroom to ask Julie where she should go next. "Where's Sharon?" asked Julie.

"Out on the front porch," said Katie. "I think she's texting her husband."

Julie went to get Sharon. "Remember, if you finish a room early, come ask me for your next instructions – or give me a hand if I'm in the last room," she admonished. Sharon sighed audibly as she came in to help Katie clean the spare bath.

As Julie and Brad finished up in the master bedroom and moved on to the master bath, Brad asked, "Am I doing okay? I'm so much slower than the others."

"You're doing just fine, Brad," said Julie. "You've improved since yesterday. Eventually, I would like to see you work without having to look at your notes."

"I just have to read things a few times before they really sink in," said Brad.

"That's okay," said Julie. "I know you'll do fine once you've had a little more experience. You're a hard worker and you're doing your best; I can tell."

"Try not to compare your work to each other's," Julie told the team when they'd completed the house. "Instead, work to beat your *own* record. Just try to improve a little bit each day. That's the best way to earn good marks on the score sheet."

At the end of the day, Julie asked Sharon to stay behind after the others had left. "Sharon, do you really want this job?" Julie asked her.

Sharon looked taken aback. "Of course I do," she said.

"That's not evident to me," responded Julie. "You don't follow the system, and you're not paying attention to my instructions."

"Honey, I've been cleaning houses since you were in diapers," retorted the older woman. "I know what I'm doing. I know cleaning – inside and out."

"Sharon, I'm sorry, but that's not the point," said Julie. "Clean Home Solutions has adopted the Swift System for one simple reason: because it works. When all the cleaning techs are working exactly the same way, there's no guesswork. We always know just what to do. That ensures that every home we serve is cleaned to the highest standard. Client complaints are kept to a minimum, and that's why we have such a great reputation in the community.

"If you can't accept that this is how we do things and learn to follow the system exactly, then maybe you're not a good fit for this job."

Sharon back-pedalled. "Oh, no, I didn't mean it that way," she said hastily. "I really need this job. I'm sorry. I'll try to do it your way, honestly I will."

Julie nodded. "You'll have to do better than try," she warned. "Have you read the entire Swift System book yet?"

"Well," Sharon confessed, "I sort of skimmed through it."

Julie recognised that statement: it was code for I haven't even picked it up. "Please read it by tomorrow," she said firmly.

Sharon nodded her agreement and went home. Julie tapped on her boss's door before leaving for the day. She wanted to give the owner an update on the three new techs.

"Come in," said Karla Knox. As Julie went inside, she saw a distinguished gentleman sitting in Karla's guest chair. "Oh, I'm sorry, I didn't know you had a visitor," said Julie.

"Julie, I'd like to introduce the Admiral," said Karla genially. "I had hoped you were still here so you two could meet. The Admiral is an expert in psychometric personality evaluations. I've called him in because I've decided I'd like to start using personality measures as part of our screening process for new hires."

"Oh, what a great idea," exclaimed Julie. "I wish we had used something like that before hiring my three new trainees."

"Please, do elaborate," said Karla. "I'm very interested to know how your training programme is working, and perhaps the Admiral may have suggestions."

Julie gave them a brief recap of how training was going and of the trainees' vast differences in work style. "Katie is a keeper, I'm fairly sure," she added, "even though she talks all the time. Brad still needs a lot of supervision and has to consult his notes frequently, and he's slow. But in time I think he'll be just fine."

"What about Sharon?" Karla asked. "She has the most experience, as I recall."

"Her experience may be getting in the way," said Julie. "She refuses to follow the system; she thinks her way is better. I spoke with her about it just now and asked her to read the Swift book by tomorrow. I can't tell if she's having trouble understanding the system or if she has a respect problem because I'm younger and less experienced than she is."

"If I may offer a suggestion," said the Admiral, "this group of new hires might be a good place to test out your psychometric strategy. At first blush, it appears to me that there may be some issues related to learning."

"Learning?" Julie asked.

"Yes," the Admiral continued. "It's easy to understand and accept that people have different personalities. We observe those differences all the time, and we use our observations to help us choose which people we enjoy being around, form friendships with, or even hire. But what many people don't realise is that personality also partly determines the type of work we choose and how we learn to do our jobs.

"Personality measures can identify the ways in which people prefer to take in new knowledge, which are called *learning styles*. Understanding the learning styles of new employees can guide the design of appropriate training and development programmes."

"That makes sense," said Julie.

The Admiral went on, "Building awareness of a team's characteristics and strengths enables team members to grow and move forwards. Understanding how people choose to learn, work, and interact with others helps you improve teamwork and reduce conflict."

"I'm excited to see how this works," said Karla. "How should we proceed?"

"You've already formed some opinions about your trainees' attitudes and skills," said the Admiral, turning to Julie. "If we have them complete a learning style assessment, it may yield information that will help you teach them a lot faster."

Both Julie and Karla liked the idea, so they decided to administer the assessment the following afternoon – Julie would have them finish cleaning about an hour early, and the company would pay them for their time to complete the questionnaire. The Admiral would interpret the results, make recommendations, and present them to the whole group on Friday.

What do *you* think?

Julie has encountered a situation in which three new employees are absorbing work knowledge and exhibiting job skill at very different paces. While the issues with Sharon do not yet represent full-scale war, it's not hard to see how a battle might ensue if the company fails to address them. Consider a few questions:

1. Do you believe Sharon's apparent unwillingness to adopt the cleaning system represents a real problem for the company? Why or why not?
2. Do you think Julie's training programme has been adequate to reach all three of the new employees?
3. Can you identify any possible differences among the three employees' learning styles?
4. Have you ever encountered a situation similar to this one? What did you do, and how well did it work?

Kolb Learning Styles Model

The Admiral asked Julie and Karla to meet with him early on Friday prior to the presentation of the questionnaire results. Since Clean Home Solutions had no conference room, they met in the employee lounge, where the company held staff meetings.

"I wanted to give you some background in learning theory," the Admiral explained. "That'll give you a better foundation from which to understand how I've applied the assessment results."

He explained that he based his interpretations on two theoretical models and first described the Kolb Learning Styles Model. David Kolb first published his model of learning styles in 1984, but it was based on many years of prior research. After publication, the model gave rise to his Learning Styles Inventory. Kolb's model sets out four distinct *learning styles* (or preferred modes of getting information) based on a four-stage learning cycle. "You also could call it a *training cycle*," the Admiral suggested.

During the four-stage cycle, according to Kolb, ***immediate or concrete experiences*** provide a basis for ***observations and reflections***. The observations and reflections are assimilated and distilled into ***abstract concepts*** which have new implications for action that can be ***actively tested,*** in turn creating new experiences, and the cycle repeats.

"In a perfect world, each person would go through each step," said the Admiral, "in a sequence of experiencing, reflecting, conceiving, and acting. Of course, our world never reaches the ideal, and people show a preference for one part of the learning cycle or another. So the next level of Kolb's model was to combine the four stages in the cycle into combinations of two, like in this matrix." He showed them the following matrix.

	Doing (**Active Experimentation - AE**)	**Watching** (**Reflective Observation - RO**)
Feeling (**Concrete Experience - CE**)	**accommodating** (**CE/AE**)	**diverging** (**CE/RO**)
Thinking (**Abstract Conceptualization - AC**)	**converging** (**AC/AE**)	**assimilating (AC/RO)**

"By representing the learning stages this way, Kolb came up with four learning styles: ***accommodating***, which combines feeling with doing;

diverging, which is observing plus feeling; *converging*, which combines thinking and doing; and finally *assimilating*, where thinking and observing are combined." He showed them a second diagram. "This is a more visual representation of Kolb's learning theory," he said.

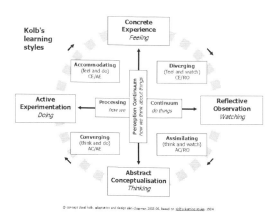

© concept david kolb, adaptation and design alan chapman 2005-06, based on *Kolb's learning styles*, 1984

"Kolb thinks that each person naturally prefers a single learning style," continued the Admiral. "Learning style preferences are influenced by various factors – like parent-child relationships, schooling, and work experience – that the person encounters throughout development.

"According to Kolb, we can't **do** and **observe** at the same time, and we can't **think** and **feel** simultaneously. So whenever a person faces a new learning situation, he or she has to make two internal decisions: whether to do or observe, and whether to think or feel. The result of these two decisions produces the person's preferred learning style. This concept has parallels in personality theory. Knowing a person's learning style helps you orient teaching materials to a person's preferred method."

Honey and Mumford's Learning Styles Theory

The Admiral went on to explain that Kolb's theory built upon the work of psychologist Carl Jung, whose theories also underpinned the Myers-Briggs Type Indicator measure of personality traits. "Other learning style models based on variations of Kolb's dimensions emerged later," he continued. "The one I asked your employees to complete was developed by Peter Honey and Alan Mumford in the 1970s. Their theory also describes four learning styles. But while Kolb's model poses that each learning style is a combination of two decisions on the learning cycle, Honey and Mumford's theory says the four styles are overlaid. Because people might prefer different methods of learning based on the situation and their experience, they move among the four learning modes rather than being locked into one."

Now the Admiral put up this diagram:

Figure 23 – Honey & Mumford's Learning Styles Model
Reproduced from Honey P & Mumford A (1982). *Manual of Learning Styles*. London: Peter Honey Publishing.

"See how the cycle is similar to yet different from Kolb's model?" he asked. "Honey and Mumford saw the four-stage learning cycle as follows: having an experience, reflecting on it, drawing one's own conclusions or theorising, and then putting one's own theory into practise to see what happens."

The Admiral explained the four learning styles identified by Honey and Mumford:

> *Activists* prefer the challenge of new experiences, involvement with others, assimilating into groups, and role playing.

> *Reflectors* prefer to learn from activities that allow them an opportunity to watch, think, and review over time.

> *Theorists* like to think problems through in logical, ordered steps.

> *Pragmatists* prefer to apply new concepts to actual practise and see first-hand how they work.

"Now I think it's time to share the results of the psychometrics," said the Admiral.

Sharing the results

They called Sharon, Brad, and Katie into the room. The Admiral started: "Before I begin, I want to remind everyone that this type of measure points up people's preferences to behave in a particular way. Your learning style is never right or wrong. People have different personalities, and one is not better than another.

"I'm going to start with Katie," he went on. "Katie, your questionnaire results are most consistent with the preferred learning style of an *activist*. Activists tend to be flexible, open-minded, and willing to try out new things. They enjoy getting involved with groups and interacting with other people, and they're good at brainstorming creative ideas. Activists often are prepared to take calculated risks in order to experiment with new and unfamiliar routines. How well do you think the description of activist fits you?"

"It sounds pretty close," replied Katie. "I think trying out new ideas is fun, and I do like working with other people."

"Okay," said the Admiral. "Brad, your results pretty closely match the traits of a *reflector*. Reflectors are usually methodical and careful. They like to learn by reading and listening, and they want to be thoroughly prepared before they make a decision or solve a problem. Reflectors might be uncomfortable when asked to rush through a job in order to meet a tight deadline. They often need lots of time to mull things over and think through how to do them better or differently. Do you see any parts of yourself in the reflector profile?"

"Yes, I do," said Brad, sounding surprised. "You could figure out all that just from my questionnaire?"

"Yes," said the Admiral. "The men who designed the questionnaire believed that most people never consciously consider how they learn. So the measure asks you about your general behavioural tendencies, and from your answers, we can make an educated guess about your learning style."

Next he turned to Sharon. "Sharon, your profile was closest to the preferred style of a *pragmatist*. In order to learn something, pragmatists usually need to see it put into actual practise in the real world to convince them that it really works. Pragmatists tend to be businesslike, practical, and down to earth. They like to adapt techniques to their own circumstances. They prefer to work in the field and to get verbal input while they work rather than written instructions to follow. Do you resonate with anything I just described?"

"That's pretty good," said Sharon. "I sure do like to know whether something works before I start using it. And I don't much like going by the book."

"All right," said the Admiral. He turned to Julie. "Julie, I'm going to suggest some training techniques that I believe may be most effective for each of your new employees, and then I'll help them decide on some action steps for effectively learning their jobs.

"Katie may benefit from small group discussions and role playing, or acting things out. She'll probably continue improving if she gets to try something new every once in a while.

"Brad is likely to learn best if he has plenty of time to read and analyse the methods you want him to adopt. Perhaps let him keep a journal, and be patient while he assimilates your techniques.

"Sharon should probably respond well to being coached on the job and receiving frequent feedback. She needs to see an obvious link between the task at hand and a specific problem."

The Admiral moved on to help the three employees come up with action plans for succeeding at their new jobs. Katie decided that her development would benefit from trying not to talk too much, thinking carefully before speaking, and concentrating on listening to others. Brad thought he could identify some actions he could take where the likelihood of grave consequences would be low and use those as learning opportunities for taking other calculated risks and acting more spontaneously.

When it came to Sharon, she drew a blank on action steps. "I thought I already knew how to clean houses," she admitted. "I didn't think I needed any training."

Julie found this statement enlightening. She'd been battling with Sharon over learning the Swift System, and now she understood more clearly what was going on – and it gave her an idea. "I see," she said. "I have a thought. Maybe it would help if you had a clearer sense of the big picture.

"You see, Clean Home Solutions is not about cleaning houses. That's not what we do. What we do is solve people's problems."

"Really?" asked Sharon doubtfully.

"Yes," Julie continued. "Think about your job. Let's say a woman hires us to clean her home. Why does she do that?"

"Because it's dirty," said Sharon.

"No," said Julie. "Her house may be filthy, sure, but that's not why she hires us. She hires us because she has a problem, and her problem is not a dirty house. What's the real problem at the root of her decision to hire a cleaning service? Maybe she's having a big party in a week or a houseful of company coming for a holiday. Maybe she doesn't have enough time to spend with her husband and kids. Or she has a demanding job and needs to focus on serving her clients. Maybe she just bought a new home and the old one needs to be cleaned for its incoming tenants. When we clean her home, we *solve her problem*."

"Wow," said Sharon. "I like that. I never thought about my job that way, but cleaning houses is really important for people, isn't it?"

This exchange sparked a big shift in Sharon's thinking. Once able to grasp that her work formed the solution to a problem, her energy and commitment to the position was renewed. In the field, Julie employed a coaching approach to show Sharon what problem she was solving for the owner of each home she cleaned. "This lady's mother-in-law is visiting next week," she would tell Sharon, "and she wants to make a good impression." Or, "This gentleman needed a Valentine's Day gift for his wife, so he gave her cleaning service for a year." Sharon's pragmatic nature thrived on making this connection, and she was able to see that the Swift System provided a paradigm within which her work became the method for solving each client's unique problem.

Katie and Brad continued improving over time as well. While the three employees had widely variant personalities and learning styles, they achieved similar success during their tenure with Clean Home Solutions. And the company thrived as Julie's training programme evolved to suit the learning needs of each new hire.

Now what do you think?

The Admiral helped Clean Home Solutions discover methods to encourage learning across multiple styles and to solve training problems by becoming more adaptive. How well do you think his solution worked, and do you think the methods are sustainable? When faced with a similar issue, do you feel competent to address it using similar techniques?

The Battle of Learning may simply result from a difference between how one is taught and how one prefers to learn. Learning to do your job right is rewarding in and of itself. But our personality differences practically guarantee that each of us will react differently to any given job training mechanism. Managers and educators would do well to take all learning styles into account when designing training programmes. And applying the principles of learning theory to teaching people job skills may enable us to address the specific needs of individuals in a way that ensures success for the company and for its employees.

CHAPTER VIII

The Battle of Change

The world is changing.

That may strike you as an obvious understatement. Today global change happens so often and so rapidly that we might fail even to notice its progress. To illustrate the point, imagine viewing the world through the eyes of a centenarian. A UK citizen aged 100 in 2012 was born into a society that relied on horse-drawn buggies for transport – a 10-mile round trip would have taken all day. Now that same person can video conference in real time with a friend in Beijing. We have never before experienced such dramatic change in such a short time.

Technology, advancement, progress – these terms are commonplace in today's changing business world. Organisational change has become the rule, the constant. No matter what career we've chosen, we can expect change to occur, probably many times within our life spans. And we can count on change both to create new, exciting opportunities and to engender chaos in our lives.

Change in the workplace comes about for many reasons. Clearly the integration of new technology and improvement in product quality cannot be accomplished without changes over time. Remaining competitive in a fluctuating global market requires dynamism in company philosophy and scope. A move towards cooperative management and employee empowerment can be sustained only when a firm leaves traditional hierarchical systems behind. And many firms cannot encourage entrepreneurial innovation or embrace diversity without making major changes to their missions or policies.

For employees, change can be scary. Sweeping company change may be met with resistance, plummeting morale, or even sabotage. Responsible leadership must recognise and plan for the challenges of implementing a major change.

Perhaps never is change more frightening than during a merger or takeover. Today's businesses routinely view acquisitions and mergers as viable growth strategies to expand into new markets or increase shareholder value. Certainly a well-planned merger can benefit a company's bottom line. But integrating two sets of employees into a seamless whole presents a nearly insurmountable challenge to all but the most creative and visionary leaders. Poor planning, underestimation of the effort needed to follow due process, and failed communication surely will derail any merger's success.

When change is handled badly, the Battle of Change can break out. Job loss, workforce demoralisation, employee turnover, lack of cooperation and teamwork, or increased stress, anxiety, absenteeism, and on-the-job errors may follow. Yet there are principles a company can follow to adequately prepare for and introduce change gradually and competently so employees get aboard the bus instead of throwing themselves in front of it.

Fear of the unknown often lies at the base of the Battle of Change. When you ask employees to embrace a future that exists only in the minds of the leaders, it can seem like a chasm is opening under their feet. And different personalities accept change differently. Some people will resist or fight back. Others might passively block or undermine the process. Still others are likely to embrace change wholeheartedly and become valuable allies in its implementation. The need for businesses to make ongoing structural changes is partly why personality instruments have included dimensions that measure employees' openness to change. If we recognise that employees are likely to adapt to changes at different paces and in different ways, we can in turn adapt our methods to ease the transition.

To set up a conceptual framework for this chapter's scenario, this diagram illustrates the unavoidable fact that different people – with different personalities – play different roles in a change process:

Figure 24 – Reacting to Change Framework
Representing concepts from 'The "four camps" of employee skills',
Roger Opie, *Reflections on the 2008 learning and development survey:
Latest trends in learning, training and development*, CIPD (2007).
Reproduced with permission of the publisher, the Chartered Institute
of Personnel and Development, London, UK (www.cipd.co.uk).

As you read the change scenario, see if you can spot any of these personae among the characters. Also, consider change situations you've experienced. Where did you fall on the Reacting to Change circle? Did you encounter cynics, dinosaurs, players, or spectators along the way?

There are lots of resources out there to aid CEOs and managers through a large organisational change. You'll find fewer materials addressing employees of all levels as they struggle to understand, become proficient, and remain productive in their new roles during a major workplace change. Yet the Battle of Change occurs at all levels. Change affects everyone. This chapter aims to illustrate how different personalities might experience – and accept – changes at work.

Scenario: Merging with Meta

If there is no struggle, there is no progress. ~**Frederick Douglass**

Action and reaction, ebb and flow, trial and error, change – this is the rhythm of living. Out of our over-confidence, fear; out of our fear, clearer vision, fresh hope. And out of hope, progress. ~**Bruce Barton**

As the all-staff meeting adjourned, the consulting team at Fishbone Financial dispersed in stunned silence. Individually or in small groups the consulting staff removed to private offices and closed their doors, either to ruminate alone or to rehash the implications of the latest news with a few close cronies. They had just learned that Fishbone was being acquired by Meta Money Management and a merger was impending.

Merging the firms made perfect sense, at least from a shareholder standpoint. Their products – full-range investment and financial consultation services – were quite similar, as were their investment philosophies. Meta was the newer but larger company; since Meta's appearance on the scene as a competitor, Fishbone had struggled to maintain market share. Leadership at both companies believed subsuming Fishbone's products and highly trained staff into the Meta ranks could only strengthen their combined capabilities and client base.

But naturally the conversation around Fishbone's office turned towards the sombre. Which employees would remain, and who was likely to be sacked? Who would run each department? How would the mission statement, systems, policies, and company philosophy change? What new expectations would they face? Meta's reputation for preserving customer satisfaction at all costs preceded them. Fishbone prided itself on more of a balance, placing equal value on employee fulfilment as on customer collaboration. Now the Fishbone sales team would have to find its way under a new regime. For many, the thought was terrifying.

Fishbone Consultation Manager Frank Ferris pondered the news in his office alone. He had a marginal acquaintance with Colin Clark, Meta Money Management's vice president for consulting. They had served on a political action committee together, so at least they had politics in common. Colin seemed a nice enough fellow but definitely all business – his professional demeanour was impeccably proper, unemotional, and detached. Frank thought they probably could work together side by side, but he didn't know how he would feel if Colin were placed above him.

As it turned out, that's exactly what happened. In the following days, the Fishbone group learned that all Fishbone managers would become direct reports to the heads of each Meta department. Colin was to be Frank's new boss. Frank considered his options. He could quit and take his chances on the open job market, but in the current economy, that seemed irresponsible; Frank was a family man. Finally he decided to swallow his pride and find out where this new venture would lead. Perhaps learning to accept a new role with Meta, even under Colin, would not be so bad. For the time being, he would stick it out. At least Meta had agreed to take on all the Fishbone personnel – no one was being sacked. But reading between the lines, Frank knew that every one of them would have to prove their worth to Meta if they wanted to keep their jobs for the long term.

The merger occurred very quickly. Preliminary conversations among leadership had been going on behind closed doors for several months while the proposal was being reviewed by legal representation for antitrust compliance. The shareholder vote for approval had taken place just prior to the employees' hearing the news. Nothing else stood in the way of the final plunge, and finalising the merger took a scant three months. Since Meta was the parent company in the transaction, former Fishbone employees were charged to move into the Meta building. But even though Meta had some room for expansion, incorporating Fishbone staff put space at a premium. Many of the acquired Fishbone workers were asked to share offices with Meta employees.

Frank's first meeting with Colin began to show him the lay of the land. Colin made his superiority perfectly clear. "I need to know I can count on you to take direction," Colin began. "Until you all get up to speed on Meta policies and systems, I'd like each of the Fishbone transfers to shadow a Meta employee working at the same level.

"Combining our staff in shared offices will be good for productivity," he added. "We encourage competition among consulting staff to build clientele."

"Really?" said Frank. "That system will be new to the Fishbone team. We emphasise teamwork over competition. Fishbone has always been more concerned with the bottom line."

"We're certainly concerned with the bottom line," said Colin. "But we believe a bit of healthy competition can only help bolster our returns."

Frank disagreed but kept his opinion to himself. He was going to have to learn to do things Colin's way, whether he liked it or not. "Now let's discuss client satisfaction," continued Colin. "Meta policy, of course, is to place the customer first. I'm sure you had a similar philosophy at Fishbone."

"Customers certainly received high priority," said Frank. "But the Fishbone method was to strike a balance between providing top-notch client service and taking care of our employees."

"You'll need to leave that behind," said Colin firmly. "You're a Meta man now, and at Meta the clients come first. At all costs.

"I would like you to provide me with some documentation," Colin went on. "I'll need a brief write-up on each of your consulting staff. Include a summary of their strengths and weaknesses and their scores at last review. I want your team to reach peak productivity in minimal time, and if there's anyone who will be unable to do that, I'd like to hear it from you first. After you've completed that task, I'll ask you to aid me in collecting some data from our current clients. I'm planning to solicit feedback from existing customers to discover how we can improve our consulting service."

Frank left Colin's office with a sinking heart. He'd just been handed a large pile of what seemed suspiciously like busywork. As one of Fishbone Financial's first employees, Frank had poured heart and soul into serving the company for twelve years. Although he was not a partner, he had felt Fishbone's ups and downs personally – he was deeply invested in the firm's well-being and believed he was a major contributor to its success. Now Fishbone was gone. Frank felt a sense of grief and mourned Fishbone, and Colin's assertion of power only highlighted his loss. Fishbone had been a congenial workplace that encouraged informal communication and disregarded traditional hierarchy. In contrast Meta drew strict, formal lines of authority, and power struggles were evident at all levels. Frank sighed miserably. This adjustment was going to be harder than he'd anticipated.

Colin's door was still open when Erin Everly approached Frank in the corridor. Erin was one of Fishbone's financial consultants, formerly one of Frank's direct reports. "Frank, I need to take the afternoon off today," confided Erin. "My son's in some trouble over at the school." Erin was a single mother whose teenage son was struggling with the challenges of puberty. "Sure, Erin," said Frank warmly. "Of course. Take whatever time you need to deal with your family issues – you know family comes first."

As Erin walked away, Colin stuck his head out the door. "Ferris – back in my office. Now," he said.

"I overheard that exchange," Colin told Frank once they were back inside. "And it was completely inappropriate – in fact, it's inexcusable. First, if Ms Everly needs personal time, she should be asking me, not you. And second, here at Meta time off is not granted without formal request. Those requests must be made in writing and given adequate time for supervisor review."

"I'm sorry," said Frank. "I was unaware of that policy. Should I call Erin back to discuss it with you?"

"No," snapped Colin. "Let it go this time. But don't let it happen again. I'm not going to let you Fishbone people take advantage of the system by claiming you don't know our policies. Ignorance is no excuse."

"I do apologise," Frank repeated. He left the room even more depressed. Fishbone had held employees' family lives as sacred; apparently Meta did not share that view. Somehow Frank had ended up in a situation where he was expected to know everything, do everything, and be everything Colin Clark wanted, without benefit of guidance to transition into or time to learn the demands of his new environment. And his Fishbone employees – who once valued and respected his leadership – now had to grasp that all his authority had been stripped away. How was he ever going to fit in?

Frank again seriously considered a job change. He had enough positive client relationships that he was sure he could bring some important assets to a competitor firm. Maybe it was time to make a new start.

*   *   *   *   *   *   *   *   *   *

Erin Everly walked quickly away from Colin Clark's office where she had just received Frank's okay to take the afternoon off. She wanted to get out the door fast, before he changed his mind or someone else intervened to stop her. Erin had fabricated the story that her son was in trouble. In reality, she simply couldn't face another minute in the office she shared with her Meta Money Management counterpart, Bill Barnes.

Erin had taken the position with Fishbone four years before, just as her divorce was finalised. The job had filled a void in her life, and she had grown to think of herself first as a Fishbone financial consultant, second as a mother, third – and least importantly – as an individual person. In other words, she defined her identity primarily by her work. The Meta merger had hit her hard. First she'd been concerned she would become jobless. When that fear didn't play out, she worried about status. At Meta she seemed to be less of everything – less respected, less valued, less important – than she'd been at Fishbone. Being asked to share an office smacked of demotion, and Erin felt even more threatened by her officemate. Bill Barnes was just so perfect.

Bill had been trying to get her to shadow him on his large accounts ever since the Fishbone team had arrived. Erin knew he had plans to make her look bad. Well, she would fix that. She would come in early one morning and beat him to the punch – she would field all his client calls and just show everyone what a good financial consultant she really was.

Bill was on the phone when Erin returned to their shared space to pick up her things. She rushed to gather herself together before he finished so she could avoid making an excuse. No good.

"Taking off?" said Bill affably, hanging up the phone.

"Yes, I must," Erin replied hastily. "I have to rescue my son from some kind of problem at his school."

"Oh, I'm sorry to hear that," said Bill. He sounded sincere enough, but Erin's suspicions rose. "I was going to show you the documentation on the Smith account. They're one of our largest clients, and we have an appointment next week. I thought that would be a good place to start going over procedures to help you get up to speed."

"Thank you so much," said Erin. "But I really must go." Bill kept insisting on interfering, ostensibly trying to help her learn the Meta standards for quoting consultation fees, writing proposals, and documenting client contacts. He put up a façade of helpful collegiality, but Erin was sure he had something more devious up his sleeve. After all, how would helping her serve *his* interests?

Bill Barnes shook his head as he watched Erin depart. Well, he'd tried. Bill had noted a good deal of hesitancy among the newly acquired Fishbone staff, but no one was as defensive and resistant as Erin. He supposed it was understandable. How would he have felt if he'd been uprooted and transferred to a completely new environment, as they had been? The transition had been no cakewalk for him, either. He now shared an office which he'd previously occupied solo. He was charged to teach Erin their client-interaction practices and documentation procedures – against which Erin balked at every turn.

Fortunately Bill possessed a calm, unflappable self-confidence. He felt grounded and secure in his financial consultant role; he had a happy, well-adjusted home life and took care to balance his workload with strong family ties and healthy leisure activity. He could afford to accommodate Erin's touchiness. She was stonewalling his offers of help because she was afraid; he could see that. He would just have to get creative in his approach and find a way to communicate that he meant her no harm.

Erin was already in the office and speaking on Bill's phone when Bill arrived the next morning. "Very well, thank you, and it was lovely to speak with you," he heard her say as she wrapped up the conversation. "I'll have that quotation to you by fax later this morning."

"Oh, did you figure out how to complete our quotation form?" Bill asked as she hung up, keeping his tone friendly. He didn't ask why she was using his desk; he'd decided to let it slide.

"I can handle it," said Erin archly. "I've been completing quotations for four years; I think I'm competent to do this one on my own."

Bill said nothing. He knew Fishbone's procedures had been very different to Meta's. But he didn't want to interfere any further with Erin's work or the wall between them would only grow. He'd been charged to help her integrate, a mission he could never fulfil if she continued to block the way.

The consultation team met that afternoon with Colin Clark at the helm. After general introductions and updates, Colin said, "Let's review where we are on the large client list so the new employees can get a feel for our status. Why don't we start with the Smith account. Bill?"

"I can address that," Erin interrupted. "I spoke with Smith early this morning. They wanted a quotation for helping them diversify a piece of their pension portfolio. I calculated the asset fees and commission and faxed it over an hour ago."

"Commission?" Colin raised his eyebrows. "But Smith is a fee-only account. Bill should have explained that to you."

Erin flushed deep red. "It's all right, Erin," said Bill, turning to Colin. "She didn't know," he told the vice president. "Erin had a family emergency yesterday, so I didn't have a chance to go over the Smith procedures with her."

"Oh yes," said Colin disapprovingly. "That reminds me that I must clarify how we go about requesting time off." He glanced sidelong at Frank before launching into a lengthy procedural description.

Colin wrapped up the meeting with the admonishment that all employees, not just the new ones but also the existing Meta staff, should revisit the Meta Employee Procedure Manual. "We're going to write a new chapter regarding integration of acquired employees," he said, and he proceeded to assign various sections of the chapter to specific staff.

"All this documentation," fumed Erin as she and Bill returned to their office. "All we're ever asked to do is write this and document that and get this other thing in writing. When do we have time to actually talk with clients? This is the worst management scheme I've ever seen."

"I'm sure it seems like a lot when you're not used to it," acknowledged Bill. "But it does back you up to have things in writing. That way there's no confusion once a decision gets made."

"I'm surprised you ever reach any decisions at all," returned Erin.

*　*　*　*　*　*　*　*　*

The next few weeks were difficult ones as the consulting teams from Fishbone Financial and Meta Money Management struggled to integrate staff and meet management expectations. Teamwork suffered as the groups failed to agree on best practices. The Meta culture was largely based on written communication; management required extensive documentation before a decision could be made. Fishbone staff had been used to a more vocal culture, where decisions were made through meetings, informal face-to-face discussion, presentations, and debate.

The resulting cultural clash sparked frustration and division. Of the Fishbone staff, the Meta group would say, "They're such mavericks! They take insane risks and make snap decisions without adequate documentation." The Fishbone group had another opinion of their Meta counterparts: "Meta is so bureaucratic that we can't get anything done! We spend so much time documenting everything that we let opportunities slip by."

At the root of the division between the two consulting groups lay a major difference in philosophy. Meta placed high value on gathering customer input to guide procedures development and to upgrade services. Fishbone had been accustomed to a more collaborative customer-service model, where employees were encouraged to develop close relationships with customers that would guide decisions. From the outside, these two strategies don't seem all that different. But from inside the struggling merger, they seemed like night and day.

At the individual level, emotions continued to run high. People were busy trying to settle their specific circumstances and decide how they fit into the new system. Concerns about personal security were rampant, and employees were challenged to re-establish order and routine in their lives. Employees complained constantly about management, and each of the two groups blamed the other for the mistakes that were inevitably made. Each group viewed the other as the enemy. Meta saw themselves as heroes fighting to conquer an infiltration. Fishbone saw themselves as victims battling to retain identity and establish rank. The more defensive each group became, the less clearly they were able to perceive the strengths of the other, and the more arrogant and exclusive they became. Shame and blame, negative exchanges, and irrational beliefs of superiority characterised the newly combined company culture. They were fighting the Battle of Change, with devastating impact on both productivity and profit.

What do *you* think?

The Battle of Change is affecting the newly merged companies Meta Money Management and Fishbone Financial on two levels. At the individual level, personalities are clashing and employees are fighting for position within a new hierarchy. At the cultural level, the merger has created a split between the two teams as they fail to agree upon a new set of company values and priorities.

What do you think is happening here, and what would you do to fix the problems? Consider a few questions:

1. What does the Johari Window look like between the conflicting staffs? Between Frank and Colin? Between Erin and Bill?
2. Where do the two companies reside on the UZOD scale?
3. Review the Reacting to Change circle presented earlier in this chapter. Are any of the characters reacting like cynics, dinosaurs, players, or spectators in this scenario?
4. Who do you think is responsible for the issues at hand? Who do you think should take steps to resolve them?
5. Which should be addressed first: problems between individual personalities or cultural conflicts?

The Admiral's entry: Backing up

Throughout this book I have followed a pattern in which the Admiral is called in after a battle has been joined, and then he works to pick up the pieces and negotiate peace between warring factions. For this scenario, I wish to diverge from that pattern. This time, I would like to show you what might have happened if leadership had taken appropriate action *before the fact* – action to avert the Battle of Change before it had a chance to start.

So let's back up to the beginning of the scenario, to the point where the leaders at Meta Money Management and Fishbone Financial are considering the possibility of merger. Let's say they called the Admiral in to provide third-party guidance before even announcing the agreement to the employees. Let's look at what he does to establish trust and ease this difficult transition from the outset.

* * * * * * * * * *

The respective leadership teams of Meta Money Management and Fishbone Financial settled into their seats in the Meta auditorium. The Admiral had been invited to present a plan that would help both companies survive the massive organisational change involved with a merger.

"Coping with organisational change is a challenge on two levels," the Admiral began. "First consider the impact on the people involved. At the individual level, your employees will be shocked and scared. Many of them will grieve the loss of a situation they've come to appreciate and enjoy. All of them will feel a sense of uncertainty and insecurity about what the future holds. A host of negative emotions will emerge. If you fail to recognise and address those emotions, you can expect to see negative results in how business is conducted. You can expect to see low morale, employee turnover, and errors. Your employees may suffer from stress, anxiety, or even illness. Absenteeism may increase while teamwork and cooperation decline. You may lose key personnel to your competitors.

"The second level to consider is your company culture. In a merger situation, *culture* is the ability of two groups to understand and work with each other's values and priorities. Two companies may do the same kind of work and undertake the same activities. But deep down, they're not the same. Culture is really a set of expectations – it's what employees mean when they say, 'This is the way we do things around here.' And a company's underlying values run deep. If you don't work towards combining your cultural values into a mutually acceptable whole, a de facto culture might emerge that does not serve your company's mission and purpose. Instead, you want to help your two constituencies to understand and learn from each other so the emerging culture represents the best of both worlds."

"How do we do that?" asked the CEO of Meta Money Management.

"We start with measurement," said the Admiral. "Let me show you a couple of diagrams. The first one shows the five mental models encountered during a merger. These ideas came from a company called Axialent, a consulting group that promotes a philosophical base they call *conscious business*." He projected this diagram on the screen.[14]

Five Mental Models for a Merger

1	My way is the *only* way	Ignorance that other organisations are not like mine
2	My way is the *best* way	Arrogance, superiority
3	You have some good ways too	Understanding, objective observation, respect
4	Let me learn from your ways	Openness, realisation of benefits
5	Let's build a new way together	New identity, best of both

Reprinted from Taylor, Carolyn (2010). *Mergers and Acquisitions: Emotions at work.* Axialent, Inc.

"You want your two organisations to combine, adapt, and grow into a culture that achieves your mission and goals. In order for that to happen, your employees must go through at least the first four mental models. Most of them will begin at level 1 or 2, even your senior staff who already know their jobs are secure. But individuals have different personalities and will adapt at different paces.

"Some employees will spend only a few days at levels 1 or 2. Others might still remain stuck at level 2 five years after the merger. Some people have enough inner confidence to respond to a change appropriately, moving through the levels with ease. Some are more insecure and will find the change personally threatening.

"That's why you have to address individuals' emotions concurrently with the evolution of your new company culture. You need to help individuals move through the mental models as quickly as possible so they can get back

---

14 Carolyn Taylor, *Mergers and Acquisitions: Emotions at Work* (Key Biscayne, FL: Axialent Inc., 2010).

to making useful contributions to the company's success. As leaders, you can take important steps to make that happen."

The Admiral turned back to his notes and presented another diagram. "Here's another model that I think will interest you," he continued. "I recommend that we conduct a Cultural Comparison Assessment to learn how your two organisations correlate with one another. The Cultural Values instrument was developed by Richard Barrett of Barrett Values Centre. Barrett advocates building a vision-guided, values-driven corporate culture that focuses not only on financial success but also on employee fulfilment.

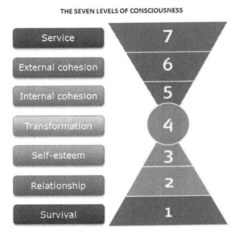

THE SEVEN LEVELS OF CONSCIOUSNESS

Figure 25 – Barrett's Seven Levels of Consciousness Model
Reproduced with kind permission from Barrett, Richard (2011).
The New Leadership Paradigm. Lulu.com.

"Barrett's model of the Seven Levels of Consciousness builds on a body of work conducted by psychologist Abraham Maslow. The basis of the model is that organisations are comprised of individuals, and thus businesses act as living entities with motivations similar to those of individuals.

"The Cultural Values Assessment tool is a simple but effective way to measure and map corporate cultures," the Admiral explained. "It's designed to diagnose and illuminate both the current and the desired cultures by asking employees how they perceive the organisation's current values, what they think the desired values are, and what their own personal values are. The measure yields results across three perspectives: the Human Perspective, the Organisational Development Perspective, and the Business Perspective."

The Admiral went on to explain that neither individuals nor organisations operate from any single level of consciousness but tend to cluster around three or four levels at once. "Individuals are usually focussed at levels 1 through 5, usually with particular emphasis on level 5. Many organisations tend to focus on the first three levels. Level 1 might stand for profit and growth, level 2 for customer satisfaction, and level 3 for productivity, efficiency, and quality. But the most successful organisations are the ones that operate from all seven levels. At level 4, learning and innovation lead to continuous renewal. At level 5 is internal cohesion, and at level 6, employee fulfilment and customer collaboration. Level 7 is where ethics and social responsibility come into play.

"Barrett's measure will map your organisations' current and desired values against what he calls the Business Needs Scorecard. You can use the information to identify where your energies are focussed and how to balance those energies across the six categories of the Business Needs Scorecard: Finance, Fitness, Client Relations, Evolution, Culture, and Contribution to Society. A comparison of the results of your two organisations will show where you share values, where you differ, where potential problem areas lie, what your mutual strengths are, and what each of you has to offer the other."

The Admiral laid out his plan. He would conduct the values assessment with the employees from both organisations. After interpreting and presenting the results, he would make recommendations for a process to effectively combine the cultures of the two companies into a unified and functional whole.

The Cultural Comparison Assessment

Two weeks later, the Admiral was ready to present the assessment results.

"Your personal values distributions are quite similar," he said, presenting the following:

Personal Value Matches
Fishbone - Meta

Creativity
Perseverance
Fun
Commitment
Ambition
Reliable

"These are the values shared by people in both organisations," he explained. "This shows that the people in both firms have similar operating principles and motivations."

Next he presented the following:

Personal Value Differences	
Fishbone	**Meta**
Co-operation	Responsibility
Honest	Independence
Balance (home/work)	Success
Enthusiasm	Positive attitude

"These are your personal value differences," he said. "Just like in a marriage, it's important to analyse differences between the parties' values. Thus you can expand each other's awareness or provide support in an area where your counterpart is less proficient. Remember that even if one group did not report values that the other group reported, that doesn't mean the first group doesn't hold or appreciate those values. They choose the values that play particular importance in their lives at this point in time. The differences need to be acknowledged and nurtured for an optimal relationship."

He went on to elaborate on the value differences. "Fishbone's people foster transparent, supportive interactions and appreciate being allowed time to attend to their personal endeavours. They have a great passion for life.

"Meta's population has a strong inner drive and sense of ownership of their actions. Doing well is important to them, and they approach life with a positive outlook."

The Admiral explained that both companies had a concentration of values at level 5 on the Levels of Consciousness Scale, with Fishbone reporting a slightly stronger focus at this level. Meta had a stronger focus at level 3 (self-esteem). "Next we'll talk about current culture values," said the Admiral. "Current culture values reflect the employees' perceptions of what their organisation focuses on and how it behaves to form a picture of the working environment, positive aspects of the business, and potential problem areas. Fishbone and Meta reported no matches in their current culture values.

"This could indicate that Fishbone and Meta have no positive values in common," continued the Admiral, "but if we look carefully at the values *differences*, we can see that there are similarities between the words each group has chosen. Here are the values each firm reported.

Current Culture Value Differences	
Fishbone	**Meta**
Professionalism	Customer collaboration
Customer intimacy	Staff engagement
Co-operation	Craftsmanship
Financial stability	Diversity
Reliable	Profit
Achievement	Results orientation
Quality	
Balance (home/work)	

"Fishbone works to provide the highest standards in their deliverables and to successfully meet their objectives. They look after the needs of their employees and customers alike. They focus on the bottom line and support one another.

"Meta solicits input from its customers to better serve the company's needs while creating a tolerant environment where employees feel connected to their work. They pride themselves on their skills and work to meet objectives. They also are focussed on the bottom line."

The Admiral continued, "When we go on to look at the potentially limiting values, we find that Fishbone and Meta report two in common: bureaucracy and short-term focus. Both companies are dealing with rigid systems and processes and a lack of forward planning.

"Only Meta reported other potentially limiting values: control and departmental interest. Meta people are frustrated by a lack of trust among colleagues within their organisation and feel decisions are made without consideration for the best interest of the organisation as a whole.

"Both firms are experiencing elevated entropy, but it's much more significant for Meta. In both cases entropy is concentrated at level 3, self-esteem, which indicates concerns in the areas of best practices and service delivery. Meta also has significant entropy at level 1, survival."

Next the Admiral presented the values matches and values differences for the two companies as related to desired culture. "The values in **bold** represent the new requests for each group," he said.

Desired Culture Value Matches Fishbone - Meta
Customer intimacy
Reliable
Professionalism
Staff engagement
Entrepreneurial
Fun

Desired Culture Value Differences	
Fishbone	**Meta**
Adaptability	**Continuous improvement**
Boldness	**Action orientation**
Balance (home/work)	**Creativity**
Long-term perspective	Customer collaboration
	Responsibility
	Employee recognition
	Goals orientation

"A match of six values shows me there's strong agreement between the two cultures," said the Admiral. "This is a solid indicator of potential success for your merger because the employees want to see many of the same values integrated into their joint system. Both groups want to support a sense of ownership and innovation in their work, and they also want to enjoy the time they spend in the workplace.

"Looking at the desired values differences, Fishbone wants to build resilience and display courage in a changing market, looking towards the future. Meta wants to support the development of new ideas and ways to conduct business as they keep objectives in mind. They want to be proactive.

They want people to take ownership of their endeavours, and they want to receive regular appreciation for their contributions."

The recommendations

The Admiral had the leadership teams take a short break before presenting his action recommendations for the merger process. When they reconvened, he gave them a list of action steps. "This is the progression of action steps I recommend you take to make your merger a success," he said. "I will be available at any of the steps along the way to facilitate the process, implement an action, and measure how well it's working."

Recommendations

- Find out what people from both companies mean, specifically, by each of the matched desired culture values. Ask both for a clear definition and for representative behaviour, and find out what the organisations need to do to promote, integrate, and implement these values: **customer intimacy, reliability, professionalism, staff engagement, fun**, and **entrepreneurialism**.
- Hold focus groups within each organisation to get maximum input about the direction people want the company to take to implant **fun** and **entrepreneurialism** into their joint culture.
- Facilitate discussions among Fishbone staff in various positions to understand what **adaptability, boldness**, and **long-term perspective** mean to them. Create new action steps based on their recommendations.
- Hold discussions with Meta staff to learn why they requested **continuous improvement, action orientation, creativity, responsibility, employee recognition**, and **goals orientation**. Try to determine whether these were stated in reaction to any of the trust and decision-making issues currently Meta is currently experiencing.
- Determine how Fishbone can facilitate **professionalism, customer intimacy**, and **reliability** into the new culture, as they are values that Fishbone holds now that Meta wants to embrace.
- In turn, determine how Meta can help Fishbone with **staff engagement**.
- Define a set of guiding values. Limit to a maximum of four. Hold discussions to determine buy-in for the proposed set of values. Once the list is accepted, define the behaviours each value specifically represents and what behaviours would undermine each value.

- Hold discussions that include employees from both companies. Display the agreed-upon guiding values in plain sight to guide the discussions. Give teams a forum where they can meet with, understand, and learn from each other – a chance to build respect.

"I recommend that you begin working through this list of action steps immediately upon sharing the news of the merger with your employees," the Admiral concluded. "Be sure that employees at all levels are represented in your focus and discussion groups. Listen to the negative emotions that people express as well as the positive ones. Give employees a chance to grieve and talk things out. Big change is hard on people, and letting them know that sadness, loss, and anxiety are normal and expected will go a long way towards easing the burden."

The grateful leaders took the Admiral's advice to heart. After breaking the news of the merger to their respective companies, they immediately embarked on his recommended action steps. They learned a good deal about their company cultures in the process of conducting the focus groups and internal discussions. They learned to listen and support employee needs. They gave employees an opportunity to air their grief, anxieties, and concerns for the future. They determined to give every employee a chance to provide input to guide the merger. Then they learned how to steer the discussions towards positive outcomes to achieve maximum employee buy-in for the process.

Upon completing the internal discussions, the leaders developed the following set of guiding values to submit to their staff for approval:

Guiding Values
- We adopt a model of continuous improvement by providing the flexibility to adapt quickly to changes in both customer and employee needs.
- We actively set company-wide goals and engage staff at all levels to take responsibility and be accountable for achieving those goals.
- We strive to recognise unique, creative staff contributions and encourage entrepreneurial opportunity.
- We celebrate goal achievement in a spirit of fun.

Then they held a town hall–style meeting to bring together the entire staff of both companies. The large group wholeheartedly approved the new guiding values. Each team felt a sense of ownership, and each individual felt like a contributor to the integration. Thus the merged company achieved widespread employee buy-in for a jointly developed set of realistic, achievable goals. The goal-driven system yielded ample opportunity for the new company to recognise the contributions of individual employees to a model of excellence, reliability, and customer service.

The leaders recognised that a plan to simply subsume Fishbone departments under Meta management heads would not adhere to the new guiding values. With the Admiral's guidance, they designed instead a more collaborative management approach. They built management teams for each department that would share responsibility for tracking that department's progress towards its goals. Each management team also was charged to plan celebrations to reward goal accomplishment.

Thus Frank Ferris and Colin Clark worked side by side to set goals for the consulting team. Frank learned the value of backing up decisions with written documentation, and Colin learned that a warm, caring attitude towards employees sparked creative problem-solving. The two men built mutual respect. Instead of pitting employees against each other in competition, they set up a programme whereby the whole staff earned rewards for goal achievement. This programme went a long way towards building camaraderie between Bill Barnes and Erin Everly. Erin came to welcome Bill's calm, thoughtful assistance, and Bill learned to value Erin's intuitive approach to customer relations and sharp focus. They took to bouncing ideas off each other as they worked towards their common goals. The guiding values helped build trust between colleagues and dissolve the fear, anxiety, and unrealistic expectations that could have undermined the merger's success.

Now what do you think?

By employing the assistance of a third party – the Admiral – Meta Money Management and Fishbone Financial were able not only to survive the challenges of a large merger but also to completely avoid fighting the Battle of Change. How well do you think the Admiral's strategy worked? Do you think the results were realistic and believable?

Barrett's Cultural Values Assessment can be applied to any situation where an organisation must implement an important change. Can you think of scenarios from your current situation in which this measure might guide an important transition? Even when major change is not at hand, the discovery of a set of guiding values can help a company restate its mission and focus its purpose towards ongoing success in a rapidly changing marketplace.

Today's organisations are challenged to balance the needs of customers, employees, shareholders, and society. Obtaining input from each of these sectors is essential for corporate success. Change is inevitable at a time when the personal and social contexts of a business are in flux. In our current world, who you are as an organisation and what your organisation stands for are just as important as your product. While addressing the personality needs of and differences between individuals has clear value for solving specific workplace problems, meeting the evolving needs of your organisational culture is crucial as well. Create a culture of collaboration, employee ownership, and mutual respect, and you may never have to fight the Battle of Change.

CHAPTER IX

The pacifist's task today is to find a method of helping and healing which provides a revolutionary constructive substitute for war. ~Vera Brittain, 1964

When you feel sick, you go to the doctor. In the examination room you see an array of tools laid out that the doctor will use to diagnose your ailment. During your examination, the doctor may reach for a stethoscope, thermometer, sphygmomanometer, retractor, or ultrasound machine; you might be sent for a blood test, X-ray, electrocardiogram, or MRI. The point is that the doctor has myriad instruments at his or her disposal to identify and treat your problem. The doctor probably will not rely upon a single instrument to guide the diagnosis.

In the same way, psychometric measures form a toolkit of instruments to diagnose workplace problems and recommend solutions. And like most doctors, I subscribe to a holistic approach to using the tools at my disposal: combined results from several measures helps you dig deeper into the root of the problem and illuminate more possible approaches to treatment. The instruments complement each other; they work together to point up a variety of possible steps towards healthy problem-solving and conflict resolution.

In previous chapters I presented you with a series of illustrations – scenarios designed to breathe life into problems you're likely to encounter at work. I hope you recognised some of the people in those scenarios. I hope at least one of the characters caused you to exclaim, "Oh, that's me!" or "Aha! That's just like my boss … or colleague … or friend … or teacher … or aunt."

But beyond believable character development, I hope this book has convinced you that there is more than one approach to resolving workplace conflict. By now I hope you have experienced at least a minor shift in your way of thinking. When you *are* faced with a problem at work, I'd like to think I've sparked one thought in the back of your mind: "Maybe I should consider some psychometric measurement." If any reader has added personality measures to his or her problem-solving toolkit, I will consider my book a success.

In this final section, I would like to detail the psychometric tools presented by the Admiral in previous chapters. I will offer some history and context for the instruments and outline how their results can be applied. I will provide brief information about the required certifications for administering and interpreting each measure. This may serve as a brief inventory of your toolkit – a summary of the instruments to which you may turn to solve workplace problems.

The Myers-Briggs Type Indicator (MBTI)

I present the Myers-Briggs Type Indicator (MBTI) first because of its popularity and recognition among organisational decision-makers around the globe. CPP Inc., current publisher and distributor of the instrument, calls it "the world's most trusted personality assessment."[15] Certainly, in the more than thirty years since Isabel Myers Briggs's passing, the MBTI has enjoyed growing acceptance as one of the gold standards for personality typing. Many Fortune 500 companies, including Starbucks, Pepsi, and Microsoft, rely on the MBTI for guidance. As many as 2.5 million individuals take the assessment each year, and the measure has been translated into twenty-one languages.

The MBTI has a rather different background from many other personality instruments. While its principles were based on the early personality theories of eminent Swiss psychologist Carl Gustav Jung (one of the first to propose personality in terms of *typology*), the measure's authors were not trained psychologists. During World War II, many women entered the workplace to replace their male counterparts fighting overseas. At that time two non-psychologists – who nevertheless had been studying Jung's personality theory for seventeen years – undertook to make that theory more accessible to a lay audience. Katharine Cook Briggs and her daughter, Isabel Briggs Myers, created the MBTI to help women identify the kind of war-effort jobs in which they might be most comfortable and effective despite their lack of workplace experience.

Since its introduction in 1942, the MBTI has gone through several iterations, improved and updated to reflect a wealth of research. Its reliability,

---

15   CPP Inc., "Products Index", <https://www.cpp.com/products/mbti/index.aspx>, accessed 7 Feb. 2012.

validity, replicability, and statistical significance have been extensively tested and confirmed, both by Isabel Myers herself and by professional psychometricians whose results have been published in more than 4,000 research papers. Authors from a wide range of backgrounds have written about the MBTI; hundreds of practical, easy-to-read resources about the Indicator are available.

The premise upon which Briggs and Myers based the MBTI was this: "each of us has a set of gifts, a set of mental tools that we have become comfortable using and thus reach for in the everyday business of living. Although we all have access to the same basic tools in our psychological toolbox, each of us is more comfortable with and thus prefers a particular tool (or set of tools) for a particular task. It is our unique set of these preferences that gives us our distinct personality and makes us appear similar or dissimilar to others."[16]

The MBTI is one of the few personality models that describe personality differences *positively*. Thus there are no better or worse types to be; each type has its strengths and potential pitfalls. In developing their assessment, Myers and Briggs sought to sort out personality type based on people's *preferences* to think or behave in a certain way. They did so using the three dichotomies specified in Jung's writing plus a fourth uniquely their own. The four dichotomies measured by the MBTI are as follows:

- **Extraversion (E)** versus **Introversion (I)**: differentiating people who direct their energy primarily outwards towards other people and events from people who direct their energy primarily inwards towards their inner environment, thoughts, and experiences.
- **Sensing (S)** versus **Intuition (N)**: differentiating people who take in information primarily through their five senses and immediate experience from people who take in information primarily through hunches and impressions and are more interested in future possibilities than present realities.
- **Thinking (T)** versus **Feeling (F)**: differentiating people who make decisions primarily based on logic and objectivity from people who make decisions primarily based on personal values and the effects of their decisions on others.
- **Judging (J)** versus **Perceiving (P)**: differentiating people who

---

16   Peter B. Myers, "Introduction", in Isabel Briggs Myers, *Gifts Differing: Understanding Personality Type* (Palo Alto, CA: Davies-Black Publishing, 1995).

prefer structure, plans, and achieving closure quickly from people who prefer flexibility, spontaneity, and keeping options open.

So when using the MBTI, it's important to understand what is meant by *type* and *preference*. Here are some of the basic assumptions:

- The MBTI assesses *preferences.*
- Everyone uses all eight preferences.
- The preferences are not the same as abilities or skills.
- All preferences are equally important and valuable, and there are no better or worse types to be.
- People themselves are the best judges of their types – hence the MBTI is an *indicator,* not a test.
- The indicator is used to open up possibilities, not to limit individuals.

The MBTI has many applications; new versions and interpretations have been developed to guide various types of decisions. People use the indicator to improve individual and team performance, explore careers, reduce workplace conflict, build management and leadership, develop teaching and learning strategies, improve relationships and communication, and guide personal and spiritual development. Thus there are several versions of the MBTI, and those who plan its use should choose the most appropriate version for the task at hand.

The MBTI is a restricted assessment tool. In other words, specific qualifications are required in order to administer the instrument to others. Practitioners must become certified in the use and interpretation of the questionnaire. To prepare for certification, one can either study personality theory academically or take courses specifically designed to meet certification guidelines. Training and certification ensure the accurate and ethical use of the Indicator. In addition, such training provides the practitioner with the methods and knowledge to help clients understand MBTI results and apply those results to their lives.

The 16PF Instrument

The 16PF is a trait-based questionnaire that measures sixteen aspects – called *traits* – of a person's personality. Traits are stable clusters of behaviours, or personality constructs, which underlie how a person chooses to act when faced with a given situation. Thus the 16PF measure provides a highly accurate prediction of how a person may behave in the future.

The 16PF was the brainchild of Raymond Cattell, who was born near Birmingham in the UK in 1905. Cattell received an honours degree in chemistry from the University of London in 1921. Subsequently, his interest in intelligence research led him to redirect his focus to the study of psychology; he was awarded a PhD in that field in 1929. In 1937 Cattell moved to the United States to work on his theories of intelligence, and he joined the faculty of Harvard in 1941.

Cattell possessed superior mathematical aptitude and became well known for applying *factor analysis* to personality theory. Factor analysis is a statistical technique that seeks to identify a small number of underlying factors that can effectively describe a much larger set of variables (like those used to describe human personality). Cattell was deeply influenced by the events of World War II; he came to believe that an understanding of human nature would bring mankind closer to solving its global economic and political problems. Eventually Cattell's research yielded a framework to account for the full range of human behaviour. By using factor analysis to classify groups of behaviours associated with deep-rooted traits, he established what he believed was a set of underlying traits that could meaningfully account for all the behaviour a person might display – the 16PF measure, first published in 1949.

More than fifty years of research have gone into the development, refinement, and updating of the 16PF, and it has become one of the most widely used and well-established personality questionnaires in the world.

Cattell described each of the sixteen traits as falling along a continuum. That is, he believed everyone possesses some degree of each trait. The key to interpreting the measure's results is determining where each trait falls along a continuum for the person being measured. The sixteen traits and their opposing points on the continuum are called the primary factors, and are as follows:

Abstractedness: Imaginative versus practical
Apprehension: Insecure versus complacent
Dominance: Deferential versus dominant
Emotional Stability: Reactive versus adaptive
Liveliness: Lively versus serious
Openness to Change: Traditional versus experimental
Perfectionism: Flexible versus organised
Privateness: Forthright versus discreet
Reasoning: Abstract versus concrete

Rule Consciousness:	Expedient versus dutiful
Self-reliance:	Group oriented versus individualistic
Sensitivity:	Objective versus subjective
Social Boldness:	Timid versus adventurous
Tension:	Relaxed versus high-strung
Vigilance:	Trusting versus suspicious
Warmth:	Emotionally distant versus warm and attentive

Cattell applied further factor analysis to group the sixteen primary factors into five broader categories which he called the global factors: Extraversion, Independence, Tough-mindedness, Self-control, and Anxiety. These global factors are now known as the "Big Five", and the five-factor model has been used in the development of many personality measures subsequently developed by others.

The 16PF is a robust and powerful tool with many possible applications. In the workplace it provides useful information to guide personnel selection and recruitment, career and vocational decisions, competency development, teamwork, and executive coaching. The 16PF also offers an excellent framework in which to conduct side by side personality comparisons and thus lends itself well to relationship and couples counselling.

The 16PF questionnaire and templates for interpretive reports are available for purchase through IPAT (www.ipat.com), the company founded by Raymond Cattell, and from OPP in Europe (www.opp.eu.com). Trained counsellors and psychologists can prepare for certification to administer and interpret the 16PF by taking a two-day workshop. A variety of such workshops are held around the world.

The Fundamental Interpersonal Relations Orientation (FIRO)

In the late 1950s, William Schutz was conducting an extensive literature review for his doctoral thesis. His thesis experiment was designed to help the US Navy understand and predict how high-performance military teams could work together effectively, and where conflicts might arise based on the interpersonal needs of team members.

Schutz's research led him to identify three areas of basic human need that fell in line with the three major schools of psychoanalytic thought: Carl Jung's Extraversion versus Introversion, Alfred Adler's individual power theory, and Sigmund Freud's focus on intimacy. Based on the idea that people need people, Schutz believed people need each other in three ways (three areas of interpersonal need): Inclusion, Control, and Affection.

In Schutz's view, these three areas of need are as fundamental to sustaining life as food, water, or shelter.[17] The Schutz theory says one's level of need is developed during early childhood. Each human being requires a certain amount of contact with others, and this amount differs among people. If the need is not fulfilled, the person becomes uncomfortable and dissatisfied.

For FIRO purposes, interpersonal behaviour is any interaction that occurs between people. The FIRO model describes interactions within the three categories of interpersonal need along two dimensions: *expressed* and *wanted*. So the FIRO seeks to measure how you typically behave with other people (expressed) and how you hope they will act towards you (wanted). Everyone has different levels of interpersonal need, and there is no right or wrong amount. The key aspect of Schutz's model is *self-awareness*. That is, the FIRO instrument is optimally used to help people become aware of their own interpersonal needs, leading them to informed choices and opportunities to design new strategies. By revealing the mismatches between wanted and expressed behaviour, the FIRO can offer profound insights into a person's self-image.

Schutz's three areas of need are defined as follows:

> *Inclusion* indicates how much you generally include other people in your life and how much attention, contact, and recognition you want from others. Inclusion is about how you relate to groups, whether small or large.

> *Control* describes how much influence and responsibility you want and how much you want others to lead and influence you. Control is about one-to-one relationships and your behaviour as part of a group.

> *Affection* shows how close and warm you are with others and how close and warm you want others to be with you. Affection is about the need to establish comfort within one's one-to-one relationships.

The FIRO is meant to address the very core of one's personality to point up ambiguities that may underlie complex, difficult relationship issues.

---

17   William Schutz, *FIRO: A Three-Dimensional Theory of Interpersonal Behavior* (New York: Rinehart, 1958).

The self-awareness gained from taking the FIRO increases the chances of a person's needs being met and helps a person manage his or her interactions with others. The tool also can help people identify the type of workplace in which they're most likely to thrive.

The FIRO instrument and its business version (the FIRO-B) are suited to a variety of applications, including personal, leadership, and management development; fitness for future roles; conflict management; team development; improved interpersonal communication; and enhancement of workplace relationships. Results on the tool can generate various reports including individual profiles, business profiles, organisational interpretations, individual and business leadership reports.

To be eligible to purchase and interpret the FIRO, one must receive some training in the developmental model and in the administration, interpretation, and application of the tool. The requirements can be met either by completing a FIRO-specific certification programme or by attaining other educational and licensing credentials. For example, anyone who is already certified to administer the MBTI becomes automatically eligible to purchase and use the FIRO and the FIRO-B.

The FIRO continues to be refined and updated and has been translated into at least five languages. Culturally sensitive versions have been published for various populations. The FIRO and FIRO-B instruments are distributed by CPP Inc.

The Occupational Personality Questionnaire (OPQ)

The Occupational Personality Questionnaire (OPQ) was launched in 1984 by Saville and Holdsworth Ltd. (SHL) in the UK. The instrument was created by Peter Saville, the occupational psychologist who developed the British Standardisation of the 16PF in the 1970s and colleagues Roger Holdsworth, Gill Nyfield, Lisa Cramp, and Bill Mabey. The OPQ was the first published instrument to apply the "Big Five" five-factor model of personality measurement (see the 16PF section, above).

The initial development of the OPQ took place in the UK between 1981 and 1984. Saville and colleagues received sponsorship from more than fifty organisations in both the private and public sectors. The OPQ's creators did not subscribe to any single personality theory; rather, they adopted an eclectic approach that incorporated constructs proposed by multiple theorists, including Eysenck, Cattell, Murray, Hersey, and Blanchard, among other psychologists and management theorists.

The OPQ and its later versions (OPQ32 and OPQ32i) provide

occupational models of personality that describe dimensions of people's preferred or typical styles at work. The OPQ Technical Manual (released in 2006) represents a major research undertaking supported by data collected from tens of thousands of people worldwide. The OPQ was designed to comprehensively cover all possible personality variables while being exclusively limited to content related to the world of work. The measure is meant to yield in-depth information on how individuals fit within a work environment, how they work with others, and their performance potential across important job competencies. SHL, the distributing organisation for the OPQ, maintains an international perspective for psychometric measurement, and the OPQ is available in more than thirty languages.

The OPQ's creators believed there were thirty-two specific personality characteristics underpinning job performance, and these characteristics are measured on the questionnaire. The following table summarises the constructs.

Relationships with People	
Influence	Persuasive, controlling, outspoken, independent minded
Sociability	Outgoing, team building, socially confident
Empathy	Modest, democratic, caring
Thinking Style	
Analysis	Data rational, evaluative, behavioural
Creativity and change	Conventional, conceptual, innovative, variety seeking, adaptable
Structure	Forward thinking, detail conscious, conscientious, rule following
Feelings and Emotions	
Emotions	Relaxed, worrying, tough minded, optimistic, trusting, emotionally controlled
Dynamism	Vigorous, competitive, achieving, decisive

The OPQ is designed to help organisations increase productivity and profitability by maximising the use of their human resources. Many organisations use the OPQ in the hiring and selection process. Further applications include training-needs analysis, individual management development, succession planning, career counselling, team building, and addressing organisational change. Different versions of the OPQ exist to serve specific purposes. These versions are the Management/Professional, Sales Report, Customer Contact Style, and Work Style questionnaires.

As with most personality measures, specialised training and certification are required to administer and interpret the OPQ. Training programmes and certification are offered exclusively by SHL, which has offices worldwide.

The Mayer-Salovey-Caruso Emotional Intelligence Test (MSCEIT)

Emotional intelligence (EI) is one's ability to use emotions to gather information and to reason – that is, how well a person identifies, assesses, and controls his or her own emotions and the emotions of others. Emotional intelligence theory has roots as far back as Charles Darwin, who studied the role of emotions in the survival and adaptation of species. Several human EI models emerged in the 1980s and 1990s. The one discussed here was introduced by psychologists John D. Mayer and Peter Salovey in 1990.

Mayer and Salovey based their theory, developed from more than a decade of stringent research, on an *ability* model of emotional intelligence. In other words, they believe emotional intelligence is the ability to reason with, and about, emotions. Mayer and Salovey[18] say that EI combines feeling with thinking and can be described by four related but different abilities:

- *Perceiving* **Emotions**: the ability to recognize how you and those around you are feeling.
- *Using* **Emotions**: the ability to generate emotions and to use emotions in cognitive tasks such as problem-solving and creativity.
- *Understanding* **Emotions**: the ability to understand complex emotions and emotional "chains" (i.e. how emotions transition from one stage to another).
- *Managing* **Emotions**: the ability to intelligently combine emotions (your own and others') with reason to devise effective strategies that help you to achieve positive outcomes.

---

18   John D. Mayer and Peter Salovey, "What is Emotional Intelligence?", in Peter Salovey and DJ Sluyter (Eds.), *Emotional Development and Emotional Intelligence* (New York: Basic Books, 1997, pp. 3-31).

Together with their colleague David R. Caruso, Mayer and Salovey developed a psychometric measure of these four abilities; the result was the Mayer-Salovey-Caruso Emotional Intelligence Test (MSCEIT). The MSCEIT is guided by three underlying principles:

- Emotions are critical to our success.
- People's emotional skills vary.
- These emotional skills can be measured objectively.

Unlike some other personality measures, the MSCEIT is not based on self-perceptions or self-awareness. Instead, the respondent takes an ability test measuring his or her ability to determine how people feel, to understand the cause of emotions, and to determine optimal emotional strategies across a series of practical tasks, as delineated in the following table.

Ability	Test Sections	Question Type
Accurately identify emotions in people and objects	Faces	Identify subtle emotions in faces
	Pictures	Identify emotions in complex landscapes and designs
Generate an emotion and solve problems with that emotion	Facilitation	Knowledge of how moods impact thinking
	Sensations	Relate various feeling sensations to emotion
Understand the causes of emotions	Changes	Multiple choice questions about how emotions change over time
	Blends	Multiple choice vocabulary definitions
Stay open to emotions and blend with thinking	Emotion Management	Indicate effectiveness of various solutions to internal problems
	Emotional Relations	Indicate effectiveness of various solutions to problems involving other people

Thus the MSCEIT is a skills test, which may instil additional confidence in its results – since the answers are based on ability, not self-perception, they cannot be faked, or deliberately misreported. Effective work performance centres on being able to integrate and use available information to constructively direct one's relationships in ways consistent with one's goals, values, and well-being. Emotions are one source of information, and an extremely important one. Emotions give us clues about how things are progressing for us and for others and can guide necessary changes. Emotional skill is a strong determinant of how successfully a given person will negotiate many challenges of work and leadership.

MSCEIT results can be applied in various ways. The test has been used to inform employee selection and promotion decisions, assist with career selection, guide executive coaching and leadership development, and aid counselling and therapy sessions.

Those interested in learning about EI or administering the MSCEIT can achieve certification upon completing a two- or three-day course. David Caruso, co-author of the MSCEIT, currently presents workshops himself. Some online study programmes are also available.

Leadership Value Assessment (LVA)

Richard Barrett, current leader of the management consulting firm Barrett Values Centre, was born in the UK in 1945. He received a first honours degree in civil engineering in 1966 from Manchester University. Barrett worked for World Bank in various roles between 1986 and 1997. From 1967 to 1997, Barrett also pursued independent study in psychology, spirituality, physics, and personal transformation. His personal studies led him to develop coaching models for promoting self-awareness, personal transformation, and leadership.

In 1997 Barrett conceived the Seven Levels of Consciousness model. This model's distinguishing feature is its evolutionary nature. The levels of consciousness provide a framework for understanding the developmental stages of both individual and group consciousness. The model covers both the internal dimensions of consciousness (our inner journey to self-knowledge and meaning) and the external dimensions of consciousness (the gradual expansion of our sense of identity in terms of who and what we care about).

Today Barrett is perhaps best known for his book *The New Leadership Paradigm*, published in 2011. His leadership paradigm, which applies the Seven Levels of Consciousness to the stages of leadership development, has been widely read and is enjoying great popularity among leaders and organisational coaches around the globe. And the Seven Levels of Consciousness model applies not only to individuals but to all human groups, including organisations, communities, and nations (see the CVA, described below).

Barrett espouses a value-driven approach to leadership and organisational success. He feels that leaders grow and develop only when they are given regular feedback. Leaders need to know what others appreciate about them; what advice their bosses, peers, and subordinates would give them for improvement; and how they contribute to the cultural entropy of the organisation. The Leadership Values Assessment (LVA) was designed to offer such feedback.

The LVA is used as a coaching tool to promote self-awareness and guide leaders towards actions that will allow them to realise their full potential. The measure is a tool that compares a leader's perception of his or her operating style with the perceptions of superiors, peers, and subordinates. The resulting LVA analysis emphasises the leader's strengths, areas for improvement, and opportunities for growth.

The LVA reveals the extent to which a leader's behaviours help or hinder organisational performance and to what degree fear influences the leader's decision-making. The LVA also measures the personal entropy and authenticity of a leader. Barrett Values Centre offers customisation of the measure template to reflect the cultural attributes of a given organisation. The survey may be taken online, and the questionnaire and questionnaire data plots are available in multiple languages. However, the written reports of the results are provided only in English.

Cultural Values Assessment (CVA)

The Cultural Values Assessment (CVA) is another tool created by Richard Barrett of Barrett Values Centre (see LVA, above). Barrett realised that, with some minor modifications, the great psychologist Abraham Maslow's Hierarchy of Needs theory could be adapted to a model for mapping the evolution of consciousness both in individuals and in all human groups – organisations, communities, nations. By 1998, Barrett completed his model, and it formed the foundation of his Cultural Transformation Tools (CTT) to map the values of organisations and their leaders.

In the mid 1990s Barrett came to realise that the role of organisations is changing. He advocates that organisations must become vision guided and values driven in order to succeed in today's global business climate. In other words, an organisation's identity and what it stands for have become just as important as what the organisation sells. An organisation's values are important to a variety of stakeholders including existing and potential employees, shareholders, and society as a whole.

Barrett also believes that corporate performance is strongly correlated with employee fulfilment. As he says, "The only way companies are going to increase market value in the twenty-first century is by focusing on their intangible assets – the components of cultural capital."[19] And cultural capital can be gained only by developing human capital, customer capital, and societal capital.

The Cultural Values Assessment is designed to offer a comprehensive diagnostic of company culture; to date, the CVA has been used by more than 2,000 organisations. The instrument provides a detailed understanding of employees' personal motivations, their experiences within the organisation, and the direction the company should be headed. Results on the measure can be used to generate deep, meaningful conversations about an organisation's purpose, priorities, and strategies and the well-being of all the stakeholders. The CVA can provide a roadmap for encouraging high performance, building resilience, and promoting sustainability.

The Strong Interest Inventory (SII)

Students choosing an academic major, people just entering the workplace, or those currently employed pursuing a career change can benefit from completing the Strong Interest Inventory (SII). The SII was developed in 1927 by psychologist E. K. Strong Jr. as a tool to assist ex-military personnel in locating civilian jobs. It has been revised several times; the modern version of the SII is based on an occupational typology model (the Holland Codes) created by psychologist John Holland. Rather than measuring personality, the SII is an indicator of one's *interests*.

Today the SII has become a valuable career-planning tool. A respondent's results on the assessment are compared to those of people with similar demographics who have already achieved satisfying careers. The results are used to generate a list of the top ten occupations the respondent is likely to find rewarding.

The SII measures interests, not skills or abilities. The results can guide a person towards not only rewarding careers but also the work activities, educational programmes, and leisure pursuits he or she is likely to find most fulfilling – all based on reported interests. The SII is used in a variety of applications:

- Achieving work satisfaction
- Identifying career options consistent with one's interests

---

19   Richard Barrett, "Building a Vision-Guided, Values-Driven Organization", *Power Projects Inc.*, <www.power-projects.com>, accessed 8 Feb. 2012.

- Choosing appropriate education and training
- Maintaining healthy balance between work and leisure activities
- Understanding personality aspects most closely associated with one's interests
- Determining preferred learning environments
- Illuminating one's preferences for leadership, risk taking, and teamwork
- Shaping a career direction
- Deciding on a focus for the future
- Directing one's career exploration at various life stages

The SII organises the respondent's results into several sections: General Occupational Themes, Basic Interests, Occupational Scales, Personal Style, Profile Summary, and Response Summary. Each section concludes with a set of recommended action steps to guide a person towards a satisfying life.

The SII can prove useful for career counsellors, psychologists, and educators. Certification in administering and interpreting the tool requires completion of coursework specific to the measure's history, interpretation, and basic testing concepts. Then, those seeking certification must pass a multiple-choice examination.

Career Anchors Profile

Edgar Schein, professor emeritus at the MIT Sloan School of Management, obtained his PhD in social psychology from Harvard University. He has conducted extensive organisational consultation focussing on organisational culture, development, and process as well as on career dynamics. His clients have included Apple, Citibank, General Foods, Motorola, Hewlett-Packard, Shell, and Con Edison.

Dr Schein's original research in career development was conducted in the mid-1970s. He identified a set of *career anchors*, which are a person's self-concept of talents and abilities, basic values, and his or her evolved sense of motives and needs as they pertain to career. Career anchors only evolve as the person gains occupational and life experience. But once a self-concept has formed, it functions as a stabilising force – thus prompting Schein to choose "anchor" as his descriptive metaphor. Anchors can be imagined as those values and motives a person will not give up if forced to make a choice.

Most of us are unaware of our career anchors until we face choices pertaining to self-development, family, or work. Becoming aware of our anchors can help us choose wisely.

Schein theorised that people's self-concepts revolve around five categories that reflect one's basic values, motives, and needs:

- Autonomy/independence
- Security/stability
- Technical/functional competence
- General managerial competence
- Entrepreneurial creativity

Schein performed additional research of a wider range of occupations in the 1980s, leading to three additional career anchor categories:

- Service/dedication to a cause
- Pure challenge
- Lifestyle

Schein based his Career Anchor Assessment on the following assertions:

1. Individuals need to do a better job of analysing their careers.
2. Organisations need to do a better job of analysing and designing the work they ask job incumbents to take on.

In 1996 Dr Schein sought to update his career anchor theory to meet the changing demands of twenty-first-century organisations. In an article published that year, he stated that

job/role planning will become an ever more critical task for everyone. As technologies change, as organizations attempt to become more competitive, as information technology makes new organizational forms possible, and as social values shift priorities, it is becoming more and more difficult to discern what a given job should consist of and how one should hire and train people for the ambiguous and changing roles that will emerge Jobs are increasingly becoming dynamic rather than static, so job descriptions are relatively useless unless they become a regular part of a dynamic job/role planning process.[20]

The Career Anchors instrument is used by professional career counsellors, outplacement firms, human resource professionals, and

---

20   Edgar H. Schein, *Career Anchors Revisited: Implications for Career Development in the 21st Century* (Cambridge, MA: MIT Sloan School of Management, 1996).

educational advisors. One may take the Career Anchors profile assessment online and receive one's own results for a modest purchase price. In addition, you can purchase multiple licences at graduated volume discounts to gather assessment results for others you serve, or you can meet certain qualifications to become an authorised distributor.

Thomas-Kilmann Conflict Mode Instrument (TKI)

The Thomas-Kilmann Conflict Mode Instrument (TKI) was created by Kenneth W. Thomas and Ralph H. Kilmann in the early 1970s. The instrument is loosely based on the 1964 Managerial Grid Model of leadership style posed by Robert R. Blake and Jane Mouton. Placing "concern for production" on the x-axis and "concern for people" on the y-axis of a grid, Blake and Mouton created a plot that yielded five managerial styles. Many conflict-style inventories that emerged later were founded upon this model.

Kenneth Thomas made important theoretical adjustments to the Managerial Grid to guide development of the TKI, changing the axes to reflect the dimensions "assertiveness" and "cooperativeness". The result was a five-category schema classifying the primary modes in which people handle conflict: competing, collaborating, compromising, avoiding, and accommodating. In designing the instrument, Thomas and Kilmann carefully matched pairs of statements to ensure that no one conflict-handling mode appeared more attractive than the others. While everyone is capable of employing all five modes, individuals will show clear preferences for one or two modes in a given interaction.

> *Competing* is assertive and uncooperative, a power-oriented mode. When competing, an individual pursues his or her own concerns at the other person's expense, using whatever power seems appropriate to win his or her position. Competing might mean standing up for your rights, defending a position you believe is correct, or simply trying to win.

> *Collaborating* is both assertive and cooperative. When collaborating, an individual attempts to work with the other person to find a solution that fully satisfies the concerns of both. It involves digging into an issue to identify the underlying concerns of the two individuals and finding an

alternative that meets both sets of concerns. Collaborating between two persons might take the form of exploring a disagreement to learn from each other's insights, resolving some condition that would otherwise have them competing for resources, or confronting and trying to find a creative solution to an interpersonal problem.

Compromising happens when parties wish to find an expedient, mutually acceptable solution that partially satisfies them all. Compromising falls on a middle ground between competing and accommodating, and the solution requires parties to give up more than when competing but less than when accommodating. Likewise, it addresses an issue more directly than avoiding but doesn't explore it in as much depth as collaborating. Compromising might mean splitting the difference, exchanging concessions, or seeking a quick middle-ground position.

Avoiding is unassertive and uncooperative. When avoiding, an individual does not immediately pursue his or her own concerns or those of the other person. He or she does not address the conflict. Avoiding might take the form of diplomatically sidestepping an issue, postponing an issue until a better time, or simply withdrawing from a threatening situation.

Accommodating is unassertive and cooperative – the opposite of competing. When accommodating, an individual neglects his or her own concerns to satisfy the concerns of the other person; there is an element of self-sacrifice in this mode. Accommodating might take the form of selfless generosity or charity, obeying another person's order when you would prefer not to, or yielding to another's point of view.

During its use, the TKI has become quite popular, leading CPP Inc. to claim that it is "the leading measure of conflict-handling behaviour."[21]

---

21   CPP Inc., "History and Validity of the Thomas-Kilmann Conflict Mode Instrument (TKI)", <https://www.cpp.com/Products/tki/tki_info.aspx>, accessed 10 Feb. 2012.

Individuals who complete the instrument receive their raw scores as well as the percentile in which they fall in comparison to a normative sample of other employed adults who have taken the TKI. Between 2002 and 2005, the instrument's distributor, CPP Inc., used online TKI responses to draw a sample of 4,000 males and 4,000 females aged 20 to 70 who were employed full-time in the United States and representative of the US population in terms of organisational level and race and ethnicity.

The TKI is applied by human resources professionals, organisational development consultants, or anyone who seeks to understand and catalyse discussion about how conflict-handling styles affect personal and group dynamics. In addition to direct conflict resolution, the TKI can be used for training in management, supervision, negotiation, or safety; team building; and leadership development. There are no special qualifications required to administer the instrument, and it is available online in self-scorable format. However, the guidance of a professional will enhance the measure's interpretation and tailor its applicability to specific situations.

Belbin Team Role Theory

Meredith Belbin received his PhD in psychology of ageing in industry from Cambridge University in the late 1940s. Twenty years later, he was invited to apply the results of a team simulation game run during managerial training at what is now Henley Business School to his research on team behaviour. Dr Belbin enlisted mathematician Bill Hartston, anthropologist Jeanne Fisher, and occupational psychologist Roger Mottram to collaborate on his studies. Over the course of seven years, Dr Belbin's group continued to run the business games at the rate of three per year with eight teams in each game, and they observed, categorised, and recorded the various contributions of team members.

The outcome of the research was the finding that team balance, rather than intellect, determined the success or failure of any given business team. Successful teams were those whose members filled a balance of compatible roles; unsuccessful teams were those subject to internal role conflict. The researchers learned that, using psychometric measurement, they could predict the roles individuals were likely to play on a team and whether a team comprised of certain people was likely to succeed.

They discovered that the most successful groups combined a mix of people representing a range of behaviours. Eight behavioural clusters were identified to guide the balance of roles, and a ninth was identified later based on field tests of the model. Ever since the Belbin theory was solidified in

1976, organisations across the world have been using the nine team roles to guide team-building efforts.

The NINE Belbin Team Roles

Team Role	Contribution	Allowable Weaknesses
Plant	Creative, imaginative, free-thinking. Generates ideas and solves difficult problems.	Ignores incidentals. Too preoccupied to communicate effectively.
Resource Investigator	Outgoing, enthusiastic, communicative. Explores opportunities and develops contacts.	Over-optimistic. Loses interest once initial enthusiasm has passed.
Co-ordinator	Mature, confident, identifies talent. Clarifies goals. Delegates effectively.	Can be seen as manipulative. Offloads own share of the work.
Shaper	Challenging, dynamic, thrives on pressure. Has the drive and courage to overcome obstacles.	Prone to provocation. Offends people's feelings.
Monitor Evaluator	Sober, strategic and discerning. Sees all options and judges accurately.	Lacks drive and ability to inspire others. Can be overly critical.
Teamworker	Co-operative, perceptive and diplomatic. Listens and averts friction.	Indecisive in crunch situations. Avoids confrontation.
Implementer	Practical, reliable, efficient. Turns ideas into actions and organises work that needs to be done.	Somewhat inflexible. Slow to respond to new possibilities.
Completer Finisher	Painstaking, conscientious, anxious. Searches out errors. Polishes and perfects.	Inclined to worry unduly. Reluctant to delegate.
Specialist	Single-minded, self-starting, dedicated. Provides knowledge and skills in rare supply.	Contributes only on a narrow front. Dwells on technicalities.

©2010, R. Meredith Belbin. Reproduced by kind permission of Belbin Associates—www.belbin.com.

Belbin Team Role theory is not a psychometric test but rather a method of describing behaviour – what people in a group see and experience. Through Self and Observer Assessments, the theoretical model helps illuminate people's tendencies and preferences to behave in certain ways in a group situation. It becomes easier to work effectively with people when you have some expectations about their behaviour as well as your own.

The theory can be applied in several ways. You can use the results to understand how to manage yourself in a team, to create working partnerships, to recognise the potential of groups working together, to encourage interdependence among team members, or to clarify how a team should fit into the overall organisation. The Belbin Team Role measure is copyrighted, and there is no self-scoring format. Results reports can be generated on the website for the inventory, www.belbin.com. Accreditation is not required to use the reports, but a two-day accreditation course will prepare professionals to interpret the reports for individuals or teams and to teach the model to others. Both Dr Belbin and I strongly recommend accreditation for those wishing to use the Belbin model for training or consultancy.

Kolb's Learning Theory and the Honey and Mumford Learning Styles Questionnaire (LSQ)

In 1984, educational theorist David A. Kolb published his learning styles model, the result of more than ten years of research. This model later led to the development of his experiential learning theory (ELT) and learning styles inventory (LSI). Influenced by psychology greats Carl Rogers, Carl Jung, and Jean Piaget, Kolb's ideas provide the fundamental concepts behind our current understanding of human learning behaviour and have given rise to a host of subsequent learning models. Peter Honey and Alan Mumford's model is one of those inspired by Kolb's theories.

However, while Honey and Mumford's Learning Styles Questionnaire (LSQ) does derive directly from Kolb's theory, Honey and Mumford found that Kolb's LSI measure had low face validity when administered to employees in management roles. Reasoning that most people do not consciously consider how they really learn, Honey and Mumford designed their questionnaire to probe general behavioural tendencies rather than directly asking people to describe how they learn.

Similar to Kolb's work, the researchers identified a cycled-stage model describing how people learn and four learning styles directly aligned to each stage in the cycle. These are the four stages through which people progress when they learn:

- Having an experience
- Reflecting on it
- Drawing their own conclusions (theorising)
- Putting their theory into practice to see what happens

Based on the results, learners can then move through the cycle again, jump in at any part of the cycle, or quit when they deem themselves successful (i.e. they have learned the task or material). The cycle of stages is represented by this model:

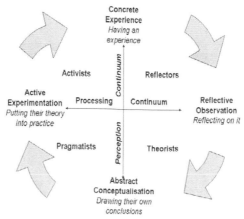

Reproduced from Honey P & Mumford A (1982).
Manual of Learning Styles. London: Peter Honey Publishing.

As represented, the cycle of learning yields the following four learning styles:

Activists prefer the challenge of new experiences, involvement with others, assimilation into groups, and role-playing. An activist likes anything new, problem-solving, and small group discussions.

Reflectors prefer to learn from activities that allow them opportunities to watch, think, and review over time. Reflectors like journals and brainstorming, and they will learn from lectures if lectures provide expert explanations and analysis.

Theorists like to think problems through in logical, ordered steps. They like lectures, analogies, systems, case studies, models, and readings. Talking with experts is normally not helpful to theorists.

Pragmatists prefer to apply new concepts to actual practise and see first-hand how they work. Pragmatists enjoy laboratories, fieldwork, and observations. They benefit from feedback and coaching and prefer an obvious link between the task at hand and a specific problem.

Honey and Mumford also believed that people prefer different methods of learning depending on the situation and their experience. People move among the four modes of learning rather than being locked into a single dominant mode. The LSQ is used to help managers strengthen their underutilised learning styles so they may become better equipped to learn from a wide range of everyday experiences. And understanding the learning preferences of trainees has clear potential to aid the development of effective training materials and delivery methods.

There are two copyrighted versions of the Honey and Mumford Learning Styles Questionnaire, one with eighty items and one with forty. Single users may complete an online self-assessment at the Peter Honey Publications website and receive an immediate diagnosis (for a fee) of current learning-style preferences. Groups may purchase multiple questionnaires and diagnoses according to a graduated fee schedule. The measure is also available as a licence to print in PDF format. The LSQ is available in English, French, and German.

CONCLUSION

Conflict is inevitable, but combat is optional. ~**Max Lucade**

The Friday-afternoon near breakdown that sparked my inspiration to write this book happened some twenty years ago. Today I look back on the experience with the fondness and satisfaction that springs from having done a job well. You see, that meltdown and subsequent epiphany changed my career. Not only that, it was a gift that I continue to give across the organisations I serve in the UK and around the globe.

Using personality measurement to manage and avert workplace battles has become more and more popular with companies over the past two decades. Yet having employees fill out a questionnaire will never eliminate the fact that people with very different personalities will be asked to work together or ensure that challenges and unproductive interpersonal clashes won't occur. What I hope you take away from this book is the notion that the same personality differences that so easily impede communication, create conflict, and reduce productivity can just as readily be turned into organisational assets simply by changing focus.

The trick to making this magical focal shift is to view each individual personality objectively, to home in on each person's fortes, and to train those strengths on accomplishing organisational goals. Accepting and honouring personality differences builds respect and encourages positive communication. And if you do it, others will follow. No matter where you fall within the organisational hierarchy, you can do your part to bring your work team into the UZOD – that place where ideas blossom, innovation is born, and productivity soars.

It all starts with letting go of your ego. Recognising that your way is not the only way to do things is a step towards opening the Johari open windowpane. Let other ideas in; different personality types perform best in different situations. The most productive workplaces will be those that allow individuals at least some autonomy to explore and experiment with different approaches to completing projects. If you promote open, non-judgemental communication (and such promotion starts with modelling), you help build an environment where reciprocal ideas flow and the expression of suggestions, constructive criticism, and concerns is both encouraged and accepted. Help others understand that combining different personality types – with their various perspectives – leads to creative solutions and improved products and services.

How should you go about recognising, honouring, and accepting the multiple personality types around you? Clearly, I recommend psychometric tools as an excellent springboard. And as I hope the Admiral has illustrated for you within these pages, the available measurement toolkit is robust and powerful. Relying on a single measure may be a mistake given the rich data that can be collected. Enough valid, reliable personality measures are available to suit the management of every possible workplace battle.

The Admiral also appears in this book to help you appreciate the value of third-party objectivity and professional training to interpret personality measures. Confident interpretation of results on a psychometric test can only be assured when undertaken by an expert. An educated and certified professional will serve as a reliable guide to help your organisation receive maximum knowledge and benefit from personality testing.

Of course, you may decide to become an expert yourself. In fact, encouraging more certified professionals to enter the field is one of my goals in writing this book. And if you do become well versed in psychometric interpretation, you will recognise ways to tease out personality type without necessarily turning to the measures in every instance. Instead of making assumptions about the reasons and motives behind your colleagues' or employees' behaviour, you will ask pointed questions that can improve your understanding of each individual. When you take the time to understand the personalities that make up your workplace, you can make better decisions regarding assignment, management, delegation, collaboration, and team formation.

The final point I'd like to make is just this: battle is never unavoidable. War is always a choice. That's not to say that we should walk away from every conflict or ignore every challenge. Instead, I advocate turning every potential war zone into the Uncomfortable Zone of Debate – where challenges are welcomed, entertained, and overcome. Positive conflict is indeed possible. And such positive conflict results in role clarification, respect among team members, and a relaxed, confident, forward-thinking, dynamic, successful, peaceful workplace.

BIBLIOGRAPHY

ARGYRIS, CHRIS, PUTNAM, ROBERT W., and SMITH, DIANA MCLEAN, *Action Science: Concepts, Methods, and Skills for Research and Intervention* (San Francisco: Jossey-Bass, 1985).

ALLPORT, GORDON W., *Personality: A Psychological Interpretation* (Oxford: Holt, 1937).

BARGER, NANCY J., and KIRBY, LINDA K., *The Challenge of Change in Organizations: Helping Employees Thrive in the New Frontier* (Palo Alto, CA: Davies-Black Publishing, 1995).

BARR, LEE, and BARR, NORMA, *Leadership Development: Maturity and Power* (Austin, TX: Eakin Press, 1994).

BARRETT, RICHARD, "Building a Vision-Guided, Values-Driven Organization", *Power Projects Inc.*, <www.power-projects.com>, accessed 8 Feb. 2012.

—— *Building a Values-Driven Organization: A Whole System Approach to Cultural Transformation* (Oxford: Butterworth-Heinemann, 2006).

—— *The New Leadership Paradigm* (Raleigh, NC: Lulu.com, 2011).

BELBIN, R. MEREDITH, *Management Teams: Why They Succeed or Fail, 3rd ed.* (Boston: Butterworth Heinemann, 2010).

CARUSO, DAVID R. (2002). "All About the Mayer-Salovey-Caruso Emotional Intelligence Test" [white paper], <http://www.rossresults.com/library/MSCEIT_White_Paper.pdf>, accessed 21 Oct. 2011.

CATTELL, RAYMOND B., *Personality: A Systematic, Theoretical, and Factual Study* (New York: McGraw-Hill, 1950).

——, EBER, H. W., and TATSUOKA, M. M., *Handbook for the Sixteen Personality Factor Questionnaire (16PF)* (Champaign, IL: Institute for Personality and Ability Testing, 1980).

COVEY, STEPHEN R., *The 3rd Alternative: Solving Life's Most Difficult Problems* (New York: Free Press, 2011).

CPP INC., "History and Validity of the Thomas-Kilmann Conflict Mode Instrument (TKI)", https://www.cpp.com/Products/tki/tki_info.aspx>, accessed 10 Feb. 2012.

—— "Products Index", <https://www.cpp.com/products/mbti/index.aspx>, accessed 7 Feb. 2012.

—— *CPP Global Human Capital Report: Workplace Conflict and How Businesses can Harness it to Thrive* (Mountainview, CA: CPP Inc., 2008).

HEATHFIELD, SUSAN M. "Twelve Tips for Team Building: How to Build Successful Work Teams", *About.com* [website], <http://humanresources.about.com/od/involvementteams/a/twelve_tip_team.htm>, accessed 12 Feb. 2012.

HONEY, PETER, AND MUMFORD, ALAN, *The Learning Styles Questionnaire, 80-Item Version* (Maidenhead, UK: Peter Honey Publications, 2006).

JOHNSON, GERRY, AND SCHOLES, KEVAN, *Exploring Corporate Strategy, 5th ed.* (Harlow, UK: Prentice-Hall, 1999).

KEIRSEY, DAVID, *Please Understand Me II: Temperament, Character, Intelligence* (Del Mar, CA: Prometheus Nemesis Book Company, 1998).

KOLB, DAVID A., *Experiential Learning: Experience as the Source of Learning and Development* (Englewood Cliffs, NJ: Prentice-Hall, 1984).

LOPACH, JAMES J., AND LUCKOWSKI, JEAN A., *Jeannette Rankin: A Political Woman* (Boulder, CO: University Press of Colorado, 2007).

LUFT, JOSEPH, AND INGHAM, HARRINGTON, "The Johari Window, a Graphic Model of Interpersonal Awareness", *Proceedings of the Western Training Laboratory in Group Development* (Los Angeles, CA: UCLA, 1950).

MAISTER, DAVID, GREEN, CHARLES, AND GALFORD, ROBERT, *The Trusted Advisor* (New York: Free Press, 2000).

MAYER, JOHN D., AND SALOVEY, PETER, "What is Emotional Intelligence?", in Peter Salovey and DJ Sluyter (Eds.), *Emotional Development and Emotional Intelligence* (New York: Basic Books, 1997, pp. 3-31).

MERRIAM-WEBSTER, *Merriam-Webster's Collegiate Dictionary, 11th ed.* (Springfield, MA: Merriam-Webster Inc., 2008).

MYERS, ISABEL BRIGGS, AND MYERS, PETER B., *Gifts Differing: Understanding Personality Type* (Palo Alto, CA: Consulting Psychologists Press, 1980).

——, MCCAULLEY, MARY H., QUENK, NAOMI L., AND HAMMER, ALLEN L., *MBTI Manual (A Guide to the Development and Use of the Myers Briggs Type Indicator), 6th Ed.* (Palo Alto, CA: Consulting Psychologists Press, 1998).

MYERS, PETER BRIGGS, "Introduction", in Myers, Isabel Briggs and Myers, Peter B., *Gifts Differing: Understanding Personality Type* (Palo Alto, CA: Davies-Black Publishing, 1995).

OPIE, ROGER, "The "Four Camps" of Employee Skills", in The Chartered Institute of Personnel and Development, *Reflections on the 2008 Learning and Development Survey: Latest Trends in Learning, Training and Development* (London: The Chartered Institute of Personnel and Development, 2007).

SAVILLE, PETER ET AL., "A Demonstration of the Validity of the Occupational Personality Questionnaire (OPQ) in the Measurement of Job Competencies over Time", *Applied Psychology*, 45/3(1996): 243-62.

SCHEIN, EDGAR H., *Career Anchors Revisited: Implications for Career Development in the 21st Century* (Cambridge, MA: MIT Sloan School of Management, 1996).

SCHUTZ, WILLIAM, *FIRO: A Three-Dimensional Theory of Interpersonal Behavior* (New York: Rinehart, 1958).

—— *FIRO: A Three-Dimensional Theory of Interpersonal Behavior* (Tucson, AZ: Pan Publishing, 1999).

STANOVICH, KEITH E., AND WEST, RICHARD F., "Individual Difference in Reasoning: Implications for the Rationality Debate?", *Behavioural and Brain Sciences*, 23(2000): 645–726.

TAYLOR, CAROLYN, *Mergers and Acquisitions: Emotions at Work* (Key Biscayne, FL: Axialent Inc., 2010).

THORNE, AVRIL, AND GOUGH, HARRISON G., *Portraits of Type: An MBTI Research Compendium* (Gainesville, FL: Center for Applications of Psychological Type, 1999).

INDEX